Lecture Notes in Computer Scie

T0237865

Commenced Publication in 1973
Founding and Former Series Editors:
Gerhard Goos, Juris Hartmanis, and Jan van Leeuwen

Editorial Board

David Hutchison
Lancaster University, UK

Takeo Kanade
Carnegie Mellon University, Pittsburgh, PA, USA

Josef Kittler
University of Surrey, Guildford, UK

Jon M. Kleinberg
Cornell University, Ithaca, NY, USA

Alfred Kobsa
University of California, Irvine, CA, USA

Friedemann Mattern
ETH Zurich, Switzerland

John C. Mitchell
Stanford University, CA, USA

Moni Naor
Weizmann Institute of Science, Rehovot, Israel

Oscar Nierstrasz
University of Bern, Switzerland

C. Pandu Rangan
Indian Institute of Technology, Madras, India

Bernhard Steffen
University of Dortmund, Germany

Madhu Sudan
Microsoft Research, Cambridge, MA, USA

Demetri Terzopoulos
University of California, Los Angeles, CA, USA

Doug Tygar
University of California, Berkeley, CA, USA

Gerhard Weikum
Max-Planck Institute of Computer Science, Saarbruecken, Germany

Miquel Oliver   Sebastià Sallent (Eds.)

The Internet of the Future

15th Open European Summer School and
IFIP TC6.6 Workshop, EUNICE 2009
Barcelona, Spain, September 7-9, 2009
Proceedings

 Springer

Volume Editors

Miquel Oliver
Universitat Pompeu Fabra
Roc Boronat 138
08018 Barcelona, Spain
E-mail: miquel.oliver@upf.edu

Sebastià Sallent
Universitat Politècnica de Catalunya (UPC)
Esteve Terrades 7, Castelldefels
08860 Barcelona, Spain
E-mail: sallent@entel.upc.es

Library of Congress Control Number: 2009932259

CR Subject Classification (1998): C.2.5, C.2.6, C.2, D.4, H.4, K.4, C.4

LNCS Sublibrary: SL 3 – Information Systems and Application, incl. Internet/Web and HCI

ISSN   0302-9743
ISBN-10   3-642-03699-6 Springer Berlin Heidelberg New York
ISBN-13   978-3-642-03699-6 Springer Berlin Heidelberg New York

This work is subject to copyright. All rights are reserved, whether the whole or part of the material is concerned, specifically the rights of translation, reprinting, re-use of illustrations, recitation, broadcasting, reproduction on microfilms or in any other way, and storage in data banks. Duplication of this publication or parts thereof is permitted only under the provisions of the German Copyright Law of September 9, 1965, in its current version, and permission for use must always be obtained from Springer. Violations are liable to prosecution under the German Copyright Law.

springer.com

© Springer-Verlag Berlin Heidelberg 2009
Printed in Germany

Typesetting: Camera-ready by author, data conversion by Scientific Publishing Services, Chennai, India
Printed on acid-free paper   SPIN: 12736867   06/3180   5 4 3 2 1 0

Preface

Ten years ago, the 5th edition of the EUNICE Summer School took place in Barcelona with the motto "Broadband for all." This year, with the broadband promise already fulfilled in the city, the international workshop returned to Barcelona in its 15th edition and focused on a polyhedrical approach to the Internet of the future.

The Internet is shaping the twenty-first century information society. It has deeply transformed the way we learn, work and interact. All kinds of institutions, from universities to businesses, have been shaken by the wave of digital innovation. Leisure and social networks also have their place in the virtual world, and the younger generations cannot imagine a time when they could not be in permanent contact with friends around the globe, interchanging messages and multimedia content.

The challenge of classifying, ranking and interpreting the massive amounts of information that are being generated is breathtaking. Furthermore, the Internet is moving beyond the computer to reach mobile phones, smart gadgets and sensor networks. The pervasiveness of the Internet fundamentally changed existing business models, and the business models themselves are driving the evolution of the Internet. In this scenario of relentless change, our aim is to foresee and design the networks and applications of the future.

We received more than 60 submissions for the conference. After the review process, 23 full papers were accepted for presentation at the workshop, together with 11 posters. Every submission received at least three reviews from the members of the Technical Program Committee and/or external reviewers. Our gratitude goes to all the reviewers for their efforts.

We would like to take this opportunity to express our thanks to the sponsors and supporters of the 15th EUNICE Summer School / International Workshop: the Department of Telematics Engineering at the UPC, the Spanish Ministry of Science and Innovation, the Euro-NF Network of Excellence (funded by the European Commission), the Catalan Autonomous Government (Generalitat de Catalunya), IFIP TC6 Working Group 6.6, the i2CAT Foundation, the Universitat Pompeu Fabra (UPF), and the Universitat Politècnica de Catalunya (UPC).

September 2009

Miquel Oliver
Sebastià Sallent

EUNICE - Member Charter

European Network of Universities and Companies in Information and Communication Engineering

Mission

The European universities and companies signing this present charter are anxious to improve in a permanent manner the quality and relevance of their teaching and research in the field of information and communication technologies. They declare their desire to cooperate in the following ways:

- By jointly developing and promoting the best and compatible standard of European higher education and professionals in information and communication technologies.
- By increasing scientific and technical knowledge in the field of telecommunications and developing their applications in the economy.

Membership

The network is made up of European Universities within the European Union and outside it, whether from Western, Central or Eastern Europe. These universities are involved at their own appropriate organization level, taking into account the mission of the network. The parties signing the present charter will be the "founding partners." Other universities, very limited in number, might be invited to join the network as "members."

Transnational companies, working together with the universities on information and communication technologies, and representatives from the relevant commission of the European Union, will be offered the opportunity to be associate members. No institution can apply for membership.

Education

The partners will seek the development of high-level compatibility of the existing or commonly developed courses and programs, in order to facilitate their recognition by employers independently of their geographical location in Europe. To achieve this goal, the partners will, inside the network, work on mutual recognition of these courses and programs. To develop interculturality, these courses and programs will be accessible in such a way as to encourage, as far as possible, long-duration mobility for students and faculty members from one country to another (i.e., several months).

To set compatible standards, shorter-duration operations will be conducted such as:

- Summer schools for young faculty members and PhD students
- Intensive seminars, in limited numbers, for students
- Short-duration mobility for faculty members for teaching assignments
- Use of new technologies in education

Finally, the partners will take advantage of the network of relations set up as described above to develop common modules for on-site training, for the world industry.

Research

The partners will also take advantage of this network to collaborate on research and development projects which could be carried out in common by several of them and which could lead to marketable applications in particular.

Organization and Structure

To achieve the above-mentioned aims, the institutions concerned will form a flexible structure whose role will be to think about and decide on joint actions. It will be called the steering group and will meet twice a year. The network would have no legal status. However, the network may authorize a member or set of members to act on its behalf. Concrete propositions in education and research will be worked out in small working groups of at least two partners, chosen by the steering group as opportunities arise. Finally, a permanent secretariat, located at France Telecom University, will be established to co-ordinate all the information relevant to the network's activities.

Means and Finance

The institutions concerned will provide the specific financial and/or inkind support necessary for the smooth running of the network, notably human resources (research lecturers, engineers, administrators, etc.).

The partners in the network will share information about funding opportunities and seek, as often as necessary, financial aid from public authorities for its actions:

- Within each country
- From bilateral programs at a country level, whenever such financial aids exist
- At the European level by means of community schemes (ERASMUS, COMETT, TEMPUS, RACE, ESPRIT, scientific and technological co-operation with Central and Eastern Europe, human resources and mobility, etc.)

All things being equal regarding a specific action within the scope of the network, a member will prefer co-operation with other members of the network.

EUNICE Member Institutions (as of February 2009)

Finland

- Department of Information Technology, Tampere University of Technology

France

- TELECOM Bretagne (Brest)
- École Nationale Supérieure des Télécommunications (ENST Paris)
- Laboratoire Lorrain de Recherche en Informatique et ses Applications (LORIA) at the University Henri Poincaré
- Nancy Telecom INT, Evry

Germany

- Cooperation and Management (Institute of Telematics) at the Universität Karlsruhe
- Institute of Communication Networks at the Technische Universität München (TUM)
- Institute of Communication Networks and Computer Engineering at the Universität Stuttgart

Hungary

- Department of Telecommunications and Media Informatics, Budapest University of Technology and Economics

Italy

- Telecommunication Networks Group, Politecnico di Torino

The Netherlands

- Centre for Telematics and Information Technology, University of Twente

Norway

- Department of Telematics, Norwegian University of Science and Technology (NTNU), Trondheim

Russia

- St. Petersburg State University of Telecommunications

Spain

- Departamento de Ingeniería Telemática, Universidad Carlos III, Madrid
- Department of Telematics Engineering, Universitat Politècnica de Catalunya (UPC), Barcelona
- ETSI de Telecomunicación, Technical University of Madrid (UPM)
- NeTS Research Group, Universitat Pompeu Fabra (UPF), Barcelona

UK

- University of Sussex
- Department of Electronic & Electrical Engineering, University College London

EUNICE Website

http://www.eunice-forum.org

Organization

EUNICE 2009 was co-organized by the Network Technologies and Strategies (NeTS) Research Group at the Universitat Pompeu Fabra (UPF), and by the Broadband Networks (BAMPLA) Research Group at the Universitat Politècnica de Catalunya (UPC).

http://www.nets.upf.edu/

http://plone.upc.edu/grupbampla

Technical Program Committee Co-chairs

Miquel Oliver   Universitat Pompeu Fabra, Spain
Sebastià Sallent   Universitat Politècnica de Catalunya, Spain

EUNICE 2009 Technical Program Committee

Finn Arve Aagesen   NTNU Trondheim, Norway
Sebastian Abeck   University of Karlsruhe, Germany
Rolv Braek   NTNU Trondheim, Norway
Jörg Eberspächer   Technical University of München, Germany
Olivier Festor   INRIA Nancy, France
Maurice Gagnaire   TELECOM ParisTech, France
Annie Gravey   TELECOM Bretagne, France
Sebastian Gunreben   University of Stuttgart, Germany
Edit Halász   Budapest University of Technology and Economics, Hungary
Jarmo Harju   Tampere University of Technology, Finland
Yvon Kermarrec   TELECOM Bretagne, France
Paul Kühn   University of Stuttgart, Germany
Xavier Lagrange   TELECOM Bretagne, France
David Larrabeiti-López   University Carlos III of Madrid, Spain
Maryline Laurent-Maknavicius   TELECOM SudParis, France
Ralf Lehnert   TU Dresden, Germany
Maurizio Munafò   Politecnico di Torino, Italy
Aiko Pras,   University of Twente, The Netherlands
David Ros   TELECOM Bretagne, France
Burkhard Stiller   University of Zurich, Switzerland
Robert Szabo   Budapest University of Technology and Economics, Hungary
Marten van Sinderen   University of Twente, The Netherlands

Local Organization

Accommodation	Jorge Infante, Núria García (UPF)
Keynote speeches	Boris Bellalta (UPF)
Proceedings	David Remondo, David Rincón (UPC)
Publicity	Jaume Barceló (UPF)
Social events	Anna Sfairopoulou (UPF)
Submissions	David Rincón, Frederic Raspall (UPC)
Sponsors	Johan Zuidweg (UPF)
Web	Cristina Cano (UPF)

Referees

Finn Arve Aagesen
Sebastian Abeck
Anna Agustí-Torra
Jesús Alcober
Esteve Almirall
Karine Amis
Jaume Barceló
Marc Barisch
Boris Bellalta
Jozsef Biro
Christian Blankenhorn
Roland Bless
Giovanni Bodini
Eduard Bonada
Rolv Braek
Daniel Camps Mur
Cristina Cano
Marisa Catalán
Miguel Catalán
Laurent Ciarletta
József Máté Csorba
Ángel Cuevas Rumin
Frederic Cuppens
Hamza Dahmouni
Pieter-Tjerk de Boer
Mari Carmen Domingo
Idilio Drago
Joerg Eberspächer
Jan Ellenbeck
Azadeh Faridi
Guillem Femenias
Olivier Festor

Tiago Fioreze
Maurice Gagnaire
Elisabeth Georgieva
Carles Gomez i Montenegro
Visvasuresh Victor Govindaswamy
Annie Gravey
Manel Guerrero Zapata
András Gulyás
Sebastian Gunreben
Christian Guthy
Lluís Gutiérrez
Edit Halász
Jarmo Harju
Christian Hartmann
Sofiane Hassayoun
David Hay
Poul Heegaard
Peter Hegyi
Marko Helenius
Bjarne Helvik
Juan Hernández-Serrano
Xavier Hesselbach
Zalan Heszberger
Jorge Infante
Yuming Jiang
Georgios Karagiannis
Yvon Kermarrec
Wouter Klein Wolterink
Svein Knapskog
Jochen Kögel
András Korn
Frank Alexander Kraemer

Paul Kühn
Oivind Kure
Xavier Lagrange
Samer Lahoud
Charlotte Langlais
David Larrabeiti-López
Maryline Laurent-Maknavicius
Ralf Lehnert
Olga León
Ángel Lozano
Patrick Maillé
Michel Marot
Jorge Mataix-Oltra
Michela Meo
Xavier Mestre
Dmitri Moltchanov
Miklos Molnar
Maurizio Munafò
Miquel Oliver
Antoni Oller
Harald Overby
Javier Ozón
José Ramón Piney
Frederic Raspall
Erwin Rathgeb
David Remondo
Francesc Rey
André Rios
David Rincón

Gerson Rodríguez de los Santos López
Ricardo Romeral
David Ros
Ramin Sadre
Diego Sáez-Trumper
Dolors Sala
Sebastià Sallent
Marc Sánchez Artigas
Joachim Scharf
Isaac Seoane
Kamal Singh
Vidar Slatten
Miguel Soriano
Burkhard Stiller
Norvald Stol
Samer Sulaiman
Robert Szabo
János Tapolcai
Geraldine Texier
Manuel Uruea
Emiel Martijn van Eenennaam
Marten van Sinderen
Sandrine Vaton
Rolland Vida
Attila Vidács
Rafael Vidal
José Yúfera
Johan Zuidweg

Technical Sponsors

Euro-NF Network of Excellence
International Federation for Information Processing (IFIP) TC6 WG 6.6

Sponsoring Institutions

Universitat Pompeu Fabra
Universitat Politècnica de Catalunya
Departament d'Enginyeria Telemàtica, UPC
Fundació Innovació i Internet Avançat a Catalunya, i2CAT
Ministerio de Ciencia e Innovación
Agéncia de Gestió d'Ajuts Univ. i de Recerca (AGAUR), Generalitat
    de Catalunya

Table of Contents

Technical Session 1: Traffic Engineering for the Internet

Quantifying the Uncertainty in Measurements for MBAC 1
  Anne Nevin, Peder J. Emstad, Yuming Jiang, and Guoqiang Hu

Ring Flushing for Reduced Overload in Spanning Tree Protocol
Controlled Ethernet Networks 11
  *Dániel Horváth, Gábor Kapitány, Sándor Plósz,
  István Moldován, and Csaba Lukovszki*

A Distributed Exact Solution to Compute Inter-domain
Multi-Constrained Paths 21
  *Gilles Bertrand, Samer Lahoud, Géraldine Texier, and
  Miklós Molnár*

Technical Session 2: P2P and Multimedia

Classification of P2P and HTTP Using Specific Protocol
Characteristics 31
  John Hurley, Emi Garcia-Palacios, and Sakir Sezer

Network Awareness in P2P-TV Applications 41
  Stefano Traverso, Emilio Leonardi, Marco Mellia, and Michela Meo

Enhancing Progressive Encryption for Scalable Video Streams 51
  Viktor Gergely and Gábor Fehér

Technical Session 3: Advanced Applications for Next Generation Networks

Characterizing User Groups in Online Social Networks 59
  László Gyarmati and Tuan Anh Trinh

Route Prediction on Tracking Data to Location-Based Services 69
  Attila István Petróczi and Csaba Gáspár-Papanek

Context Aware Programmable Trackers for the Next Generation
Internet 78
  Pedro Sousa

Technical Session 4: Future Internet Architectures and Models

The Metalist Model: A Simple and Extensible Information Model for the Future Internet   88
  Éric Renault and Djamal Zeghlache

On Designing for Tussle: Future Internet in Retrospect   98
  Costas Kalogiros, Alexandros Kostopoulos, and Alan Ford

NIT: A New Internet Topology Generator   108
  Joylan Nunes Maciel and Cristina Duarte Murta

Technical Session 5: Pervasive Wireless Networks and Protocols

Resource Allocation in MIMO-OFDMA Wireless Systems Based on Linearly Precoded Orthogonal Space-Time Block Codes   118
  Borja Dañobeitia, Guillem Femenias, and Felip Riera-Palou

On the Influence of Packet Scheduling on the Trade-Off between System Spectral Efficiency and User Fairness in OFDMA-Based Networks   128
  Emanuel B. Rodrigues, Michael L. Walker, and Fernando Casadevall

RSSI-Based Forwarding for Multihop Wireless Sensor Networks   138
  Azlan Awang, Xavier Lagrange, and David Ros

Technical Session 6: Innovative Algorithms for Network-Related Problems

A Pipelined IP Address Lookup Module for 100 Gbps Line Rates and beyond   148
  Domenic Teuchert and Simon Hauger

Comparative Study of Multicast Protection Algorithms Using Shared Links in 100GET Transport Network   158
  Samer Sulaiman, Abdelfattah Haidine, Ralf Lehnert, and Stefan Tuerk

Implementation and Evaluation of the Enhanced Header Compression (IPHC) for 6LoWPAN   168
  Alessandro Ludovici, Anna Calveras, Marisa Catalan, Carles Gómez, and Josep Paradells

Technical Session 7: Disruptive Technologies for Future Services

Primary Transmitter Discovery Based on Image Processing in Cognitive Radio 178
    Liliana Bolea, Jordi Pérez-Romero, Ramón Agustí, and Oriol Sallent

A Flexible Framework for Complete Session Mobility and Its Implementation 188
    Marc Barisch, Jochen Kögel, and Sebastian Meier

A Model-Driven Approach for Telecommunications Network Services Definition 199
    Vanea Chiprianov, Yvon Kermarrec, and Patrick D. Alff

Technical Session 8: Traffic Analysis

Detecting Spam at the Network Level 208
    Anna Sperotto, Gert Vliek, Ramin Sadre, and Aiko Pras

Consistency Analysis of Network Traffic Repositories 217
    Elmer Lastdrager and Aiko Pras

Author Index 227

Quantifying the Uncertainty in Measurements for MBAC

Anne Nevin, Peder J. Emstad, Yuming Jiang, and Guoqiang Hu

Centre for Quantifiable Quality of Service in Communication Systems (Q2S)*,
Norwegian University of Science and Technology (NTNU), Trondheim, Norway
{anne.nevin,peder.emstad,yuming.jiang,guoqiang.hu}@q2s.ntnu.no

Abstract. In Measurement Based Admission Control (MBAC), the decision of accepting or rejecting a new flow is based on measurements of the current traffic situation. An in-depth understanding of the measurement error and its uncertainty is vital for the design of a robust MBAC. In this work, we study the measured parameters used by the MBAC and characterize their error. Our work differs significantly from previous work in that we find how the uncertainty in the measurements varies with the length of the observation window.

Keywords: MBAC, QoS, Measurements, Error, Uncertainty, Gaussian distribution.

1 Introduction

Measurement Based Admission Control (MBAC) has long been recognized as a promising solution for providing statistical Quality of Service(QoS) guarantees in packet switched networks. An MBAC does not require an *a priori* source characterization that in many cases may be difficult or impossible to attain. Instead, MBAC uses measurements to capture the behavior of existing flows and uses this information together with some coarse knowledge of a new flow, when making an admission decision for the requesting flow.

Consider a system where all parameters of the flows are known. Given the proper characteristics of a flow and the available bandwidth c, it is possible to determine the maximum average rate the system can handle and at the same time minimize the QoS violation such as loss/delay probability [1]. In the following this maximum average rate will be termed uc, where c denotes the total capacity of the system and u, which is a number between $[0,1]$ is a tuning parameter which varies with the flow characteristics. Using the simplest MBAC algorithm, the measured sum MBAC algorithm [2], a new arriving flow, with a bandwidth requirement ν, will be accepted by the MBAC if:

$$\hat{E}[R] + \nu \leq uc. \tag{1}$$

---

* "Centre for Quantifiable Quality of Service in Communication Systems, Centre of Excellence" appointed by The Research Council of Norway, funded by the Research Council, NTNU and UNINETT. http://www.q2s.ntnu.no

M. Oliver and S. Sallent (Eds.): EUNICE 2009, LNCS 5733, pp. 1–10, 2009.
© Springer-Verlag Berlin Heidelberg 2009

$\hat{E}[R]$ in (1) is the measured average rate which includes statistical error [3]. Though much research has been done on determining uc and an overview can be found from [2] and [4], less attention has been given to the added uncertainty due to the measurement process. This measurement error may cause a flow to be accepted in error which again may cause increased QoS violation beyond what is actually predicted by the MBAC algorithm. Thus, an in-depth understanding of the measurements themselves and how they are affected by the underlying traffic is vital for the design of a robust MBAC. Particularly, measurements are improved when they are taken over longer intervals. However, flows generally only stay in the system for a limited time. There is a tradeoff between the accuracy and the validity of measurements. We state the question: How long do we need to measure in order to accept a flow with a certain degree of accuracy? The issue of measurement error exists naturally in all MBAC schemes, which makes the question even more appealing.

The objective of this paper is to quantify the uncertainty of measurement and provide answer to the question. In the study, both correlation characteristics of flows and flow dynamics will be taken into account A proper setting of the length of the measurement period has been of general concern in the MBAC literature. Based on simulations, the only conclusion that can be drawn is that different settings are needed for different traffic scenarios. A deeper analytical understanding of the measurement process and its error has been sought in [5] and [6]. Our work differs significantly from previous work in that we find how the uncertainty in the measurements vary with the length of the observation window.

The reminder of the paper is organized as follows. In the next section, the system model with assumptions and a framework considering flow arrivals and departures is given. Then follows the method of obtaining the measurements in Section 3 before the estimation error is treated in detail in Section 4. Section 5 presents an analytical evaluation before the conclusion is given in Section 6.

2   System Model, Assumptions and Performance Measures

Flows compete for a limited resource, which is a link with capacity c controlled by the MBAC that makes its admission decision based on the average aggregate rate of admitted flows (1). The flows, link and MBAC together form the system.

At the rate level, it is assumed that each flow is a stationary rate process $X_i(t)$ described by its mean and auto covariance function and that these are known parameters. All flows are independent such that the aggregate rate $R(t) = \sum_{i=1}^{n} X_i(t)$. A mixing of flow classes will cause increased complexity for the MBAC algorithm and also the measurement process. To simplify, only the homogenous case where flows belong to the same class will be considered. With the knowledge of the mean aggregate rate of the individual flows ξ, the current average aggregate rate can be specified by the current number of flows. The maximum number of flows the system can handle is thus $n_{max} = uc/\xi$.

At the flow level the system is dynamic in the sense that flows arrive and leave after some time. It is assumed that new flows arrive according to a Poisson process with parameter λ. The number of flows in progress can then be regulated by varying the flow arrival rate and/or flow lifetime. The offered traffic at flow level is the Erlang load denoted by A. With the arrival rate of new flows λ and the expected flow lifetime $E(T_L)$, A in terms of number of flows is then given by:

$$A = \lambda \cdot E(T_L). \tag{2}$$

To be able to see the effect of flow dynamics on measurement error, we define a framework at flow level similar to what is in [7]. A new arriving flow will be accepted by the MBAC with probability q_i in state i, where i is the number of flows in the system. It is assumed that new flows arrive according to a Poisson process with mean $1/\lambda$, and that the flow lifetime T_L, also a Poisson process, has mean $1/\mu$.

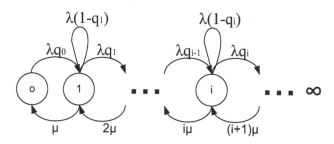

Fig. 1. State diagram of the number of sources accepted by the MBAC

Then the number of flows currently accepted by the MBAC follows a continuous-time Markov chain, see Fig. 1 and the probability, $P(i)$ of having $N = i$ flows in the system is:

$$P(i) = \frac{\frac{A^i}{i!} \prod_{x=0}^{i-1} q_x}{\sum_{j=0}^{\infty} \frac{A^j}{j!} \prod_{x=0}^{j-1} q_x}. \tag{3}$$

Implied by (3) and as also discussed in [7], the distribution $P(i)$ is indeed insensitive to the distribution of flow lifetime and only depends on the expected flow lifetime.

Upon the arrival of a flow, the decision process will make a correct or wrong admission decision. From a flow point of view, the performance measures related to the decision process are stated:

- **Probability of false acceptance, denoted by** P_{FAcc}, is defined as the probability of accepting a flow when it should have been rejected.
- **Probability of false rejections, denoted by** P_{FRej}, is defined as the probability of rejecting a flow when it should have been accepted.
- **Blocking Probability, denoted by** P_B, is the overall blocking probability.

With the continuous-time Markov system defined above, analytical expressions become:

$$P_{FAcc} = \sum_{i=n_{max}}^{\infty} P(i) \cdot q_i, \; P_{FRej} = \sum_{i=1}^{n_{max}-1} P(i) \cdot (1-q_i), \; P_B = \sum_{i=1}^{\infty}(1-q_i)P(i).$$

The q_is are yet to be determined and the reminder of the paper will give a deep insight into how the probability of accepting the requesting flow, i.e. q_i, is determined by the measurements. The way we shall use in determining q_i, where correlation between samples and the measurement errors are included, makes our framework significantly different from the work in [7].

3   Measurement Process

In this section, the method of obtaining the measured statistics will be given. The individual flow rate process $X(t)$ is observed every time slot Δ, where X_i is the observation at the end of time slot i. A measurement window w, consists of m observations of the process, $w = m\Delta$. (See Fig. 2, where $R_t = \sum_i^n X_i(t)$)

The rate process has mean ξ and is assumed to be covariance stationary with covariance function $\rho(h)$:

$$\begin{aligned}\rho(h) &= cov(X_i, X_{i+h}) \\ &= E\{(X_i - E[X_i])(X_{h+i} - E[X_{h+i}])\} \\ &= E(X_i X_{h+i}) - \xi^2.\end{aligned} \quad (4)$$

3.1   Measurement Method 1: Equidistant Sampling

An instant measurement of the rate $X(t)$ is taken at every $t = \Delta i$. X_i is the measured rate at the end of time slot i given by $X_i = X(t_i)$. The measured sample $X = X_1, X_2, ..., X_m$ will be identically distributed but correlated observations, where the X_is have a sample mean, $\bar{X}$ given by

$$\bar{X} = \frac{1}{m} \sum_{i=1}^{m} X_i. \quad (5)$$

A general expression for the variance of $\bar{X}$, $Var(\bar{X})$, is given by [8]:

$$\begin{aligned}Var(\bar{X}) &= E[(\bar{X} - \xi)^2)] \\ &= \frac{1}{m^2} \sum_{i=1}^{m} \sum_{j=1}^{m} E[(X_i - \xi)(X_j - \xi)],\end{aligned} \quad (6)$$

and with a covariance stationary process:

$$Var(\bar{X}) = \frac{1}{m^2} \sum_{h=1-m}^{m-1} (m- \mid h \mid)\rho(h). \quad (7)$$

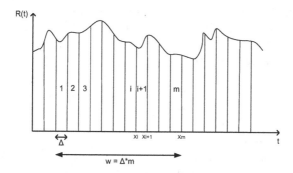

Fig. 2. Aggregate rate R(t) vs time

3.2   Measurement Method 2: Continuous Observation

The average rate over the window can also be found by continuous observation by letting the sampling rate go towards infinity. In practical sense this can be done by observing the time of change between busy and idle state on the incoming links. Let now $\Delta \to 0$ and $m \to \infty$ keeping the product $m\Delta$ constant such that $t_i = i\Delta \Rightarrow t$ then:

$$\bar{X} = \frac{1}{m}\sum_{i=1}^{m} X_i \Rightarrow \lim_{\Delta \to 0 | w = m\Delta} \frac{1}{m}\sum_{i=1}^{m} X_i = \frac{1}{w}\int_0^w R(t)dt. \tag{8}$$

Using limit considerations known from the literature, the time variance of the sample mean, $\zeta^2(w)$ can be found:

$$\zeta^2(w) = \lim_{\Delta \to 0 | w = m\Delta} Var(\bar{X})$$

$$= \lim_{\Delta \to 0 | w = m\Delta} (\frac{\Delta}{w})^2 \sum_{i=1-m}^{m-1} (m - |i|)\rho(t_i)$$

$$= \frac{1}{w^2}\int_{-w}^{w} (w - |t|)\rho(t)dt$$

$$= \frac{2}{w^2}\int_0^w (w - t)\rho(t)dt. \tag{9}$$

Note that $\zeta^2(w)$ only depends on the window size and the auto-covariance function $\rho(t)$.

4   Estimation Error

In the following a detailed analysis of the estimation error will be presented to give an in-depth understanding of the accuracy of the measurement. A new flow is accepted based on measurements over a complete measurement window w and we will assume that flows do not leave during this window. Each flow has a rate process $X_i(t)$ with mean ξ. The variance of the measured average rate of the flow rate process, $\zeta^2(w)$, given by (9), decreases as the window size increases.

With $N = n$ flows in the system,

$$Y = \sum_{i=1}^{n} \frac{1}{w} \int_0^w X_i(t),$$

is an estimator of the aggregate mean $n\xi$. According to the MBAC algorithm, (1) as long as $Y \leq \xi n_{max} - \nu$ a new flow will be admitted. When $N = n_{max}$, additional flows should be rejected but due to measurement error, underestimation of the aggregate rate will cause a flow to be admitted erroneously and constitutes a false acceptance. The probability of false acceptance for a flow P_{FAcc} depends on the state probabilities and thus requires the inclusion of the reference system defined in Section 2. Here we will only consider a static system remaining in state n_{max} excluding the impact of flow dynamics. The requirement is to keep the probability of a false acceptance in state n_{max} below a performance target value ε where typically $\varepsilon = 0.05$. Conditioning on being in the state n_{max} the conditional performance target can be written:

$$P(Y + \nu \leq \xi n_{max} \mid N = n_{max}) \leq \varepsilon. \tag{10}$$

The probability of underestimating the aggregate mean increase as the measurement window size decreases. Because the measurement window size in general is very limited, it may be impossible to meet the required performance target given in (10). To cope with this problem, we reduce the maximum allowable bandwidth ξn_{max} by a number of levels l of size ξ, such that a new flow will only be accepted if:

$$Y + \nu \leq \xi n_{max} - l\xi , \quad l = 0, 1, ... n_{max}. \tag{11}$$

Dividing the bandwidth $n_{max}\xi$ evenly between the flows, $\nu = \xi$ and the performance requirement is rewritten:

$$P(Y + \xi \leq \xi n_{max} - l\xi \mid N = n_{max}) \leq \varepsilon , \quad l = 0, 1, ... n_{max}. \tag{12}$$

The task is now to determine l. This requires the distribution of Y which can be found analytically for some simple sources. When the number of flows is large (say $n > 30$), the sum of the time averages of the flows will be close to a normal distribution thus $Y \sim N(n\xi, n\zeta^2(w))$. Conditioned on being in state $N = n_{max}$ we have that:

$$\left(\frac{Y - \xi n_{max}}{\sqrt{n_{max}}\zeta(w)} \leq z_\varepsilon \right) = 1 - \varepsilon, \tag{13}$$

where z_ε is the $\varepsilon - quantile$, $F_z(z_\varepsilon) = 1 - \varepsilon$. Rearranging the terms gives:

$$P(Y \leq \xi n_{max} + \sqrt{n_{max}}\zeta(w)z_\varepsilon) = 1 - \varepsilon. \tag{14}$$

and due to symmetry in the normal distribution:

$$P(Y \leq \xi n_{max} - \sqrt{n_{max}}\zeta(w)z_\varepsilon) = \varepsilon. \tag{15}$$

Comparing (15) and (12), the performance target (10) will be met if l and $\zeta(w)$ satisfy:

$$\xi(l+1) = \sqrt{n_{max}}\zeta(w)z_\varepsilon. \tag{16}$$

Since l is an integer, the requirement can be expressed:

$$l+1 = \left\lceil \frac{\sqrt{n_{max}}\zeta(w)z_\varepsilon}{\xi} \right\rceil. \tag{17}$$

For a given quantile and known $\zeta(w)$, this equation determines the required number of levels l in the refined admission control algorithm (11).

With the introduction of levels, there will be a region between n_{max} and $n_{max} - l$ where a flow may be admitted in error according to the condition given in (11) but will not necessarily be a false acceptance as defined in Section 2. We define the region between n_{max} and $n_{max} - l$ the critical region and we define a Hazardous Admission to be the act of admitting a flow when the number of accepted flows is above $n_{max} - l$ (See Fig. 3.).

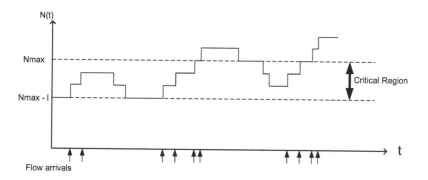

Fig. 3. Illustration of the critical region

Note again that (12) gives the probability of false acceptance conditioned on the system being in state $N = n_{max}$. The probability of false acceptance for a flow P_{FAcc} can only be found using the reference system defined in Section 2. With the assumption of $Y \sim N(n\xi, n\zeta^2(w))$ and $\nu = \xi$, the conditional accepting probability q_i required in the reference system is written as:

$$q_i = P(Y \leq uc - (l+1)\xi \mid N = i)$$
$$= \frac{1}{\zeta(w)\sqrt{2\pi i}} \int_{-\infty}^{uc-(l+1)\xi} e^{-\frac{(x-i\xi)^2}{2i\zeta^2(w)}} dx, \tag{18}$$

A study of the reference system will be addressed in a separate work where also dependence of the q_is at arrival is discussed.

5   Case Study Using the MMRP Source Model

In the following all flows belong to the same class and are of type Markov modulated rate process (MMRP), which is a process $X(t) = rI(t)$ where $I(t)$ alternates between states $I = 0$ and $I = 1$. The duration of the 0 and 1 states follow a negative exponential distribution with mean $1/\alpha$ and $1/\beta$ respectively. Each flow is sampled by means of continuous observation. The auto-covariance of the MMRP process is given by:

$$cov(X_i, X_{i+\tau}) = \frac{r^2 \alpha \beta}{(\alpha + \beta)^2} e^{-\tau(\alpha+\beta)}. \tag{19}$$

Using (9) the expression for the variance of the sample mean is given by:

$$\zeta^2(w) = var(\bar{X}) = \frac{2}{w^2} \int_0^w (w - t)\rho(t)dt$$
$$= \frac{2r^2 \alpha \beta}{w^2(\alpha + \beta)^3} \left(w - \frac{1}{\alpha + \beta}(1 - e^{-w(\alpha+\beta)}) \right). \tag{20}$$

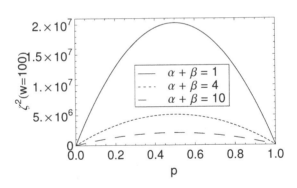

Fig. 4. Variance of sample mean as a function of p

$\zeta^2(w)$ approaches 0 as the window size increases. How quickly it tends to zero, depends on the sum $\alpha+\beta$ and also the relative difference between α and β. Processes with long time constants ($\alpha + \beta$ small) increase the value of $\zeta^2(w)$ resulting in less accuracy. The burstiness of the sources can be described by the activity parameter $p = \frac{\alpha}{\alpha+\beta}$. Keeping $\alpha+\beta$ constant, $\zeta^2(w)$ reaches its maximum value when $p = 0.5$. This is shown in Fig. 4 for a window size of 100s.

With the knowledge of the variance of the sample mean we now turn to a discussion of the accepting probability given that the system is in state n_{max}.

Accepting a flow in this state is considered an error and a false acceptance. To emphasize the state-dependency, this error probability is termed $q_{n_{max}}$. It can be seen from (17), that with a given confidence level and l fixed, the required window size will depend on the values of α and β. As α and β increase, the required window size or critical region can be reduced. Also as the activity parameter p approaches one a more accurate decision can be made.

As n_{max} increases, the impact of one single flow on the aggregate will be reduced. This causes again an increase in $q_{n_{max}}$ as the difference between n_{max} and $n_{max} + 1$ becomes more and more negligible. To state this another way, the size of the critical region must be increased when the aggregation level goes up to keep the level of confidence at a certain value.

To check (17) we run a simple simulation with $n_{max} = 50$ flows with mean rate $\xi = 32000 bps$. An admission decision is made based on measurements of a complete measurement window. With $l = 1$, Fig. 5 shows how $q_{n_{max}}$ is reduced as the window size is increased. The simulated results follow closely what is theoretically predicted.

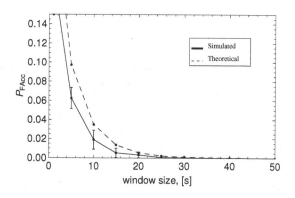

Fig. 5. Conditional probability of false acceptance in state n_{max}

6   Conclusion

Measurement error is a critical aspect in measurement-based research [9]. However, there is in the literature of MBAC, unfortunately very limited work focusing on the impact of this error. An MBAC algorithm no matter how advanced, will be of little use if the measured parameters used by this algorithm include error of unknown quantity. This error causes uncertainty in the decision process and the degree of uncertainty abates with the length of the observation window. In this paper we have set up an analytical framework to analyze the measurement error. With analytical tractable sources with known covariance function, we are able to state the uncertainty of the decision process up front.

If on the other hand the covariance of the sources is unknown it must also be measured. Our work in progress extends this study to situations with only partial knowledge of the auto-covariance function. This work also includes the analysis of non-homogeneous flows.

The framework defined in this paper, considers the flow dynamics such that the influence of flow arrival and departure can be studied. A separate work will discuss this in more detail where attention also will be given to the effect of correlation at arrival points causing a cascade of false admissions. If the number of flows remains constant, increasing the window size will only improve performance. However, in reality this is not the case since flows may leave within a measurement window. Measuring too long will cause the number of connection to be changing at a rate causing instability in the measurements. With the help of simulations, errors not explained by the above reference system, can be revealed to get a more complete picture of the estimation errors. This current work sheds light on a more in-depth understanding of how measurement uncertainties and flow dynamics impact the admission decision in MBAC.

Acknowledgments. The helpful comments from anonymous referees are highly appreciated.

References

1. Knightly, E.W., Shroff, N.B.: Admission control for statistical QoS: Theory and practice. IEEE Network, 20–29 (March/April 1999)
2. Breslau, L., Jamin, S., Shenker, S.: Comments on the performance of measurement-based admission control algorithms. In: IEEE INFOCOM (2000)
3. Grossglauser, M., Tse, D.N.C.: A framework for robust measurement-based admission control. IEEE/ACM Trans. Networking 7(3), 293–309 (1999)
4. Moore, A.W.: Measurement-based management of network resources. Technical report, University of Cambridg, Cambridge CB3 OFD, United Kingdom (April 2002)
5. Grossglauser, M., Tse, D.N.C.: A time-scale decomposition approach to measurement-based admission control. IEEE/ACM Trans. Networking 11(4), 550–563 (2003)
6. Dziong, Z., Juda, M., Mason, L.G.: A framework for bandwidth management in ATM networks - aggregate equivalent bandwidth estimation approach. IEEE/ACM Trans. Networking 5(1), 134–147 (1997)
7. Key, P.B., Gibbens, R.J., Kelly, F.P.: A decision-theoretic approach to call admission control in atm networks. IEEE Journal on Selected Areas in Communications (JSAC) 13(6), 1101–1114 (1995)
8. Brockwell, P.J., Davis, R.A. (eds.): Introduction to Time Series and Forecasting, 2nd edn. Springer, Heidelberg (2002)
9. Krishnamurthy, B., Willinger, W.: What are our standards for validation of measurement-based networking research? Performance Evaluation Review 36(2), 64–68 (2008)

Ring Flushing for Reduced Overload in Spanning Tree Protocol Controlled Ethernet Networks

Dániel Horváth, Gábor Kapitány, Sándor Plósz, István Moldován,
and Csaba Lukovszki

Dept. of Telecommunications and Media Informatics
Budapest University of Technology and Economics
Budapest, Hungary
{horvathd,kapitanyg,plosz,moldovan,lukovszki}@tmit.bme.hu

Abstract. Flooding causes serious problems to the scalability of Ethernet networks. Recent proposals to overcome this problem, such as SEATTLE [5], usually require significant changes in different network layers, making the realistic chance of their deployment questionable. In this paper, we propose Ring Flushing, a practical method to reduce the burden of flooding during topology changes. The basic idea behind our approach is to locate stale forwarding information in an efficient way. Ring Flushing abolishes the broadcast-like spreading of topology change information thus shrinking the flushing domain. We implemented Ring Flushing in OMNeT++ simulation environment and evaluated its performance in different topologies and parameter settings. Our simulations show that the Ring Flushing has clear advantage over the approach of standard Rapid Spanning Tree Protocol (RSTP) in terms of throughput during network recovery. Furthermore, the Ring Flushing diminishes overall network overload during topology changes as the network size increases.

Keywords: ring flushing, flooding, spanning trees, rstp, Ethernet.

1 Introduction

The Ethernet became dominant technology in wired local area networks during the last two decades. This trend is supported by the development of new related standards. Ethernet has many advantages making it an appealing candidate in flat and homogeneously managed networks, such as Metropolitan Area Networks. The popularity of Ethernet technology resides in its low cost, ubiquity and easy management, without the need of error-prone manual configuration. A network topology is formed by connecting devices called bridges or switches.

The frame forwarding model in Ethernet did not change as the technology evolved; each bridge has a unique identifier called Media Access Control (MAC) address, used to address the device. The bridges have to learn the MAC addresses of the hosts and end devices in the network. Upon frame arrival a bridge stores the frame source address in conjunction with a timer and the port number the frame has arrived on, in a table called the Forwarding Database (FDB). Bridges rely only on

M. Oliver and S. Sallent (Eds.): EUNICE 2009, LNCS 5733, pp. 11–20, 2009.
© Springer-Verlag Berlin Heidelberg 2009

the FDB at forwarding incoming frames. If the bridge has no information about the destination yet stored, it floods frames causing partially unnecessary traffic.

The purpose of the spanning tree protocols is to exclude redundant links from the active topology, which can otherwise form loops in the network. They construct one or more spanning trees in the network with a distributed algorithm. The elimination of loops is vital because the forwarding of frames is based on flooding and the lack of Time-to-Live field in the Ethernet header can cause the frames to remain in the network thereby congesting it. The Rapid Spanning Tree Protocol (RSTP) [1] is the most applied spanning tree protocol.

By the usage of a spanning tree protocol on Ethernet level the scope of this technology extends tremendously getting acceptance in more demanding networks, like backbone networks, where speed, reliability and easy manageability are primary requirements. The spanning tree protocols fulfill these requirements while keeping the benefits of the plain-old Ethernet technology. Drawbacks of such plain and well-distributed technology reveals while examining its capabilities in terms of scalability.

The classical Ethernet has several drawbacks. First of all, it does not forward traffic on the shortest path because of the use of a spanning tree (e.g. RSTP). This causes poor load balancing and inefficient resource usage. There are existing solutions for this problem, like Multiple Spanning Tree Protocol (MSTP) [2], Shortest Path Bridging [3] and Spanning Tree Alternate Routing (STAR) [4]. The other main problem with Ethernet is the scalability. The scalability of Ethernet is severely affected by the high number of broadcasts necessary for its operation. Kim et al. also considers scalability as the biggest problem of the Ethernet technology [5]. Proposals were made to eliminate spanning trees by applying link-state based algorithm instead of distance-vector algorithm, like CMU-Ethernet by Myers et al. [6].

To overcome the scalability shortage of Ethernet, service providers split the network to subnets by IP routers. By doing this efficiency increases because of the smaller broadcast domains and more optimal paths, on the other hand, the need for manual configuration arises. This approach does not solve the main disadvantage of Ethernet, simply avoids it. The flooding in Ethernet was also targeted by several papers in the recent literature. R. Perlman developed the Rbridges, a method of interconnecting links that combines the advantages of bridging and routing [7]. Moreover, the Scalable Ethernet Architecture for Large Enterprises (SEATTLE) network architecture by Kim et al. learns MAC addresses only on edge ports improving control plane scalability [5].

The main cause of flooding is the flushing of FDBs after a network failure. The solution for flooding applied in the original RSTP and MSTP standards is not optimal since it causes a large amount of unnecessary traffic on the network by flushing the FDBs of every bridge. This paper introduces Ring Flushing, which has a novel approach to flush ports containing stale entries only. In Ring Flushing the topology change information is propagated as unicast and not flooded. Moreover ports of a bridge are selectively flushed.

The paper is structured as follows. In Section 2, the RSTP is introduced, and its inefficiency problem is explained. In Section 3, we present our solution, the Ring Flushing Method. Simulation analysis and validation is shown in Section 4. Finally, in the Section 5, the paper is concluded.

2 Inefficient Address Removal of RSTP

The RSTP builds an overlay tree of the bridges in the network rooted at a bridge, called Root Bridge. The port roles calculations in the network are distributed. Each port providing the shortest path towards the Root Bridge is set to be Root Port. Each port of a bridge which provides the shortest path towards the attached LAN segment is elected to be a Designated Port. The roles of the rest ports are set to Alternate role.

The spanning tree protocols use link-local frames called Bridge Protocol Data Units (BPDU) to spread information to each bridge in the network.

Port state is assigned to each port besides port role on bridges. The Root Port and the Designated Ports are in forwarding state while the Alternate Ports are in discarding state in a stable topology. The forwarding ports transmit and receive all frames while discarding ports transmit and receive only BPDUs [1,9] thus pruning the network to a simple tree topology.

The most significant drawback of the spanning tree protocols is the inefficient address removal. The learnt addresses can be removed from the FDB via aging or flushing. Each entry in the FDB has an age attribute. An entry is removed on timeout unless its age is renewed by an ingress frame with the same source MAC address. This is called aging. Flush may be invoked on a bridge by RSTP after a change in the physical topology.

The current version of these protocols use a 1-bit flag called Topology Change (TC) bit to indicate the start of flushing. A BPDU with TC-bit set is called TC message. On reception of a BPDU the TC flag is polled. If it is set then all ports are flushed except the one which received the BPDU and those ports to where one end-device is attached only. The flush initiates a re-learning period. During the re-learning period all the devices forward packet by flooding therefore multiplying the traffic on the network. This is severely inefficient. The bigger the network the bigger the overload will be on certain links depending on the topology. These links can be overloaded, unable to transfer all data, resulting in packet losses. At present it is a major problem of Ethernet which diminishes its scalability.

3 Our Proposed Solution: The Ring Flushing Method

We start with a motivational example. In a topology which is redundant enough to remain connected after a topology change a ring can be identified where all the stale forwarding information reside. The idea is illustrated by an example topology in Fig. 1. The squares symbolize the bridges. The Root Bridge is marked with R. The cross indicates a failure of a link. The ports represented in grey indicate the old forwarding information to be stale. The out-dated forwarding information can be located easily. It resides in the ring defined by the recently failed link and the link which has become part of the active topology and the links connecting them in both directions. As a result, locating the stale information in an effective way would reduce unnecessarily flooding of messages. Any other possible end device attached to this topology would also have had stale forwarding information in this ring only. This ring always exists because the newly activated link has not been part of the previous topology.

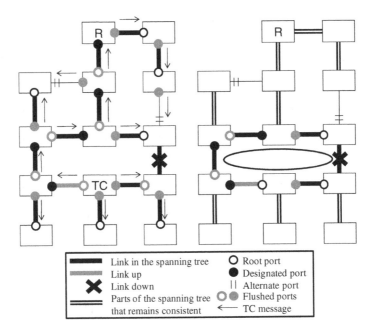

Fig. 1. Flushed ports by the standard flushing method are shown on the left figure. The ports that are needed to be flushed reside along a ring identified by the recently inactivated and activated links.

We state that bridges along the ring are affected by the change only. Indirectly, suppose a bridge which is not in the ring has at least one stale forwarding entry. Suppose also that there is no link state change outside the ring. There are two kinds of ports on bridges which are not part of the ring: ones which forward frames towards the broken link, and the ones which forward frames in the opposite direction. The forwarding entries in the port of the first kind can point to a destination whose path is changed. The path of the entries, whose destination's reachability is changed, traverses a part of the ring. The ring contains the old and the new path to that destination therefore the entries are valid. The forwarding entries of the port of the second kind are always point to a destination whose path has not changed. Therefore these entries are valid also. Then all entries are valid, which is a contradiction therefore implying that the considered bridge should have been the part of the ring..

Even in the ring not all entries in the FDB are needed to be deleted. The stale forwarding information is present in ports which are in the direction of the failed link in the original spanning tree. Therefore only this subset of the ports on the ring should be flushed, which can be seen on the right side of Fig. 1. The standard flushing method is presented on the left side. The number of ports unnecessarily affected by the standard ring flushing can be seen in this example network in Fig. 1.

3.1 How It Works

As illustrated above, the basic idea of our approach is the efficient removal of the entries. The current standard prescribes the removal of all entries with some exceptions whose validity can be verified by rules. These rules are not fully comprehensive. The standard leaves the ports untouched by the flush, which receives the TC message and the ones to which only an end-station is attached. Our approach is to remove the stale entries only by isolating the affected part of the topology. We introduce the notation Branching Bridge for the closest bridge to the Root Bridge on the ring defined by the link-down and the link-up event. If the Root Bridge resides in the ring then the Root Bridge is the Branching Bridge. Three sectors of the ring can be distinguished. Each sector is an alternating series of bridges and links which starts and ends with a bridge {bridge$_a$, link$_{ab}$, bridge$_b$ ... bridge$_m$, link$_{mn}$, bridge$_n$}. Every link in these series is part of the active topology. The sectors of the ring in the example and the relevant port roles in the final topology are shown in Fig. 2.

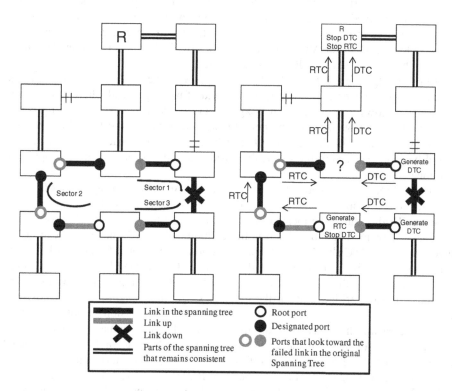

Fig. 2. The three sectors of the ring are shown in the left figure and the spreading of the RTC and DTC messages in the Ring Flushing implementation is presented in the right figure

The first sector is the path from the bridge having a link which is recently inactivated, to the Branching Bridge. It does not contain the newly enabled link. In this sector only Designated Ports should be flushed. The second sector starts at a bridge which has a forwarding port that has been discarding before the topology change and ends at a bridge which has the Branching Bridge as its Designated Bridge. In this sector, only Root Ports should be flushed. At last, the third sector is between the recently inactivated and activated links. In this sector, only Designated Ports should be flushed.

A sector of a ring may contain one bridge only. Nor the second nor the third sector contains the Branching Bridge. The second and the third sectors may overlap in their first and last bridge, respectively. The newly inactivated and activated ports do not need explicit flushing. The newly inactivated ones are flushed anyway at inactivation time, and the newly activated ones do not contain any entries.

3.2 Practical Issues on Implementation

Port table flushing is needed only on the ring. Additional control messages are required in order to flush the appropriate port tables. We define Root Topology Change (RTC) and Designated Topology Change (DTC) messages. These are handled the following way. A bridge receiving either an RTC or a DTC propagates it on its Root Port. If the received message is a DTC then the port table of the receiver port is flushed. The role of the receiver port is always Designated because the sender port is always a Root Port or an Alternate Port. Further on, if the message is an RTC message then the port table of the Root Port is flushed.

With the help of the RTC and DTC messages, and the definitions of the sectors, one can easily see, where to generate which kind of messages, and where to terminate them. Fig. 2 shows that one RTC message should be generated at the link-up event, and should be propagated until the penultimate bridge before the Branching Bridge. Two DTC message should be generated at both side of the inactivated link. Either should be propagated until the Branching Bridge and the other should be propagated until the end of the third sector.

One DTC message is needed to traverse until the Branching Bridge, one RTC message should be terminated at a neighbor of the Branching Bridge. However, the Branching Bridge cannot be located in topology change time, where a DTC should be terminated. Nor its neighbor, which is the endpoint of the second sector, can be located, where the RTC should be terminated. A bridge could only find out of being the Branching Bridge if received both an RTC and a DTC message from different directions. It is unlikely that these messages met in the Branching Bridge. Without the demand to make a bridge wait for the other message this recognition is not possible. Applying timer however would only slow down the transmission in both directions thereby increasing the delay without any gain. The flushing domain is therefore extended to the path between the Branching Bridge and the Root Bridge. The Root Bridge does not have Root Port therefore these messages are terminated there. The RTC and DTC messages traversing to the Root Bridge are presented on Fig. 2.

The flushing domain is a set of bridges which have to flush at least one port table. The flushing domain of the RSTP is by definition the whole topology except when the topology got partitioned during the topology change. The flushing domain of Ring Flushing is the ring and the path between the Branching Bridge and the Root Bridge.

The advanced removal is enabled by the existing 2-bit TC flag of the Bridge Protocol Data Unit (BPDU) headers. We use the TCAck flag of the BPDU header as well which is unused by RSTP. One of the 2-bit flag indicates RTC and the other indicates DTC. Setting both bits is possible which makes the receiver bridge behave like it received an RTC and DTC message independently. No additional fields required in the BPDU header but kept for compatibility with STP, therefore the size of the BPDUs remains the same.

RTC and DTC messages are triggered by network events. Transitions between RSTP port states initiate the RTC and DTC message by means of the following rules. A bridge that has a Discarding Port changing to Forwarding transmits an RTC message on its (new) Root Port. A bridge losing its Forwarding Port transmits a DTC message on its (new) Root Port.

The proposal-agreement mechanism temporarily sets some forwarding ports to discarding and later back to forwarding. This causes a lot of unnecessary DTC and RTC messages unless we detect and bypass these in the Ring Flushing algorithm.

We were intent on minimizing the modification needed on the implementation advocated by the standard thereby contributing to the easy integration of our method into existing architectures.

4 Performance Evaluation

In order to be able to measure the performance of RSTP protocol, we implemented it in a simulation environment following the standards. Measurements of properties of real devices like PDU construction and processing times were added to authenticate our simulator. To verify its proper operation several scenarios were worked out to deploy the simulator against real networks. These protocols are deterministic besides some exceptional transient behavior hence allowing mathematical verification in simple scenarios. Ring Flushing method has been added in the RSTP implementation followed by verification. The simulations are implemented in the OMNeT++ environment [8].

We implemented an MSTP module and used existing modules slightly modified to create an Ethernet based bridge. Interconnecting these bridges and a number of hosts we could easily measure differences between the standard and our proposal. The simulation scenario presented in this paper uses the following properties.

- Traffic:
  - Packet size is 1500 byte (including all headers)
  - Packet transition frequency is 0.01s
  - Each Host communicate with one other host

- Delays:
  - Each bridge has a BPDU construction time which is uniformly distributed between 0.1ms and 1ms
  - Each bridge has a BPDU processing time which is uniformly distributed between 1ms and 10ms

- Other RSTP specific settings are set to default according to 802.1D

An example network we used during investigation consists of a main circle (link 1, 2, 15, 19) and sub trees that connect to this circle. The left side of Fig. 3. shows the spanning tree (thick line), the link failure (cross on a line), the new link (grey thick line), as well as ports flushed. The standard flushes ports marked with black or grey. Flushing of all these ports is not necessary. The black ports are flushed unnecessarily. The Ring Flushing removes entries only in the ports marked with grey. In this scenario, each bridge has one host attached that sends traffic into the network.

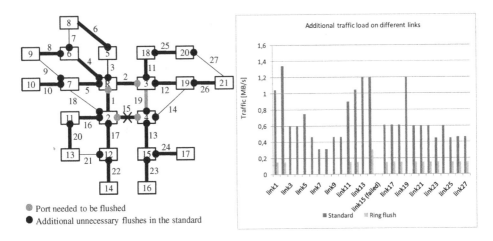

Fig. 3. An example network can be seen on the left. On the right the overhead caused by the flooded traffic is shown during re-learning which is smaller when Ring Flushing is used.

The right side of Fig. 3. shows the overhead of the traffic caused by flooding in each link after the failure. It can be seen that the less port flushed the less the traffic overhead will occur during the relearning period. In this example, most of the traffic avoids the main circle, which gives reason for the big difference of the amount of flooded traffic during the relearning period.

Fig. 4. An example topology of inner circle of 6 bridges and outer circles of 5 bridges. This means an additional 3 bridges per outer circles, and a total of $6 + 3 \times 6 = 24$.

Additionally a topology was investigated which had an inner circle, shown as a dashed circle in Fig. 4., and several outer circles, indicated with solid circles, connected to the inner circle. Simulations were made with different number of bridges. Each bridge has one host that sent traffic to the Root Bridge which is located in the inner circle. Each host transmitted traffic at a constant rate. We measured the peak value of the traffic load on each link after the failure. The network traffic is the sum of the link loads at a given time instant. We compared the peak value of the network load to the constant value of the network load after the relearning period.

Table 1. The simulation results shows diminishing of overhead during broadcast storm

Traffic load comparison: inner-outer ring topology				
Number of bridges			Additional traffic load on network	
In the inner circle	Per outer circle	total	Standard flushing	Ring flushing
3	1	6	64%	43%
3	2	9	48%	16%
4	3	16	50%	31%
5	4	25	60%	13%
6	5	36	50%	11%
7	6	49	55%	4%
8	7	64	67%	9%
9	8	81	69%	1%
10	9	100	67%	1%

For example when the traffic load on the network is 320Mbps before link failure, 600Mbps the peak value, and 400Mbps after the relearning then the additional traffic load on the network is (600-400) / 400 × 100%= 50%. The mean values of the additional traffic load of 30 simulations are presented in Table 1. As can be seen, using the Ring Flushing method the traffic overload caused by flooding diminishes in each scenario. Increasing the number of bridges in the network the standard solution greatly overloads the network, while Ring Flushing decreases the overload.

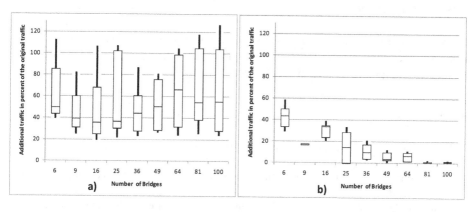

a)   Number of Bridges

b)   Number of Bridges

Fig. 5. The simulation results for 30 runs with different random delays. a) shows the maximum traffic load on the network during the relearning period using the standard method. b) shows the maximum traffic load on the network during the relearning period using the Ring Flushing method.

The results of simulations can be compared in Fig. 5. Thirty simulations were made for the standard method (shown on the left side), and for the ring flushing method (shown on the right side) for each size of the network. The box-plots show the 10 percentiles, first quartiles, the medians, the third quartiles and the 90 percentiles of the maximum traffic overload during relearning period. The median values of the standard method (50%, 39%, 35%, 37%, 44%, 50%, 66%, 54% and 55%) do not have obvious trend and are approximately constant. The values for the Ring Flushing method (43%, 16%, 33%, 11%, 10%, 1%, 6%, 1% and 1%) show a downtrend with the increasing network size, therefore the burden of the traffic overload diminishes.

To summarize, the standard method operates with the same efficiency usually generating flood of more than 50% overhead. Meanwhile, the efficiency of Ring Flushing method is increasing with the increasing size of the network because the flushing domain to whole network ratio diminishes causing proportionally less FDB entry removal. In larger networks more link will be unaffected by the relearning in the ring flush method, while in the standard, always all links are affected.

5 Conclusion

We presented Ring Flushing, a practical method for reduced overload in spanning tree controlled Ethernet networks. By keeping all the benefits of Ethernet while dealing locally with events previously considered to be network-wide, our proposal flushes fewer ports in most cases but still slightly more than necessary. We implemented the algorithm into OMNeT++ simulation environment to investigate the performance of our Ring Flushing algorithm. The presented results showed significant improvement over the approach of standard RSTP in different network topologies and parameter settings.

Acknowledgement

We would like to express gratitude to Ericsson Hungary Ltd. for supporting our work. Moreover, we would like to thank to the reviewers for their useful advices and comments which helped us to improve this paper.

References

1. IEEE Standard for Local and Metropolitan Area Networks: Media Access Control (MAC) Bridges, 802.1D (2004)
2. IEEE Standard for Local and Metropolitan Area Networks: Virtual Bridged Local Area Networks, 802.1Q (2005)
3. Virtual Bridged Local Area Networks — Amendment 9: Shortest Path Bridging, IEEE draft standard 802.1aq-D0.3 (2006)
4. Lui, K., Lee, W., Nahrstedt, N.: STAR: A Transparent Spanning Tree Bridge Protocol with Alternate Routing. ACM Sigcomm Computer Communications Review (2002)
5. Kim, Ch., Ceasar, M., Rexford, J.: Floodless in SEATTLE: A Scalable Ethernet Architecture for Large Enterprises. ACM SIGCOMM Computer Communication Review (2008)
6. Myers, A., Ng, T.S.E., Zhang, H.: Rethinking the Service Model: Scaling Ethernet to a Million Nodes. In: Proceedings of HotNets III (2004)
7. Perlman, R.: Rbridges: Transparent Routing. In: INFOCOM (2004)
8. OMNeT++ Community Site, http://www.omnetpp.org
9. Pallos, R., Farkas, J., Moldovan, I., Lukovszki, C.: Performance of rapid spanning tree protocol in access and metro networks. In: Access Networks & Workshops (2007)

A Distributed Exact Solution to Compute Inter-domain Multi-constrained Paths

Gilles Bertrand[1], Samer Lahoud[2], Géraldine Texier[1], and Miklós Molnár[3]

[1] Institut TELECOM, TELECOM Bretagne, RSM
{gilles.bertrand,geraldine.texier}@telecom-bretagne.eu
[2] IRISA - Université de Rennes 1
samer.lahoud@irisa.fr
[3] IRISA - INSA de Rennes
molnar@irisa.fr

Abstract. The fundamental Quality of Service (QoS) routing problem, which consists in determining paths subject to multiple QoS constraints, has been extensively investigated in the intra-domain context. However, few solutions exist for the inter-domain case, despite the importance of this problem to enable the delivery of services with QoS across domain boundaries. We propose a method that distributes the operations to compute inter-domain constrained paths. This method relies on a per-domain formulation that is compatible with the path computation element framework. It enables us to propose the first algorithm that guarantees to find optimal paths subject to an arbitrary number of constraints. These paths ensure the best QoS performance with respect to the constraints.

1 Introduction

The computation of constrained inter-domain paths is a highly investigated topic: it enables the operators to take control over the routing and facilitates the delivery of Quality of Service (QoS) across domain boundaries. Inter-domain applications typically impose constraints on several QoS metrics (for example, delay, jitter, packet losses). Nevertheless, computing the corresponding inter-domain paths subject to multiple QoS constraints has long been considered as impracticable because of the required communication overhead and because of confidentiality constraints. Thus, in the current Internet, inter-domain routing is based solely on basic connectivities and operator policies. However, recent initiatives propose connection-oriented solutions based on multiprotocol label switching to allow the computation of constrained inter-domain paths without breaking the confidentiality constraints of the domains [1]. In particular, the Path Computation Element (PCE) framework [2] enables the collaboration of multiple domains to setup inter-domain constrained paths.

The present paper investigates the problem of computing inter-domain Multi-constrained Paths (MCPs) in the PCE framework. As the MCP problem has many important applications, the literature describes several solutions for the *intra-domain* case [3, 4, 5, 6]. However, these solutions cannot be used to solve

M. Oliver and S. Sallent (Eds.): EUNICE 2009, LNCS 5733, pp. 21–30, 2009.
© Springer-Verlag Berlin Heidelberg 2009

the *inter-domain* MCP problem because they rely on centralized computations and break the confidentiality constraints of the domains. Alternatively, Saad and others [7] propose an approximate solution to the inter-domain MCP problem. Nevertheless, their study is limited to the problem with two constraints.

We analyze the required inter-domain information exchanges to solve the inter-domain MCP problem exactly. This study enables us to present a method to distribute the path computation. In particular, we describe a per-domain formulation that is compatible with the PCE framework. This formulation allows us to introduce the first solution that guarantees to find a path satisfying the considered QoS constraints if such a path exists in the network. Moreover, the computed paths are the furthest from the constraints, and thus, ensure the best resistance to changes in the QoS conditions.

The remainder of the paper is organized as follows. In Section 2, we present the requirements for inter-domain MCP computations and related work. The proposed path computation method is described in Section 3 and followed by a discussion on its performance in Section 4.

2   Background

2.1   Requirements for Inter-domain Path Computations

The Internet relies on the inter-connection of networks administrated by various network operators and called *domains*, as illustrated in Fig. 1. The domains interconnect through domain border routers, which exchange mainly connectivity information to preserve the scalability of the routing protocols.

The domains represent network operators, which are bound by competitive relationships. In particular, the operators preserve the confidentiality of their network state and topology. As a result, in every domain, only internal entities possess enough information about the network state of the domain to allow the computation of constrained paths inside this domain. Moreover, the domains (*e.g.*, BGP autonomous systems) have a wide autonomy. To summarize, there is no central coordination entity with global state and topology information on the traversed domains.

With distributed procedures, every domain controls its internal paths. We think that the computation of inter-domain paths must typically be distributed

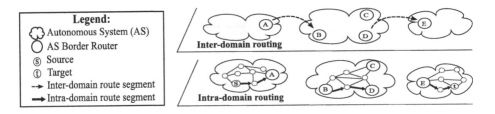

Fig. 1. Routing relies on a two-level hierarchy with a separation between intra-domain and inter-domain operations

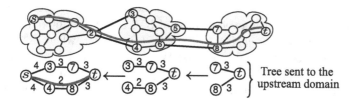

Fig. 2. Operations of the BRPC procedure to compute an inter-domain path from s to t and that traverses the lowest number of links

among the domains, to preserve both the autonomy of the domains and the scalability of the routing protocols. Therefore, we present a novel method to distribute the computation of inter-domain constrained paths.

2.2 The BRPC Procedure

Reference [1] describes a Backward Recursive PCE-based Computation (BRPC) procedure to compute constrained inter-domain traffic engineered label switched paths. BRPC uses multiple PCEs to compute these paths along a determined domain sequence and preserves the autonomy of the domains.

We illustrate the operations of BRPC in Fig. 2. Starting from the destination domain, each domain computes a shortest-path tree with respect to a specific objective function. The root of this tree is the destination node of the considered path computation request. Its leaves are the entry Border Nodes (BNs) of the domain. Then, the domain forwards this tree to the previous domain in the considered sequence of traversed domains. Note that the advertised tree does not necessarily include all the computed shortest paths: the domain selects the paths that it wants to advertise to the upstream domain. The upstream domain uses the information contained in the tree to compute a similar shortest-path tree from its entry BNs towards the destination (t) of the request. This process is repeated until the source node (s) is reached.

Note that BRPC requires that the domains exchange information about the computed paths. This information might divulge confidential details about the internal topology of the traversed domains. This problem is solved by the use of path keys [8], which enable the domains to advertise only the entry BNs and information about the path performance. The BRPC procedure specifies the protocol exchanges among the domains; however, it does not describe the algorithm that must be used in each traversed domain to compute the paths.

2.3 The MCP Problem

To define the MCP problem, we consider a network represented by a valued graph $G = (V, E, w)$. The set V of vertices represents the nodes of the considered network. The set E of edges corresponds to the network links. The function $w : E \to \mathbb{R}$, where $\mathbb{R}$ denotes the set of the real numbers, provides the value of the considered link metrics for every link: to model multiple QoS metrics, each link l in E is associated with a vector $\boldsymbol{w}(l)$ of $K \in \mathbb{N}$ link weights. We denote the k-th weight of the link l as $w_k(l) \in \mathbb{R}^+$, with k in $[1..K]$, where $\mathbb{R}^+$ represents the set of the nonnegative real numbers. We define the weights of a path $\mathbf{p}$ as the sum $w_k(\mathbf{p}) = \sum_{l \in \mathbf{p}} w_k(l)$ of the link weights on this path. This means that we consider only additive metrics. Nevertheless, we can treat the constraints on bottleneck metrics (*e.g.*, bandwidth) by computing a path in a graph from which we have removed the links that break the constraints. In addition, positively-valued multiplicative constraints can be transformed into additive constraints by using a logarithm function.

We consider two non-empty paths $\mathbf{p}$ and $\mathbf{s}$. We say that $\mathbf{s}$ is a *suffix* of $\mathbf{p}$ if there is a path $\mathbf{q}$ such that $\mathbf{p}$ is the concatenation of $\mathbf{q}$ and $\mathbf{s}$. We denote the set of paths from a node s to a node t as $P_{s \to t}$. Similarly, we denote as $P_{D \to t}$ the set of paths whose source is in the subset D of V and whose destination is the node t in V. We consider a *path computation request*, which specifies a source s and a destination t in V, as well as K constraints W_k in $\mathbb{R}^{+*}$, with k in $[1..K]$ and $\mathbb{R}^{+*}$ representing the set of the positive real numbers. The constraints represent maximum bounds W_k on every weight $w_k(\mathbf{p})$ of the requested path: to be acceptable, a path $\mathbf{p} \in P_{s \to t}$ must satisfy $w_k(\mathbf{p}) \leq W_k$ for all k in $[1..K]$. We call *feasible path* any path that fulfills the constraints of the request; the MCP problem consists in determining a feasible path. For instance, the problem of finding a path whose end-to-end propagation delay is below fifty milliseconds and which traverses less than fifteen links is an MCP problem.

The literature describes several brute-force algorithms [3, 5] as well as heuristics [4] and approximation algorithms [6] for the *intra-domain* MCP problem. These algorithms typically assume that the network uses link-state routing (every router maintains a complete view of the network) and require centralized path computation operations. For inter-domain path computation, these assumptions imply that every domain involved in the computation operations has complete information about the state of other domains, which is usually unacceptable for confidentiality and communication overhead reasons. In addition, centralized path computation operations are incompatible with the required autonomy of the domains. Consequently, we investigate distributed methods for multi-constrained inter-domain path computation. To the best of our knowledge, our work is the first to present an exact distributed solution to the inter-domain MCP problem.

2.4   The Inter-MCP Problem

We consider a mathematical partition $\mathcal{D}$ of the set of nodes V, that is a division of V into a finite number of non-overlapping and non-empty sets. We call every element of this partition a *domain*. We define the Inter-MCP problem as follows:

Problem 1 (Inter-MCP). Given a finite loop-free sequence $\mathbf{S} = (D_1, D_2 \ldots)$ of $|S| \in \mathbb{N}$ domains, a source node $s \in D_1$, a destination node $t \in D_{|S|}$, and a set of K end-to-end constraints W_k with $k \in [1..K]$, find a *feasible* path from s to t that traverses the sequence $\mathbf{S}$ of domains.

Our definition of the Inter-MCP problem relies on the assumption that the domain sequence crossed by the path is predetermined. This assumption is commonly adopted in relevant work of the domain, as in [1], to reduce the complexity of the problem.

Wang and Crowcroft [9] have shown that the MCP problem is $\mathcal{NP}$-complete. As the MCP problem is a special case of the Inter-MCP problem, the Inter-MCP problem is $\mathcal{NP}$-complete too [10]. Thus, some of its instances cannot be solved exactly in polynomial time (if $\mathcal{P} \neq \mathcal{NP}$) [10]. However, previous work on the MCP problem shows that most instances of the MCP problem can be solved exactly in polynomial time [4, 11].

The contribution of our paper is to propose a method to distribute the computation of inter-domain MCPs. We provide two mechanisms, the first is a method to distribute end-to-end computation operations among the traversed domains, and the other one is an algorithm to perform the per-domain calculations. In particular, we propose a solution, named ID-MCP (Inter-Domain MCP), which is the first to enable the distributed exact computation of inter-domain MCPs considering an arbitrary number of constraints. We use BRPC to propagate the computation results and to permit the selection of optimal end-to-end paths.

3   Proposition of a Distributed Exact Solution

3.1   Distribution of the Computations among the Domains

Inter-domain path computations must be distributed among the traversed domains so that the domains keep their autonomy. Therefore, our solution defines the per-domain computations of the inter-domain MCP problem for every traversed domain. The result of these per-domain computations is a set of paths that our algorithm will use to find a feasible end-to-end path.

We use the concept of *dominance*, which expresses the idea that a solution is "better" than another, to reduce the complexity of the computations inside each domain. A path $\mathbf{p}$ is *dominated* if there is a path $\mathbf{p}'$, with the same source and destination, such that $w_k(\mathbf{p}') \leq w_k(\mathbf{p})$ for all considered weights $w_k, k \in [1..K]$ and such that there is a k in $[1..k]$ for which $w_k(\mathbf{p}') < w_k(\mathbf{p})$. In this case, we say that $\mathbf{p}'$ dominates $\mathbf{p}$. For instance, consider two paths $\mathbf{p}_1$ and $\mathbf{p}_2$ between the same nodes and such that $\boldsymbol{w}(\mathbf{p}_1) = (4,3)^T$ and $\boldsymbol{w}(\mathbf{p}_2) = (3,3)^T$, then, $\mathbf{p}_2$ dominates $\mathbf{p}_1$. Concretely, a dominated path is never a good solution to an MCP problem: there is a better candidate solution between the same nodes. Thus, we are interested in computing only non-dominated paths. In particular, previous work on the intra-domain MCP problem [5] shows that, to compute MCPs exactly, intermediate nodes should memorize only feasible non-dominated intermediate paths. We can apply this result: to compute inter-domain MCPs, it is sufficient that every domain computes non-dominated feasible paths from its entry BNs to the destination of the request. This method allows us to transform the Inter-MCP problem into a specific MCP problem for every traversed domain.

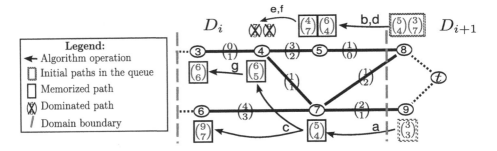

Fig. 3. Simplified operations of the extended RDA in a domain, considering the constraints $W_1 = 11$ and $W_2 = 14$

Problem 2. [Per-Domain Problem] Given an instance of the Inter-MCP problem, a domain D_i in the sequence $\mathbf{S} = (D_1, D_2 \ldots)$, and a set $P^* \subset P_{D_{i+1} \to t}$ of paths from the entry BNs of the next domain D_{i+1} to t, find all the non-dominated feasible paths from the entry BNs of D_i to t that have a suffix in P^*.

3.2   Solution to the Per-domain Problem

For the per-domain operations of ID-MCP, we propose a novel extended reverse Dijkstra's algorithm (RDA) [12] that memorizes all non-dominated feasible intermediate paths. Figure 3 depicts the operations of this algorithm: the purpose of the operations is to find the non-dominated feasible paths from the entry BNs 3 and 6 to the destination t of the request. To compute these paths, the algorithm uses a queue structure that contains the shortest paths from every intermediate node to t. This queue is initialized with paths from the entry-BNs of the neighboring downstream domain, nodes 8 and 9, to t. In the example, the queue starts with two different paths from 8 to t and a path from 9 to t. The calculation progresses from the right to the left of Fig. 3.

The algorithm runs a loop. During each iteration of the loop, the algorithm picks among the paths of the queue a path **p** whose weights are the furthest from the constraints. In the example, the first path selected starts from node 9 and its weights are $(3, 3)^T$ because the alternative paths in the queue (two paths from node 8) are closer to the constraints. Then, the algorithm *relaxes* **p**: it evaluates the weights of the paths from the neighboring nodes (node 7) of the source of **p** (node 9) that have **p** as suffix. The algorithm adds the discovered paths to the queue if they are feasible and not dominated by any path in the queue. In the example, the path from node 7 with weights $(5, 4)^T$ is added to the queue. If a new path dominates one or more paths of the queue, then the dominated paths are discarded. The loop is repeated while the queue contains at least one element that has not been relaxed or discarded (operations b to g). Finally, the algorithm finds the feasible non-dominated paths from the entry BNs 3 and 6. For example, it discovers the path with weights $(6, 6)^T$ from the entry BN 3 to t through the nodes 3-4-7-9. During its operations, the algorithm does not discard

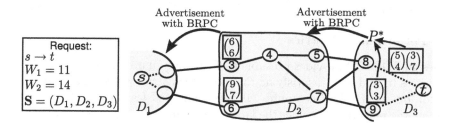

Fig. 4. Propagation of the per-domain results for an inter-domain MCP problem with two integer-valued metrics

any non-dominated feasible path. Thus, it guarantees to solve the Problem 2. The termination of the algorithm is guaranteed as it relaxes one path during each iteration of the loop and the number of paths in a domain is finite.

3.3 Propagation of the Per-domain Computation Results

Figure 4 illustrates the Inter-MCP problem on a simple example with two integer-valued link weights. We use BRPC to forward the non-dominated feasible paths computed by every traversed domain to a PCE of the previous domain in the considered sequence of crossed domains. An intermediate domain (D_2) receives a set P^* of paths from the downstream domain (D_3). P^* includes the feasible non-dominated paths from the entry-BNs (8 and 9) of the downstream domain to the destination t of the request. The intermediate domain extends its local vision of the network topology with the paths in P^* and uses this information to compute the non-dominated feasible paths from its own entry-BNs (3 and 6) to t using our algorithm. Then, it advertises these paths to its neighboring upstream domain (D_1), which is the source domain and is able to compute an end-to-end feasible path. Note that a path-key mechanism [8] can be used to preserve confidential information: it enables the BNs to advertise only path performance information and a path-key that identifies a specific path. The key is later translated into an explicit path during signaling operations.

Our algorithm requires the two following extensions of the PCE framework. First, with our method, more than one non-dominated feasible paths from the same entry BN can be advertised to the previous domain. This case was not considered for the original BRPC procedure, thus, our algorithm requires an extension of the virtual shortest-path tree structure defined in [1] to enable the forwarding of several paths with the same source. This extension of the BRPC procedure is conceptual: it does not require any modification of the PCE protocol (PCEP) [2], which already provides the objects required to carry such paths. Second, the path computation requests and replies should indicate that every traversed domain must use our algorithm. This information can be carried thanks to an objective function object [13] of PCEP [2], for example.

4 Discussion

4.1 Performance Metrics

By design, ID-MCP provides provable performance guarantees. In particular, it guarantees to find a path satisfying the request constraints if such a path exists. In addition, as ID-MCP computes all non-dominated feasible paths, it enables selecting the path that provides the largest performance margin compared to the request constraints. This feature is important to maximize the chances that a computed path can be successfully setup, as the state of the network can change between the computation of a path and its setup. Simulations provide additional information about the performance of our algorithm and the amount of signaling overhead that it introduces in the network.

We evaluate the following performance metrics. The number of feasible non-dominated paths returned by ID-MCP is denoted as NP. This number enables us to evaluate the available path diversity in the simulated scenario. More-over, we consider the cost (C), defined as the lowest value of the function $c(\mathbf{p}) = \max_{k \in [1..K]} \left(\frac{w_k(\mathbf{p})}{W_k} \right)$ among the computed paths. Furthermore, we define a function c' as $\mu_{k \in [1..K]} \left(\frac{w_k(\mathbf{p})}{W_k} \right)$, where μ denotes the arithmetic mean operator. We call multi-dimensional cost (MC) the value of c' for the end-to-end path that has the lowest value of c' among the computed paths. MC helps to evaluate the quality of the returned paths considering all metrics, whereas C indicates their performance margin with respect to the most restrictive metric.

Previous work [4, 5] has shown that the complexity of MCP computations inside a domain depends on the maximum number α of paths memorized for a single node. Thus, we measure α to estimate the time complexity of ID-MCP. In addition, α helps us to determine the number of paths exchanged by the domains during inter-domain path computation operations, and thus, the signaling overhead.

4.2 Evaluation Scenario

We present results for topologies representing extreme cases for the algorithm, to assess its performance in a worst-case situation.[1] We consider lattice domain topologies (square grids) made up of 25 nodes, as represented in Fig. 5. We interconnect the domains to build a domain sequence along which we compute inter-domain MCPs. In FM (Full Mesh), every node of an intermediate domain is connected to every node in the next and in the previous domain of the sequence. In SL (Single Link), only the bottom-right node of every domain is connected to the top-left node of the next-domain. We generate the values of two random uniformly distributed link-weights for every simulation run. We consider the following path computation requests. The source is the top-left node of the first domain and the destination is the bottom-right node of the last domain. We compare the outputs of ID-MCP for two different set of constraints. First, we

---

[1] Simulations on real topologies provide similar results [14].

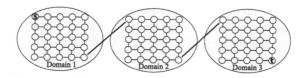

Fig. 5. The lattice topology with single-link domain inter-connections (SL)

define *strict constraints* so that, in average, there is a feasible path for less than 70% of the simulated requests. Second, we define *loose constraints* so that there is a feasible path for every simulated request.

4.3   Simulation Results

Table 1 presents the results of the simulations. For loose constraints, the performance of the optimal path computed by ID-MCP is much better than requested (C and MC are below 20%). This indicates that ID-MCP finds paths that will remain feasible even in case of variations in the network state. In addition, ID-MCP manages to find several feasible non-dominated paths (NP is greater than 3) even when the optimal performance of the network is close to the constraints (for strict constraints, C and MC are greater than 60%).

The complexity of the computations remains reasonable for the simulated scenario (α is lower than 10). However, the size of the simulated topology is relatively limited compared to real networks, which can include several hundreds of nodes. In addition, the MCP problem is $\mathcal{NP}$-complete. Thus, the complexity of the computations on larger topologies would be typically prohibitive. This scalability concern underlines the need for a trade-off between the complexity of the calculations and the performance of the computed paths. In particular, our algorithm provides the theoretical basis for future heuristics with a reduced complexity. We will study these heuristics in forthcoming work.

Table 1. Simulation results with loose and strict constraints

Constraints	C [%]		MC [%]		α		NP	
	SL	FM	SL	FM	SL	FM	SL	FM
Loose	19.2	13.9	18.7	11.4	10	7	7	3
Strict	89.3	72	86.5	60.1	8	2	5	1

5   Conclusion

In this paper, we have studied the inter-domain MCP problem, whose applications are more and more important with the recent advances in inter-domain traffic engineering. The main contribution of the paper is the distribution of the MCP computation operations among the traversed domains. In particular, we have analyzed the required information exchanges among the domains to solve the inter-domain problem. This study has enabled us to introduce ID-MCP, the first solution to the considered problem that guarantees to find a feasible path if such a path exists in the network. In particular, ID-MCP is based on distributed per-domain computations that are compatible with the PCE framework and that allow computing optimal end-to-end paths. These paths are the furthest from the constraints, thus, they ensure the best resistance to future variations of the QoS conditions. As the considered problem is $\mathcal{NP}$-complete, the complexity of the computations is prohibitive for large topologies. However, our solution provides the theoretical foundation for future heuristics with a reduced complexity.

References

1. Vasseur, J., Zhang, R., Bitar, N., Roux, J.L.: A Backward-Recursive PCE-Based Computation (BRPC) Procedure to Compute Shortest Constrained Inter-Domain Traffic Engineering Label Switched Paths. RFC 5441, IETF (2009)
2. Vasseur, J., Roux, J.L.: Path Computation Element (PCE) Communication Protocol (PCEP). RFC 5440 (2009)
3. Korkmaz, T., Krunz, M.: Multi-constrained optimal path selection. In: IEEE INFOCOM, vol. 2, pp. 834–843 (2001)
4. Yuan, X.: Heuristic algorithms for multiconstrained quality-of-service routing. IEEE/ACM Trans. Netw. 10(2), 244–256 (2002)
5. Van Mieghem, P., Kuipers, F.A.: Concepts of exact QoS routing algorithms. IEEE/ACM Trans. Netw. 12(5), 851–864 (2004)
6. Xue, G., Sen, A., Zhang, W., Tang, J., Thulasiraman, K.: Finding a path subject to many additive QoS constraints. IEEE/ACM Trans. Netw. 15, 201–211 (2007)
7. Saad, T., Mouftah, H., Nouroozifar, A.: Constraint-based routing across multi-domain optical WDM networks. In: Canadian Conference on Electrical and Computer Engineering, vol. 4, pp. 2065–2068 (2004)
8. Bradford, R., Vasseur, J.P., Farrel, A.: Preserving Topology Confidentiality in Inter-Domain Path Computation Using a Key-Based Mechanism. draft-ietf-pce-path-key-06, work in progress, IETF (2009)
9. Wang, Z., Crowcroft, J.: Quality-of-Service Routing for Supporting Multimedia Applications. IEEE J. Sel. Areas Commun. 14, 1228–1234 (1996)
10. Garey, M.R., Johnson, D.S.: Computers and Intractability; A Guide to the Theory of NP-Completeness. W. H. Freeman & Co., New York (1979)
11. Kuipers, F., Van Mieghem, P.: The impact of correlated link weights on QoS routing. In: IEEE INFOCOM, vol. 2, pp. 1425–1434 (2003)
12. Ahuja, R., Magnanti, T., Orlin, J.: Network Flows: Theory, Algorithms, and Applications. Prentice-Hall, Inc., New Jersey (1993)
13. Le Roux, J.L., Vasseur, J.P., Lee, Y.: Encoding of Objective Functions in the Path Computation Element Communication Protocol (PCEP). draft-ietf-pce-of, work in progress, IETF (2008)
14. Bertrand, G., Lahoud, S., Molnár, M., Texier, G.: Inter-Domain Path Computation with Multiple Constraints. Technical Report 1902, IRISA (2008),
   `http://hal.inria.fr`

Classification of P2P and HTTP Using Specific Protocol Characteristics

John Hurley, Emi Garcia-Palacios, and Sakir Sezer

The Institute of Electronics, Communication and Information Technology (ECIT),
Queens University of Belfast
jhurley03@qub.ac.uk, e.garcia@ee.qub.ac.uk,
s.sezer@ecit.qub.ac.uk

Abstract. A key aspect of traffic classification is the early identification of individual flows which may utilise strategies such as ephemeral ports and transport later encryption to 'hide' on the network. This paper focuses on P2P and HTTP – the two main producers of network traffic – to determine the characteristics of their individual flows. We propose a heuristic based classification system to distinguish HTTP and P2P flows using only the structure of how packets are passed and the lengths of the individual packets. The classification system is then tested on real network traffic and results presented to show it can accurately detect P2P and HTTP within the early part of a TCP flow.

Keywords: Traffic Classification, P2P, HTTP.

1 Introduction

ISPs (Internet Service Providers) and network administrators have seen a huge increase in high bandwidth consuming traffic in recent years [1]. In order for them to deploy effective bandwidth management and quality of service (QoS) policies a traffic classification strategy must be in place.

The original concept of traffic classification was applied on a per packet basis and took into account the port numbers stipulated at the transport layer [2]. Well known port numbers were connected to specific applications (e.g. port 80 for HTTP). However, many applications now use random (or ephemeral) ports to complete data transfer and some even try to avoid detection by masquerading as another application. For example, HTTP traffic mostly travels to port 80, but some P2P protocols can masquerade as HTTP by also using this port [3], thereby confusing a classifier.

To overcome the ineffectiveness of port based classifiers, packets can be considered on a 'per flow' basis rather than individually [4]. A flow is defined as all the packets involved in a single process or task and identified by a 5 tuple value (source and destination IP address, source and destination port number, and transport layer protocol) [4, 5]. On a 'per flow' classification only one packet within the flow requires classifying to enable the identification of the protocol that has generated all packets from the flow.

M. Oliver and S. Sallent (Eds.): EUNICE 2009, LNCS 5733, pp. 31–40, 2009.
© Springer-Verlag Berlin Heidelberg 2009

To identify one packet within a flow, application signatures can be used [6, 7]. These are ASCII stings or a byte series that appear in the transport layer payload of certain signalling packets from specific protocols. However, protocols wishing to avoid detection can apply encryption to their payloads negating the use of signatures. This strategy is deployed on all packets within the mainly Asian used P2P protocol Winny [8], and has also been introduced into the bitTorrent protocol [9]. It is envisaged that, as legal pressure continues to mount on ISPs to combat the transfer of copyrighted material, and as they continue to restrict the available bandwidth for P2P file swapping, more P2P protocols will utilise such classification avoidance techniques.

If port classification cannot be relied on and applications signatures are not available then flow statistics like packet lengths and packet inter-arrival times can be used to predict the underlying protocol of a flow [10, 11]. However, the use of statistics for classification has two main restrictions that must be overcome. Firstly, the statistical strategy must be accurate in its classification of traffic and, secondly, the strategy must reach a classification decision without having to examine too many packets. For example, while the total amount of data passed in a flow can be an indicator of the protocol that generated the traffic, it is of little value to an ISP as all the data would have to pass across the router unclassified before any decision can be made. This introduces the need for fast or early packet classification.

Our research aims to generate fast classifications of the two most common forms on internet traffic - HTTP web traffic and P2P file swapping [17]. We do so by examining the lengths and properties of the initial packets of a flow. We concentrate on TCP flows as the main protocol used by HTTP and P2P to exchange large data quantities (high bandwidth consumers). A series of heuristics are produced to extract 'fingerprints' that are common in either P2P or HTTP flows but not in both. This allows the differentiation between the two even in situations where transport layer encryption is in place, or where P2P flows are trying to masquerade as HTTP by travelling on port 80. Our strategy is applied to real core internet traffic and the results presented.

The rest of this paper is as follows; section 2 gives an overview of related work; section 3 gives our methodology; section 4 introduces the network data used; section 5 outlines our heuristics; section 6 introduces our classification strategy and section 7 provides the classification results.

2 Related Work

BLINC [13] has taken a unique approach to classifying traffic by examining the behaviour of the hosts on the network and connecting it to an application. This behaviour is examined in increasing levels of detail. These levels are defined as the social level (connections at a host), the functional level (hosts role on the network), and the application level (packet transport layer information). This technique can classify around 80 to 90% of all flows with a high level of accuracy. However, this approach utilises application signatures within its application level. Its effectiveness for encrypted traffic when signatures are not available is unknown.

Other classification proposals have used machine learning to test a set of discriminators for their validity in the classification process. [14] and [15] make use of 249 statistical variables in an attempt to find those most suited to traffic classification, while [16] tests machine learning techniques against training set sizes to find the most accurate classifier of P2P traffic. However, these machine learning techniques utilise discriminators based on entire flows (e.g. flow duration) and are only really applicable in data mining processes, not for real time ISP requirements.

[10] introduces a new approach to classification by considering only the first few packets in each bidirectional TCP connection. This focuses on the negotiation phase of the flows meaning that few packets will pass before a classification is determined. It takes the packet lengths of the first 5 data packet of a flow (with server to client packet marked negative) and clusters them in N-dimensional space. These clusters are then used outside their training data to classify new flows.

Our work has a similar concept but expands on the strategy [10] to overcome some of the problems inherent in it. Firstly we consider incoming and outgoing packet lengths in groups rather than individually to lower any errors that will occur through out of order packets (e.g. in retransmissions). Secondly we examine slightly more data within a flow to consider not only the initial handshake phase but to view how data transfer is progressing and to define the structure the flow is taking in an attempt to generate more accurate classifications. However, we are still classifying within the early part of a high bandwidth consuming P2P or HTTP flow. Finally, [10] only examines eDonkey and Kazaa P2P flows while we also aim to investigate and classify a wider range of P2P protocols including the extremely popular bitTorrent and Gnutella networks [17].

3 Methodology

HTTP and P2P flows tend to make use of the TCP transport layer protocol for the transfer of large amounts of data (UDP tends only to be used for signalling [12]). The connection orientated nature of TCP means that the beginning of a flow and the initiating host can easily be determined through observation of the SYN control flag within the TCP header. This is opposite to the connectionless properties of UDP where the initiator or beginning of a flow is much harder to detect. In this work we concentrate on detection of large, high-bandwidth consuming TCP flows.

We examine flow properties in a bidirectional format. This means that the packets sent from a client (flow initiator) to a server and those returned from the server to the client are considered the same flow. A bidirectional flow is recognised in a network trace by its 5 tuple value and by the reverse 5 tuple value. That is *clientIP, clientPort, serverIP, serverPort, TCP* is considered the same flow as *serverIP, serverPort, clientIP, clientPort, TCP*. Properties of these flows are examined in both directions for the maximum packet size, the number of maximum packet sizes, the minimum packet size, the number of minimum packet sizes, throughput (total data passed) , and flow structure (layout of the flow).

Each flow's bidirectional statistics are measured until one of the directions has received a limit of X data packets (those that contain a TCP payload). For experimentation in this paper we set X to 20. Through our flow analysis we determined that this value would allow a depiction of how a flow transfers data after any initial handshakes (first 5 packets in [10]) while still allowing a classification to be made 'early' within the flow. The number of acknowledgement (ACK) packets in the opposite direction is also considered to confirm all packets in both directions are received and have not been lost or chosen a different route across the network. If the number of data packets plus the number of non payload ACK's are equal in both directions then it is reasonable to say that the recorded statistics give an accurate interpretation of the early activity of the TCP flow. This validates the recording of each flow and removes any anomalies that may be present in the data.

4 Data

The research carried out in this paper has utilised real network traffic. This traffic has been taken from a core router situated in the home users ADSL network of a major European ISP in March 2007. There are approximately 20,000 ADSL modems on the network with the data recording covering half of the flows passing over the router at that time period. Different samples of traces from different time periods have been used for heuristic development and for testing.

When carrying out experiments on the core network traffic a background classification (pre-processing) of application signatures was used to determine the protocol of each flow. The application signatures used are developed from [6] and [7] along with further modern signatures not presented in these research papers (e.g. 'ajprot' signalling the use of the appleJuice P2P protocol). Although it is the purpose of this paper to provide an alternative to application signatures, the high accuracy they achieve [6] justifies their use in pre-processing. It is likely that P2P flows existing in our trace data have avoided detection in our pre-processing as they already use encryption. However, we can be confident that those flows that are selected through preprocessing have been accurately identified.

Analysis of flows longer than 20 data packets (our packet limit selection) within our sample traffic show that over 90% of flows are created by P2P and HTTP with the percentage possibly higher as some P2P flows may be unclassified by pre-processing. This figure highlights the importance of differentiation between these two protocol sets. The most popular P2P flows seen are bitTorrent, Gnutella, and eDonkey. We use a first sample trace for protocol analysis and heuristic identification (training trace). A second sample has been recorded from a different time period to ensure fairness [12], and is used to test the heuristics (test trace).

5 Heuristics

To determine the protocol of a flow as P2P or HTTP with a packet limit (20) we use the lengths, throughputs, and structure of the early packets in both directions of a bidirectional TCP flow. The structure of the flow is defined as the shape it has taken once the data packet limit has been received in either the client to server or server to client direction. In other words the number of data packets that have been passed in the opposite direction when one side reaches 20. Figure 1 gives an example of structures by showing how many packets appear in the opposite direction when 20 packets are received in either the incoming or outgoing direction from the flow initiator (client). The results are generated from our training network trace.

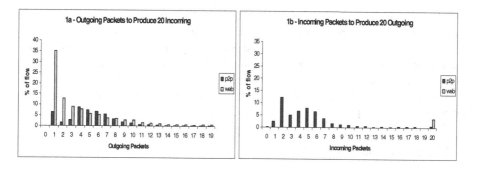

Fig. 1. The structure of P2P and HTTP flows

The most common structure of HTTP traffic shown in figure 1 sees 20 incoming packets signalled by 1 outgoing data packet (figure 1a). However, it can be seen in figure 1b that many P2P flows have structures uncommon with HTTP traffic. These structures are created when the initiator of the flow sends 20 outgoing data packets while only receiving a few incoming packets. This suggests the uploading of data from source to destination – a key aspect in the sharing nature of P2P protocols.

A further example of how packet lengths can be used to differentiate P2P and HTTP is shown in figure 2. This figure describes flows with a structure of 20 incoming packets and at least 2 outgoing. The total of these 20 incoming packets that are of the maximum size witnessed in that direction of the flow are presented.

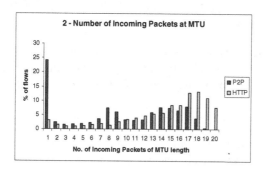

Fig. 2. Number of incoming packets at maximum size

Figure 2 indicates that most of the P2P flows with the associated structure have only 1 incoming packet of maximum length. HTTP flows are more likely to have a high number of Maximum Transmission Unit (MTU) packets with a significant portion of flows having all of their incoming packets at the maximum. HTTP over TCP can stream its data together and pass it out in all, or mostly, MTU packets enabling more efficient transfer of the data. P2P, on the other hand, normally chooses to pass its data in predefined blocks [7]. This means breaking each block into MTU slices and passing the remainder of the block in a packet of its own. This means fewer MTU packets will be viewed in P2P flows.

Furthers heuristics were proposed based on protocol properties and flow observations. All heuristics were tested in an iterative manner with variations made to 'cut off' values and structure types to optimise their results. For each heuristic a calculation was made on our training trace showing the percentage of P2P and HTTP flows that the heuristic selects. From these calculations we chose a total of 10 heuristics that we determined to select a high enough percentage of one protocol while selecting few flows from the other protocol.

6 Classification Strategy

From the 10 proposed heuristics a classification strategy was formed. Six of the heuristics detect P2P protocols with four used to define HTTP. The protocol heuristics used to define HTTP are:

Initial incoming packets of same length
   Suggests incoming data is being streamed or that the initial handshake information is large. The short handshake lengths that are common in P2P are not taking place.

All incoming packets of MTU
   Shows that all data is being streamed at a constant length (figure 2).

Large first 5 packet averages in both directions
   Assumes a structure of at least 5 packets in each direction and divides the throughput of the first 5 packets by the MTU for the flow. If both directions produce a result of above 3 then the heuristic is matched. Determines that HTTP request messages are longer than in P2P.

19 out of 20 packets at MTU with the non MTU packet occurring in the first 5
   Suggests data is being streamed in an incoming direction but that not all packets are at MTU, possibly due an initial signalling/handshake packet (figure 2).

The characteristics used to define P2P are:

Throughput ratio between outgoing and incoming (> 4 packets in lesser direction)
   At least 10 times more bytes in one direction of the flow. Based on the observation that P2P flows tend to receive more data with smaller requests than in HTTP.

Average packet length of non MTU packets < 100 bytes in both directions
   P2P tends to have small signalling messages and transfers data in blocks which are divided into MTU packets with any remainder in a small single packet. Many P2P flows consist of all small packets and MTU packets - uncommon in HTTP.

Average of first 5 packet lengths in both directions <100 bytes
   P2P flows can require many short signalling messages before passing file data greatly reducing the average of the early packets in both directions - uncommon in HTTP.

20 outgoing packets with between 0 and 5 incoming
   P2P flows are commonly used for uploading as well as downloading (figure 1).

Average packet size in the second group of 5 packets <100 bytes in one direction
   If one direction of a flow has passed more than 5 data packets and the average size
   of the next packets is small then these are likely to be short signalling packets (P2P).

Average incoming packet length more than 5 times greater than average outgoing
   Similar to the throughput ratio but does not require a structure of 5 packets or more
   in both directions. Assumes that P2P requests are small compared to responses.

7 Results

To test the validity of this classification scheme the heuristics were applied in order to
our test network trace. The results of HTTP and P2P classification are analysed
through the use of our pre-processing scheme of application signatures. We define our
results with 2 calculations (X represents either P2P or HTTP):

*Selected: percentage of the total number of protocol X in the trace data (based on our
pre-processing) that are selected by a heuristic defining protocol X*

*Misclassified: the percentage of total flow selections by heuristics defining protocol X
that are shown by pre-processing not to be generated by protocol X – i.e. the number
selected as P2P that are actually HTTP and vice versa*

   Table 1 presents the classification results on our test trace (recorded over a separate
time period from training trace).

Table 1. HTTP versus P2P classification results

Protocol	Selected	Misclassified
HTTP	82.39	0.84
P2P	77.43	2.85

   The results in table 1 show that over 82% of HTTP and over 77% of P2P traffic
flows can be identified with a low misclassification rate (at most 2.85%) using our
proposed heuristic set. However, to show how the accuracy of our classifications
compares with a similar classification technique we must apply the technique to the
same data.
   Table 2 shows the results of the k-means clustering strategy proposed in [10] when
applied to our network traces. We run the technique by generating clusters from an
equal sample of P2P and HTTP traffic in our training trace using the optimum values
of the first 5 packet lengths and 50 clusters [10]. The clusters are then used to classify
the HTTP and P2P traffic in our test trace. Because a nearest cluster strategy is used
[10] to assign flows to a protocol, all flows will be classified as either P2P or HTTP
with none remaining 'unselected'. Therefore table 2 only presents the *misclassification* rating for the strategy proposed in [10].

Table 2. HTTP versus P2P classification from strategy proposed in [10]

Protocol	Misclassified
HTTP	16.79
P2P	16.59

Comparison of our results with those achieved through the clustering strategy of [10] show that our approach is much more reliable by wrongly classifying far fewer flows. In a real-time, online classifier it is important that an ISP of network administrator falsely classifies as few flows as possible.

7.1 Variation of Results with Packet Limits

The results featured for heuristic classification in table 1 require information from the first 20 packets of a TCP flow to make a decision. Figure 3 shows how these results vary if the same (or slightly adapted) heuristics are applied with a smaller packet limit on the same flows.

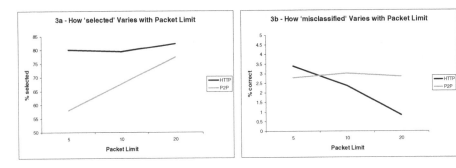

Fig. 3. How results vary when the packet limit for analysis is less than 20

Figure 3a shows how the *selected* calculation varies when the packet limit is changed from 20 data packets in one direction to 5 or 10. The number of total HTTP flows selected is almost constant (varies by approximately 3%) although there is a slight decrease when 10 packets are used as the limit. There is a large change in the number of P2P flows classified with the number selected growing almost 20% as we move from 5 packets to 20 packets. This suggests that the more packets examined within a flow, the more likely that an increasing number of P2P flows will become distinguishable.

Figure 3b signifies how the *misclassified* values vary as the number of packets used in the analysis is increased. The accuracy of the P2P classifications is approximately constant while the accuracy of the HTTP selections is increasing (misclassifications decreasing). Combining the observations from both graphs in figure 3 concludes that the more packets analysed the better the classification of HTTP and P2P. As the number of packets examined is increased the accuracy of P2P will remain constant but the number of total P2P flows selected will increase. In HTTP the number of flows selected will remain constant but the accuracy will increase. Therefore, when a higher number of packets are examined, overall, more flows are selected with a higher accuracy. However, even with this it should be noted that the misclassification rate for both P2P and HTTP never surpasses 3.5% of flows no matter how many packets are measured. This is still a big improvement on the misclassification rate generated by a similar method (table 2).

8 Conclusions and Future Research

In this paper we introduced a new strategy for classifying high bandwidth consuming TCP flows within their early stages meaning ISPs or network administrators can use the classification results for real-time bandwidth management, QoS purposes, and security policies. It was shown that by applying heuristics to analyse the structure and packet lengths of the early transactions of a flow that the two main generators of network traffic, P2P and HTTP, could be classified separately. Our approach produced misclassification rates far lower than a similar strategy [10] when applied to the same test and training data. We also show how these results varied depending on the number of packets examined and suggested that a correlation exists between the number of packets analysed and overall accuracy and detection success of the classification process.

The classification technique presented in this paper has shown accuracy in the distinction of P2P and HTTP. Although these are the main contributors of network traffic other protocols can generate high bandwidth consuming TCP flows. Future work will consider these other flows from applications including FTP, RTSP, email and instant messaging protocols to move the system towards a complete traffic classifier. Future work will also concentrate on the differentiation of the P2P network flows from HTTP through other classification strategies involving social aspects and how hosts behave on the network for situations when flow activity alone is not enough to determine the residing protocol.

References

1. Karagiannis, T., Broido, A., Brownlee, N., Claffy, K.C., Faloutsos, M.: Is P2P dying or just hiding. In: Proceedings of the 47th IEEE Globecom Conference, Dallas, TX (2004)
2. Roughan, M., Sen, S., Spatscheck, O., Duffield, N.: Class-of-Service Mapping for QoS: A Statistical Signature-based. In: 4th ACM SIGCOMM conference on Internet measurement, Taormina, Sicily, Italy, October 25-27 (2004)
3. Kazaa, http://www.kazaa.com
4. Gouda, M.G., Liu, A.X.: A model of Stateful Firewalls and its properties. In: Proceedings of the IEEE International Conference on Dependable Systems and Networks (DSN 2005), pp. 320–327 (2005)
5. Ocampe, R., Galis, A., Todd, C., Meer, H.D.: Towards Context-Based Flow Classification. Autonomic and Autonomous Systems. In: ICAS 2006, p. 44 (2006)
6. Sen, S., Spatscheck, O., Wang, D.: Accurate, Scalable In-Network Identification of P2P Traffic Using Application Signatures. In: WWW 2004 (2004)

7. Karagiannis, T., Broido, A., Faloutsos, M., Claffy, K.C.: File-sharing in the Internet: A characterization of P2P traffic in the backbone. Technical report (2004),
   http://www.cs.usr.edu/~tkarag

8. Ohzahata, S., Hagiwara, Y., Terada, M., Kawashima, K.: A traffic identification method and evaluations for a pure P2P application. In: Dovrolis, C. (ed.) PAM 2005. LNCS, vol. 3431, pp. 55–68. Springer, Heidelberg (2005)

9. BitTorrent – A technical description of the bitTorrent protocol,
   http://www.cs.chalmers.se/~tsigas/Courses/
   DCDSeminar/Files/BitTorrent.pdf

10. Bernaille, L., Teixeira, R., Akodjenou, I., Soule, A., Salamatian, K.: Traffic Classification On The Fly. ACM SIGCOMM Computer Communication Review 36(2) (2006)

11. Bernaille, L., Teixeira, R.: Early recognition of encrypted applications. In: Uhlig, S., Papagiannaki, K., Bonaventure, O. (eds.) PAM 2007. LNCS, vol. 4427, pp. 165–175. Springer, Heidelberg (2007)

12. Karagiannis, T., Broido, A., Faloutsos, M., Claffy, K.C.: Transport Layer Identification of P2P Traffic. In: Proceedings of the 4th ACM SIGCOMM Conference on Internet Measurement (IMC 2004), Italy, October 2004, pp. 121–134 (2004)

13. Karagiannis, T., Papagiannaki, K., Faloutsos, M.: BLINC: Multilevel Traffic Classification in the Dark. In: Proceedings of the 2005 conference on Applications, technologies, architectures, and protocols for computer communications, Philadelphia, Pennsylvania, USA, August 22-26 (2005)

14. Moore, A., Zuev, D.: Internet Traffic Classification Using Bayesian Analysis Techniques. In: ACM SIGMETRICS, Banff, Canada (June 2005)

15. Junior, G.P.S., Maia, J.E.B., Holanda, R., De Sousa, J.N.: P2P Traffic Identification using Cluster Analysis. In: Global Information Infrastructure Symposium. GIIS 2007, pp. 128–133 (July 2007)

16. Raahemi, B., Kouznetsov, A., Hayajneh, A., Rabinovitch, P.: Classification of Peer-to-Peer traffic using incremental neural networks (Fuzzy ARTMAP). In: Electrical and Computer Engineering, CCECE 2008, Canada, pp. 719–724 (2008)

17. Basher, N., Mahanti, A., Mahanti, A., Williamson, C., Arlitt, M.: A Comparative Analysis of Web and Peer-to-Peer Traffic. In: Proceeding of the 17th international conference on World Wide Web, China, pp. 287–296 (2008)

Network Awareness in P2P-TV Applications*

Stefano Traverso, Emilio Leonardi, Marco Mellia, and Michela Meo

Politecnico di Torino
lastname@tlc.polito.it

Abstract. The increasing popularity of applications for video-streaming based on P2P paradigm (P2P-TV) is raising the interest of both broadcasters and network operators. The former see a promising technology to reduce the cost of streaming content over the Internet, while offering a world-wide service. The latter instead fear that the traffic offered by these applications can grow without control, affecting other services, and possibly causing network congestion and collapse. The "Network-Aware P2P-TV Application over Wise Networks" FP7 project aims at studying and developing a novel P2P-TV application offering the chance to broadcast high definition video to broadcasters and to carefully manage the traffic offered by peers to the network, therefore avoiding worries to Internet providers about network overload. In such context, we design a simulator to evaluate performance of different P2P-TV solutions, to compare them both considering end-users' and network providers' perspectives, such as quality of service perceived by subscribers and link utilization. In this paper, we provide some results that show how effective can be a network aware P2P-TV system.

1 Introduction

Last years witnessed the emergency of many P2P video-streaming services (P2P-TV) on the Internet, like SopCast [1] or PPLive [2] to possibly name the most popular ones. Recently, a new and promising generation of high-definition commercial video P2P applications, such as Babelgum [3], Zattoo [4] or TVUnetworks [5], are at an advanced stage of development and testing. These systems are targeted to offer high bandwidth video streams (1 to 5 Mbit/s) to a large population of users (up to millions). These applications are seen as a good opportunity by broadcasters to both reduce the cost of providing a streaming service to the Internet, and to reach a world-wide population of users. However, the same motivations constitute a worry for network carriers since the traffic P2P-TV application can generate may potentially grow without control, causing a degradation of quality of service perceived by users or even a collapse of network functionalities. This is the main research topic of the FP7 project "Network-Aware P2P-TV Application over Wise Networks", which aims at studying a novel P2P-TV application that offers high quality service to the end-users, while guaranteeing network providers to optimize network resource usage. Therefore, to study, characterize and optimize P2P-TV service, we developed a simulator that allows us to understand the impact of

* This work was funded by the European Commission under the 7th Framework Programme Strep Project "NAPA-WINE" (Network Aware Peer-to-Peer Application over Wise Network).

these new services on network performance: the main objective of this paper is to propose a simple evaluation of P2P-TV systems, focusing on their impact on the transport network.

A preliminary distinction must be done: when using a general P2P application, two different *topologies* have to be considered: i) a *logical topology* at application level, made up by peers, which is created and updated whenever a peer joins or leaves the network; and ii) a *physical network* composed by hosts, nodes and links, which is typically given and rarely changes. In other words, each peer can be seen as a P2P application running on a PC; it establishes logical connections with other peers running on some other PCs, which are then used to exchange the content, e.g., the video in case of P2P-TV applications. The graph which is created by peers is called *Overlay topology*. Considering, instead, the physical network, it is made up by real devices like routers and links, and the graph they form is called *Underlay topology*.

Typically, the Overlay and Underlay topologies are independently set up, managed and optimized. For example, in BitTorrent, a popular P2P file sharing application, a peer selects to which peers upload the content based on the amount of data received in the past, playing the famous tit-for-tat algorithm [6]. However, if the selected peer is actually physically close or far away is not taken into any consideration. The tit-for-tat algorithm clearly optimizes application layer performance, e.g., maximizing download throughput, but it possibly causes a large waste of resources at the Underlay topology, e.g., downloading data from a high-speed peer far away, thus forcing the network to transport traffic over several links.

Similarly, P2P-TV applications transmit streaming videos on the Overlay topology ignoring information about the Underlay network, so that the Overlay topology is built "randomly", without any awareness about location or available bandwidth of hosts which run the application. In this paper we quantify the lack of efficiency due to this issue and demonstrate that the adoption of smart strategies in Overlay topology creation process can improve performance of both the application and the network. We focus our attention on P2P-TV systems, in which the Overlay topology is a generic mesh, and a swarm-like delivery of the video is adopted: a source node splits the video stream into small *chunks*, which are then transmitted to and by peers, exchanging chunks according to some scheduling scheme.

We first define a simple, yet accurate model which describes both the P2P-TV application and the transport network. Then, we compare performance of different algorithms with increasing knowledge about topological information of the network layer exploited to set up the P2P Overlay graph. Results show that it is possible to reduce the traffic the network has to carry by more than two order of magnitudes, while at the same time improving quality of service users perceive.

2   Scenario Description

In the following, we briefly describe the reference model that has been implemented in the simulator. More details are available in [7]. First we describe the model of the Underlay topology, which is assumed to be given. Then the Overlay topology and chunk scheduling algorithms are described.

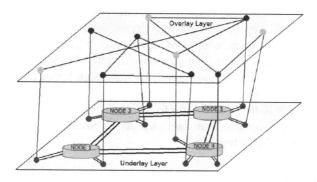

Fig. 1. Overlay and Underlay topologies (RC strategy applied)

2.1   The Underlay Topology

As already mentioned, we have to consider two different topologies: the first one is built at application level, and it is composed by peers which set up connection among them to transmit chunks. Peers are actually hosts, connected to the Internet, whose topology constitutes the Underlay topology. Here, *nodes* (or routers) are connected by means of bidirectional physical links, with a given capacity. Overlay connections correspond to "paths" at the Underlay topology, so packets forming a chunk are routed through the Underlay topology from the source host up to the destination host, following for example the shortest path.

Fig. 1 shows an example of a Underlay topology (at the bottom) in which four routers are connected forming a ring topology among them. Hosts (or users) are then connected to a router. Hosts are running the P2P-TV application, and therefore they are peers, which are connected forming the Overlay topology (at the top).

In the simulator, the chunk transmission by a host is modeled according to a fluid traffic model, so that no packet is actually routed. Instead, on all links along the path, a given amount of bandwidth will be allocated for the duration of the data transmission. Hosts transmit one chunk at a time; given the chunk size and the upload capacity of a host, an amount of bandwidth comparable to the chunk transmission speed is allocated on all links along the path to the destination for the whole chunk duration. This model allows to get therefore the actual link load at any time, given the set of chunks that are actually transmitted by peers. At the same time, it avoids the burden to simulate packet level details, therefore allowing to consider larger networks and higher number of peers. In [7], we were able to run simulations with hundreds of nodes, several thousands of peers transmitting video streams of thousands of chunks.

In this paper, we consider as Underlay topology a simplified version of the actual Telecom Italia backbone network [8]: two main routers are placed in Milano and Roma, and they are connected by 40 Gb/s links. Those two routers and links form the "backbone" of the topology. Nodes in cities in the north part of Italy are then connected to node in Milano, while nodes in the south part of Italy are instead connected to the backbone node in Roma. 10 Gb/s links are used. Nodes in each city are called "access routers", and there are twenty of them in the considered scenario. Hosts are then connected to access routers using either a xDSL link, or using higher capacity connections, like FTTH access. For the sake of simplicity, we assume that two classes of hosts are present: i) *residential* users, with xDSL connection of about 0.5 Mb/s upload capacity, and ii) *business* users, with high access bandwidth of about 5 Mb/s. We refer to residential and business peers as Low-Speed (LS) and High-Speed (HS) peers respectively in the following. In both cases, we assume the download capacity is large enough so that the bottleneck is the uplink capacity of hosts. There are 500 hosts globally, each of them randomly connected to a selected access router, so peers are uniformly distributed over the Underlay topology.

2.2   The Overlay Topology

As introduced in Sec. 1 the topology which is created at application level is a graph composed by peers and logical connections. Given a peer, there is a subset of all peers which are then connected to it, called "neighborhood".

Each peer belonging to the Overlay topology is permanently associated to a host belonging to the Underlay topology - Fig. 1. In our model, we assume each peer establishes on average k logical connections with other peers to build the graph which represents the Overlay topology; k is called "degree" of peer. In this paper, we set an avegare degree $k = 8$, independently on the Overlay topology generation strategy we adopted (see below). HS-peers are granted an additional number of neighbors k'. The intuition behind this is to offer peers with more upload capacity the chance to serve more neighbors. For the sake of simplicity, *churning* phenomenon is not considered in this paper, so the number of peers involved in simulation is fixed and never changes: no peers are expected to join or leave the system during the simulation. In this paper, we compare three different algorithms to setup the Overlay topology, which entail an increasing level of "awareness" by the peers:

- **Random Choice strategy - RC:** In this case, each peer selects on average k neighbors at random, therefore completely ignoring the actual location of hosts in the Underlay topology. This models the today typical approach in which peers ignore any information about the network layer, and Overlay topology results uncorrelated to the actual Underlay topology.
- **Location and Bandwidth Awareness strategy - LBA:** In this case peers have some knowledge about the physiognomy of the Underlay topology, so that peers are connected to the topologically closest peers in order to avoid congestion on network backbone links and to reduce the average delivery time of chunks. In particular, in this model two peers are topologically close if the corresponding hosts are connected to the same access node. Each access node represents an "isle" of peers, in which peers are connected among them using a Random Choice policy. To interconnect the island among them, HS-peers *randomly* connect between them using additional k' connections, forming therefore a hierarchical topology. In other words, the Overlay topology exploits information about the peer location to form groups of close peers, and information of peer upload capacity to interconnect different groups of peers.

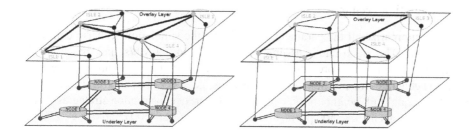

Fig. 2. Examples of LBA and NLBA Overlay topologies on the left and right figures

– **Neighbored Location and Bandwidth Awareness strategy - NLBA:** In this case, the HS-peers perform a smarter choice when selecting other k' HS-peers, so that physically closer peers are selected. The resulting Overlay topology therefore entails a greater knowledge about the Underlay topology, so that the communication between island is optimized as well.

Fig.2 shows two examples of Overlay topologies in which the LBA and NLBA policies are adopted (left and right figures respectively). HS-peers high are represented with light-coloured dots, while dark dots represent LS-peers. The NLBA topology better reflects the Underlay topology, so that HS-peers are interconnected among them mimicking the same ring topology which is present in the Underlay topology.

2.3 Chunk Scheduling Algorithm

Once the Overlay topology has been created, peers can then start exchanging video chunks. A *source* node encodes the video stream, chops it into chunks, which are regularly injected in the Overlay by transmitting them to source neighbors; then, peers that received a new chunk can upload it to those neighbors that have not yet received it, according to a "scheduling" algorithm. We assume a push mechanism, in which the transmitter selects both which chunk to transmit and to which peer. Several scheduling algorithms have been proposed in the literature (see for example [9,10,11,12]), among which we selected the simplest one since our focus is on the Overlay topology optimization rather than chunk scheduling algorithm. Therefore, we adopt a simple *random chunk/random peer* scheduling scheme: each peer selects at random one chunk among those it has received and still stores in the trading window ([12] employs a sliding window mechanism to optimize chunk transmission); then it selects at random one of its neighbors among those that have not yet received the selected chunk. The peer then transmits the chunk to the selected peer. When the transmission ends, a new chunk and a new peer are selected. In P2PTV terminology this policy is called RND-RND scheduling policy [12]. Note that the transmission time depends on the chunk size and on the transmitter upload capacity.

All the above algorithms have been implemented in the simulator. Details about the simulator design and performance are available from [7,14].

2.4 Simulation Scenario

Here we summarize all the parameters that define the simulation scenario considered in this paper. The video-rate is assumed to be equal to 0.4 Mb/s, and the chunk size is fixed to 2 Mbit. Therefore, the source node (selected at random among one of the HS-peer) generates a new chunk every 5 seconds. Each peer has an average number of neighbors equal to 8 neighbors ($k = 8$) for all Overlay construction strategies. For all tests, simulations involve 500 peers, and the simulation lasts 500 chunks, i.e., 2500s of video.

The capacity of links in the physical topology is very large (10Gb/s or 40Gb/s), so that the bottleneck link is the upload capacity of each peer. This is a typical scenario in which users are connected to the Internet with xDSL links, in which the download capacity is typically higher than the upload capacity. Upload access bandwidth is 0.5 Mbit/s for LB-peers and 5 Mbit/s for HS-peers. Download bandwidth was equal to 5 Mbit/s for every peer. The chunk scheduling algorithm is RND-RND, with a trading window size equal to 5 chunks. We run simulation then to compare the three different Overlay topology construction policies: RC, LBA and NLBA strategies. As parameter, we vary the additional degree of HS-peers k', and the number of HS-peers that are present in the Underlay topology.

As performance indexes, we select the load on actual links of the Underlay topology, i.e., the load due to chunk transmission on the physical link. We report also the average number of hops traversed by each chunk, i.e., the corresponding Underlay path length of each Overlay link. Both these two metrics are important to assess the impact on the Underlay topology of the P2P-TV traffic, so to appreciate how increasing degree of network awareness can reduce the actual traffic the Underlay network has to carry. All results presented in this paper are averaged over 10 independent runs.

To observe the impact of the different topologies on the quality of service perceived by users, we evaluate the *chunk delivery delay*, i.e., the delay from when the source emits the chunk to when a peer receives it. Indeed, assuming that there is enough capacity to deliver the video stream to all peers, the chunk delivery delay is typically considered the main performance index to be optimized in live P2P-TV systems: minimizing it means minimizing the delay since when the information is produced at the source and when it can be played at the peers, guaranteeing therefore better "live" experience; furthermore, the chunk delivery delay is also related to the startup time, i.e., the time required to a peer that "tunes" to a channel to start receiving the video data [12].

3 Results

3.1 Network-Centric Scenario

Fig.3 reports the network link load for the different Overlay topology strategies, using a log scale. Plot on the left refers to the Underlay topology backbone links, i.e., the links between Milano and Roma, while the plot on the right refers to the access links, i.e., the links between access and backbone nodes. The additional degree of HS-peers k' is used as parameter. It can be observed that both LBA and NLBA reduce the bandwidth occupation on network links of a factor of 10. In particular, forming the island between

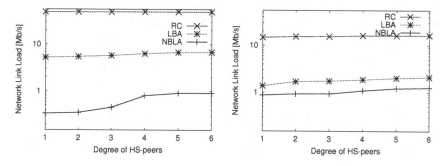

Fig. 3. Network links load adopting different strategies for varying degree k' of HS-peers. Backbone links (links between Milano and Roma spots) on the left, access links (all node-node links which are not backbone) on the right.

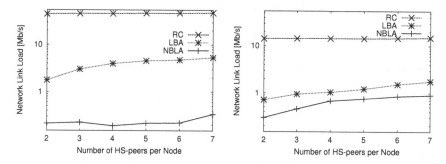

Fig. 4. Network links load adopting different strategies for varying number of HS-peers per node. Backbone links on the left, access links on the right.

peers that are connected to the same access nodes (LBA algorithms) allows to reduce the amount of traffic in backbone links from 45Mb/s (corresponding to about 115 video streams) to only 5Mb/s (or about 12 video streams). This is due to the fact that most of the chunks are transmitted between peers that are connected to the same access node, therefore avoiding crossing backbone links. Enforcing a smarter interconnection between HS-peers (NLBA algorithm) further reduces the load on backbone links, so that about 0.4Mb/s is on average transmitted, corresponding to the minimum value of a single copy of the video stream. Notice that the degree of links between HS-peers has little effects on the link load. Indeed, it is sufficient to use one additional link to already optimize the Overlay performance. Moreover, increasing k' actually reduces the benefit of the optimized topology, since two HS-peers that are far apart in the Underlay topology can possibly exchange chunks due the random peer selection policy implemented by the chunk scheduling algorithm.

Similar considerations hold when looking at the load carried on access links. In this case it is possible to note that the improvement of the NLBA and the LBA strategies are more similar. Indeed, the choice of the k' additional neighbors has been designed to reduce the traffic on the backbone links only.

Fig.4 reports the network link load versus the number of HS-peers per actual Underlay node. Also in this case it can be seen that the presence of at least one HS-peer is sufficient to optimize the Overlay topology so that traffic on the Underlay network is reduced (in this case we selected $k' = 2$). Similarly as in the previous case, increasing the number of HS-peers per nodes increases the network link load as well. This is due again to the chunk scheduling policy that allows a random selection of peers. In case a larger number of HS-peers is present, a larger number of links among them in the Overlay topology is present. During chunk scheduling, then, there is an increased probability that those links are selected to transmit a chunk between two HS-peers. Finally, in case the LBA strategy is considered, HS-peer to HS-peer connections are generated at random, possibly between two far apart nodes, so that more physical links are crossed.

To confirm this intuition, and to appreciate the better usage of Underlay resources, the number of hops traversed by each successful chunk transmission, $E[H]$, is reported. Practically, this parameter shows how many "local" transmissions a strategy can do. Simulations with configuration described above shows that the mean number of hops per each chunk tranmission adopting a RC strategy is

$$E[H]_{RC} = 3.11 \tag{1}$$

whereas much better results are reached by smart algorithms:

$$E[H]_{LBA} = 1.33, \tag{2}$$

$$E[H]_{NLBA} = 1.14 \tag{3}$$

These results confirm that most of chunks do not traverse more than one hop when location awareness is enabled. NLBA strategy gives best results because logical links among HS-peers, that connect together different islands, are mapped at most on only two hop long path, corresponding to a (host)-(node), a (node)-(node), and finally a (node)-(host) on the Underlay topology; moreover, all other links between two LS-peers or between a LS-peer and a HS-peer are mapped on (host)-(node) and (node)-(host) links, so that only one router is crossed.

3.2 User-Centric Performance

Fig. 5 reports on the left the average chunk delivery time for varying degree of HS-peers and for different strategies. The number of peers in the simulation is 1000, with 6 HS-peers for each node. Few considerations hold: first, both LBA and NLBA offer better performance than the RC policy. This is due to the presence of connections between HS-peers that form a fast backbone among HS-peers. This allows to quickly distribute the chunks on the Overlay topology [12]. Indeed, in the RC case, the additional k' connections HS-peers have are randomly spread among all peers. On the contrary, the Bandwidth awareness of LBA and NLBA strategies forces HS-peers to preferentially connect to other HS-peers. In addition, Fig. 5 shows that increasing k' improves the probability of chunks to be transmitted between HS-peers, reducing chunk delivery time.

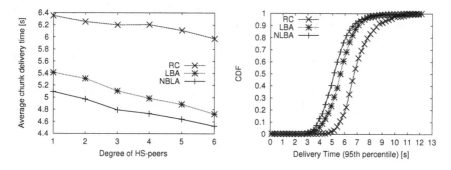

Fig. 5. Average chunk delivery time for varying degree k' of HS-peers on the left. Cumulative distribution function of the 95 percentile of the chunk delivery time for different Overlay topology strategies on the right.

To give more insight, Fig. 5 reports on the right the cumulative distribution function (among peers) of the 95th percentile of the chunk delivery time. For each peer we compute 95th percentile of the chunk delivery time (computed among all chunks), and plot its distribution among peers. We select this index as another good parameter to quantify the quality of service perceived by each user. Intuitively, it reports the delay with which peers receive the chunk with probability 0.95. The results refer to a scenario in which $k' = 2$ and the number of HS-peers per node is set to 6 as above. As we can see, again NLBA and LBA strategies obtain better performance respect to the RC topology, even if improvements are limited. This is essentially due to the fact that LBA and NLBA strategies prefer to interconnect HS-peers among themselves, forming a sort of high speed interconnection that allows to quickly spread the chunks among the islands of peers. On the contrary, the RC strategy does not explicitly exploit the peer bandwidth when interconnecting peers. Moreover, the Random peer and chunk selection ignores any peer properties, so that the resulting chunk spreading is not optimal. In more details, after six seconds both NLBA and LBA strategies guarantee that 80% of peers has already received the chunks in 95% of time. Adopting the RC strategy, after 6 seconds, only 20% of peers are assured to receive the chunk with probability 0.95.

In summary, the network aware Overlay topologies can also improve the P2P-TV performance, while at the same time greatly reducing the offered traffic the Underlay network has to carry.

4   Conclusions

In this paper we investigated the impact of P2P-TV traffic over the physical topology of a network. Since P2P-TV applications are increasingly becoming popular among users, networks operators are worried that the traffic these applications can inject in the network may cause potential congestion if not carefully controlled. We therefore developed a simulator to efficiently study the amount of traffic links of the network carry due to peers watching a P2P-TV stream. We compared then different Overlay setup strategies with increasing level of network-awareness, i.e., in which information about the physical placement of peers and their capacity is made available to the peers during the overlay topology setup.

Results, even if preliminary, show that it is possible to reduce the amount of traffic the network has to carry by up to two orders of magnitude, while, at the same time improving the quality of service perceived by users. This encourage further investigations to increase the level of network awareness of P2P-TV applications.

References

1. SopCast, http://www.sopcast.com
2. PPLive, http://www.pplive.com
3. Babelgum, http://www.babelgum.com
4. Zattoo, http://www.zattoo.com
5. TVUnetworks, http://www.tvunetworks.com
6. Cohen, B.: Incentives Build Robustness in BitTorrent (May 2003)
7. Traverso, S.: Master Thesis: Design and Implementation of an Integrated Simulator for P2P Video-streaming Application Performance Evaluation, Politecnico di Torino (2008)
8. Langellotti, A.M., Mastropietro, S., Moretti, F.T., Soldati, A.: Il Backbone IP di Telecom Italia Wireline, Notiziario Tecnico Telecom Italia Anno 13(2), Roma (2004)
9. Massouli, L., Twigg, A., Gkantsidis, C., Rodriguez, P.: Randomized decentralized broadcasting algorithms. In: INFOCOM, Anchorage, AK (May 2007)
10. Sanghavi, S., Hajek, B., Massouli, L.: Gossiping with multiple messages. In: INFOCOM, Anchorage, AK (May 2007)
11. Bonald, T., Massouli, L., Mathieu, F., Perino, D., Twigg, A.: Epidemic Live Streaming: Optimal Performance Trade-Offs. In: Sigmetrics 2008, Annapolis, ML (June 2008)
12. da Silva, A.P.C., Leonardi, E., Mellia, M., Meo, M.: A Bandwidth-Aware Scheduling Strategy for P2P-TV Systems. In: 8th International Conference on Peer-to-Peer Computing 2008 (P2P 2008), Aachen, September 8-11 (2008)
13. Liu, Y.: On the minimum delay peer-to-peer video streaming: how realtime can it be? In: ACM Multimedia 2007, Augsburg, Germany (September 2007)
14. P2PTV-Sim,
http://www.napa-wine.eu/cgi-bin/twiki/view/Public/Software

Enhancing Progressive Encryption for Scalable Video Streams

Viktor Gergely and Gábor Fehér

High Speed Networks Laboratory,
Department of Telecommunication and Media Informatics,
Budapest University of Technology and Economics
H-1117, Magyar Tudósok körútja 2., Budapest, Hungary
{gergely,feher}@tmit.bme.hu

Abstract. The technique called progressive encryption is used in many areas of content security. However, the plain algorithm itself is only applicable in real transmission scenarios where no packet loss occurs, otherwise additional error correction techniques need to be used in order to achieve maximum decodeability of network packets. The cipher-stepping method (CSM) described in this article adds error correction to progressive encryption in the case where stream ciphers are used to encrypt stream data. It is also explained how the CSM method along with progressive encryption can be used in the encryption of scalable video streams.

Keywords: progressive encryption, scalable video streaming, stream ciphers, wireless networks.

1 Introduction

Scalable video coding has been an active research area for decades. Up to now, several solutions exist for streaming multimedia over networks, especially the Internet. In order to deliver multimedia services over wired and wireless networks, efficient encryption becomes one of the main problems in scalable video streaming. The aim of the Secure Scalable Streaming technology (SSS) [4] is to enable efficient transcoding of encrypted scalable video streams also over wireless networks [3] using progressive encryption. Due to the fact that progressive encryption partially contradicts the requirement of flexible accessibility to the content of the media stream when the media is transmitted over channels that suffer from packet losses, it is desirable to converge better to this requirement by increasing the robustness of progressive encryption.

Section 2 highlights the advantages of stream ciphers that can be exploited to keep the stream cipher synchronized for proper decryption after lost packets, followed by Section 3 introducing the main idea of progressive encryption. Section 4 describes a proposal of an algorithm called cipher-stepping method (CSM) that can be used to keep the state of a stream cipher synchronized with the received packet, hereby enhancing the robustness of progressive encryption.

M. Oliver and S. Sallent (Eds.): EUNICE 2009, LNCS 5733, pp. 51–58, 2009.
© Springer-Verlag Berlin Heidelberg 2009

Robustness of packet decryption is analyzed theoretically and practically based on packet loss measurements on a wireless network, including a comparison of the CSM method to the classical progressive encryption, described in Section 5. The applicability of the CSM method for scalable video streams is presented in Section 6. Section 7 summarizes the advantage and applicability of the proposed algorithm.

2   The Stream Cipher Architecture

Before the demonstration of the CSM method, it is important to understand the main features of the stream cipher architecture. Block ciphers are the most famous types of ciphers used in symmetric encryption. They operate on fixed-length data blocks, i.e. a fixed amount of plaintext can be encrypted with a key, which produces a fixed amount of ciphertext. A typical example of block ciphers is the AES cipher [2] used in a wide range of applications.

On the contrary, stream ciphers operate on streams of arbitrary length, using a secret key and a public initialization vector as input, and output a stream of random-looking symbols, known as keystream [1]. This output is used for encrypting the data stream by applying exclusive-or (XOR) on the data symbols and the keystream, as shown in Fig. 1.

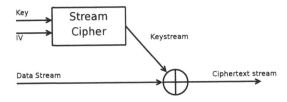

Fig. 1. Encryption using synchronous stream cipher

The stream cipher architecture implies that the state of the cipher is completely independent from the input stream, which can be utilized by the cipher-stepping method described in Section 4. It is important to note that there exist asymmetric stream cipher constructions where this independence cannot be assumed, the article only covers the usage of symmetric stream ciphers.

3   Progressive Encryption

Progressive encryption has been a widely used technique for a long time. The purpose of the technique is to increase data security by encrypting data segments (tiles) continously without reinitializing the cipher instead of encrypting tiles independently of each other and reinitializing the state of the cipher before encrypting each tile. Examples of usage cover progressive encryption and access control of JPEG 2000 images [5] or the Secure Scalable Streaming technique [3], [4] used for encryption of scalable video streams.

On the one hand, an advantage of the progressive encryption method is that ciphering a larger amount of data in one session instead of beginning a new session for each tile and ciphering them independently, encryption can be made more secure as it becomes a harder task for the attacker to get access to encrypted information. This is due to lower correlation between the transmitted packets, and solving information related to encryption requires more capacity. On the other hand, progressive encryption enables less flexible accessibility to the data stream, because data packets cannot be decrypted independently of each other.

By using progressive encryption, the time required for encryption of a certain amount of data can be reduced, due to lower number of cipher initializations, which can be rather costly in case of certain stream cipher types. Several new stream cipher types have been introduced [1] as a result of the ECRYPT Stream Cipher Project (eSTREAM) which can possibly outperform conventional stream ciphers i.e. AES in some aspects including speed measured in cycles per byte (CPB) especially for long streams. Therefore, using progressive encryption for these ciphers is essential for acceptable level of security and performance.

4 The Cipher-Stepping Method (CSM)

4.1 Keeping the Cipher State Synchronized

The aim of the cipher-stepping method (CSM) is to keep the state of the stream cipher synchronized with the received packet bytes, even if one or more packet is lost during transmission. By using a cipher for progressive encryption based on the stream cipher architecture desribed in Section 2, it can be seen that the state of the stream cipher does not depend on the value of the ciphered bytes, only the number of bytes ciphered. Therefore it is desirable to keep a record of the number of bytes ciphered in the actual session to synchronize the cipher to the correct state before decrypting each packet. This can be done by extending the header of each transmitted packet with an extra information containing the number of bytes encrypted in the current session till the current packet. Fig. 2 shows a scenario where packets are extended with the synchronization information.

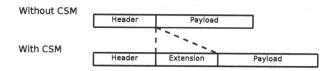

Fig. 2. Header extension for cipher state synchronization

4.2 Decryption Using Cipher Stepping

When decrypting a received packet, first the state of the cipher has to be synchronized with the actual received packet in order to decrypt the packet correctly. By investigating the header extension information in the packet, it can be determined what state the stream cipher should be in for correct decryption. If no packet loss happened after decryption of the previous packet, the number of bytes decrypted with the cipher should be equal to the header information, so the packet can be decrypted using the cipher with no additional operation. If one or more packets are lost before the actual packet, the number of bytes decrypted with the stream cipher is less than the number in the header of the actual packet. In this case, the cipher has to decrypt a number of bytes to reach the state when the received packet can be decrypted. In the CSM method the cipher should decrypt so many bytes of irrelevant information that the number of decrypted bytes is equal to the number of bytes shown in the packet header. As the state of the stream cipher only depends on the amount of information encrypted in the actual session, the bytes used for stepping the cipher to the correct state can be chosen arbitrarily. Provided that no packet disorder occurs during transmission, the cipher can be set to the correct state for each received packet.

4.3 Example Scenario

To summarize the CSM method, the following scenario is taken.

Let us take a session of packets where the first packet is N_1 bytes long, the second is N_2 bytes long, etc. Assume that the second packet is lost over the network. Let C represent the cipher state (the number of decrypted bytes after initialization), and let H_i stand for the header extension information in the i-th packet.

Initially, $C = 0$, because no packets were decrypted so far. After decrypting the first packet, $C = N_1$ holds. The second packet is lost, so after receiving the third packet, the cipher state remains the same as after decrypting the first packet. Before decrypting the third packet, $C = N_1$ and $H_3 = N_1 + N_2$, which implies that $C < H_3$. Therefore, the cipher has to be synchronized before decrypting the third packet using the CSM method, which is done by stepping the cipher with $H_3 - C = N_2$ arbitrary bytes. After synchronization $C = H_3$ holds, so the third packet can be decrypted, and the cipher moves to state $H_3 + N_3 = N_1 + N_2 + N_3$, which is the same as the state of the cipher if the second packet were not lost during transmission.

5 Robustness of Packet Decryption

A self-explanatory measurement of robustness of the cipher-stepping method is comparing the number of decodeable packets while not using any enhancement to the number of decodeable packets using the CSM method. The comparison is made both using theoretical approach and analysing measurements based on packet transmission over a wireless network. Redundancy solutions that can further increase the robustness of the method itself are over the scope of this article.

5.1 Theoretical Approach

Let us assume that a channel for data transmission has a packet loss probability p for a specific time interval. Let p_i denote the probability of receiving i packets correctly. The number of correctly received packets is represented by probability variable X. Therefore the distribution of X is

$$\mathbf{Pr}(X = i) = p_i \tag{1}$$

where

$$p_0 = p, \quad p_1 = (1-p)p, \quad p_2 = (1-p)^2 p, \quad \ldots, \quad p_N = (1-p)^N \tag{2}$$

in the case where the cipher-stepping method is not used and N is the number of packets encrypted in a session. The distribution of X is similar to geometrical distribution. The average number of decodeable packets can be derived by calculating the estimated value of this variable:

$$
\begin{aligned}
\mathbf{EX} = \sum_{i=0}^{N} i p_i &= \sum_{i=0}^{N-1} i(1-p)^i p + N(1-p)^N = \\
&= \frac{1-p}{p} - \sum_{i=N}^{\infty} i(1-p)^i p + N(1-p)^N = \\
&= \frac{1-p}{p} - N(1-p)^N - \frac{(1-p)^{N+1}}{p} + N(1-p)^N = \\
&= \frac{1-p-(1-p)^{N+1}}{p}.
\end{aligned}
$$

When using the cipher-stepping method, neither lost packet causes further decodeability problems in other packets, so the distribution of X is reduced to binomial distribution, as shown below:

$$
\begin{aligned}
\mathbf{Pr}(X = k) &= \mathbf{Pr}(k \text{ correct packets received}) = \\
&= \mathbf{Pr}(N - k \text{ packets dropped out of } N) = \\
&= \binom{N}{N-k} p^{N-k}(1-p)^k = \binom{N}{k}(1-p)^k p^{N-k}.
\end{aligned}
$$

Therefore X is a binomial probability variable with parameters N, $(1-p)$. The average number of decodeable packets is

$$\mathbf{EX} = N(1-p). \tag{3}$$

5.2   Measurement Results

The robustness of the CSM method was also analyzed using transmission measurements in real time environment. The measurement scenario was sending packets from a wired to a wireless network node through congested channel. The congestion was created by producing CBR background traffic with UDP packets of 2 kilobytes each and a time lag of 2 milliseconds. The analyzed traffic contained UDP packets of length 2 kilobytes with sequence numbering and a time lag of 7 milliseconds. Running the tests with the configuration above resulted in approximately 0.002 probability of packet loss in the analyzed stream over a WLAN channel with 54 Mbit/s bitrate.

The measurement data was derived from identifying lost packets and calculating the number of correctly received packets using progressive encryption with and without the CSM method. For comparison with the theoretical results, the packet loss probability p was estimated by calculating the rate of the number of received packets to the number of all sent packets. Calculating p for shorter periods can lead to adaptively choosing the parameters (header extension overhead and the number of tiles in a session) of the CSM method – assuming that the packet loss probability can be considered constant for the interval of estimation.

The results of the measurement are shown in Fig. 3, where *EX1* and *EX2* mean the estimated values described in Section 5.1, *Sim1* and *Sim2* mean the average number of decodeable packets in the case of using and not using the CSM method, respectively.

The difference between the theoretical and measured values is not significant when using the CSM method, as in this case, a packet loss results in no further undecodeable packets, so the packet loss probability and the number of lost

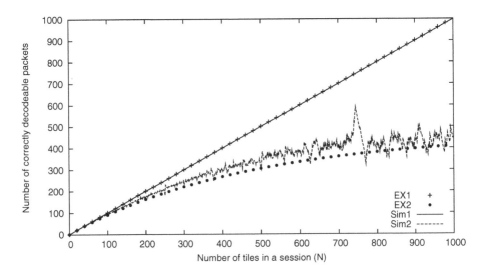

Fig. 3. Measurement results in comparison with theoretical results ($p \approx 0.002$)

packets are strictly correlated. However, when not using the CSM method, the difference of the theoretical and practical results increase if more tiles are encrypted continously in a session. This effect is due the lower number of samples from which the average number of decodeable packets is calculated when larger sessions are taken. When calculating the number of decodeable packets after a lost packet, all further packets were assumed to be corrupted. In certain application circumstances, when self-synchronizing stream ciphers are used or the state of the stream cipher can be changed adaptively to packet losses, the number of decodeable packets can be increased, even if the CSM method is not used.

Consequently, the measurement results indicate that the CSM method can be very effective in increasing the number of correctly decodeable packets when using progressive encryption with large number of tiles encrypted in a session. In this case large sessions also gain greater security of the transmitted data and produce smaller encryption time by avoiding regular initialization of the stream cipher.

6   Applicability for Scalable Video Streams

For scalable video streams it is an important requirement to have flexible accessibility to the different layers included in the video stream. During encryption, different encryption keys need to be used for the different layers to enable the customization of the video stream in the network nodes without decrypting and re-encrypting the stream. When applying progressive encryption it is desirable to arrange the video packets into different groups by the video layer information and encrypt the packet groups independently in different sessions.

The packets of different layers can differ in packet size, importance, quality or confidentiality, so the length of header extension used in the CSM method can

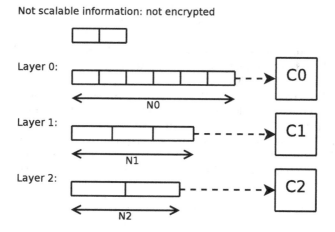

Fig. 4. Example configuration of CSM for scalable video streams

be arbitrarily chosen for each group, making the CSM method and progressive encryption flexible to adapt to the needs of specific applications. Fig. 4 shows an example of the CSM method parameters for each layer group of a scalable video stream.

7   Conclusion

In this paper, a method was introduced which can increase robustness of progressive encryption by utilizing the property of stream ciphers that the cipher state depends only on the amount of encrypted information. The synchronization of the cipher can be maintained by a relatively small overhead introduced by a header extension of the transmitted packets, making decryption resistant to packet losses over a network. Theoretical analysis and wireless network measurements confirm gain increase of the CSM method for large sessions in progressive encryption, which additionally enhances the security of the transmitted content. The proposed method can be easily adapted to encryption of scalable video streams, making the method practically useful.

Acknowledgement

This paper has been (partially) supported by HSNLab, Budapest University of Technology and Economics (http://www.hsnlab.hu) and the European Union through the OPTIMIX FP7 ICT project (http://www.ict-optimix.eu).

References

1. Bjørstad, T.E.: An Introduction to New Stream Cipher Designs. In: 25th Chaos Communication Congress (December 2008)
2. Schneier, B.: Applied Cryptography, 2nd edn. John Wiley & Sons, Inc., Chichester (1995)
3. Wee, S.J., Apostolopoulos, J.G.: Secure Scalable Video Streaming for Wireless Networks. In: IEEE International Conference on Acoustics, Speech, and Signal Processing, Salt Lake City, Utah (May 2001)
4. Wee, S.J., Apostolopoulos, J.G.: Secure Scalable Streaming Enabling Transcoding Without Decryption. In: IEEE International Conference on Image Processing (ICIP) 2001, Thessaloniki, Greece, October 7–10 (2001)
5. Haggag, A., Ghoneim, M., Lu, J., Yahagi, T.: Progressive Encryption and Controlled Access Scheme for JPEG 2000 Encoded Images. In: ISPACS 2006. International Symposium on Intelligent Signal Processing and Communications (December 2006)

Characterizing User Groups in Online Social Networks

László Gyarmati and Tuan Anh Trinh

High Speed Networks Lab
Department of Telecommunication and Media Informatics
Budapest University of Technology and Economics
{gyarmati,trinh}@tmit.bme.hu

Abstract. The users' role is crucial in the development, deployment and the success of online social networks (OSNs). Despite this fact, little is known and even less has been published about user activities in the operating OSNs. In this paper, we present a large scale measurement analysis of user behaviour, in terms of time spent online, in some popular OSNs, namely Bebo, Flixster, MySpace, and Skyrock, and characterise user groups in OSNs. We used more than 200 PlanetLab [1] nodes for our measurement, monitored more than 3000 users for three weeks by downloading repeatedly their profile pages; more than 100 million pages were processed in total. The main findings of the paper are the following. Firstly, we create a measurement framework in order to observe user activity. Secondly, we present cumulative usage statistics of the different OSNs. Thirdly, we classify the monitored users into different groups and characterise the common properties of the members. Finally, we illustrate the wide applicability of our datasets by predicting the sign out method of the OSN users.

1 Introduction

Online social networks change the way how humans connect, get in touch with each other. Novel online social networks are published almost every day but only a few of them become popular worldwide, the most of them vanish. The success of a social network – both short-term and long-term – depends on the behaviour of its users, in particular the users' activity has an important effect on the services.

The activity of the users, time spent on the OSN, is an important aspect if the value of the social networks has to be expressed. Only the operators of the OSNs have these informations although investors, seeding firms, and advertisers would appreciate and utilize this knowledge. In addition, developers of new social networks can build their systems with more incentives if they merge the properties of successful OSNs.

Measurement studies of online social networks are starting to build up in the last few years. The first group of the results deals with the topology and structure of OSNs. For example, the topological properties of several online social

M. Oliver and S. Sallent (Eds.): EUNICE 2009, LNCS 5733, pp. 59–68, 2009.
© Springer-Verlag Berlin Heidelberg 2009

networks are examined based on real world measurements in [2], including verifying the scale-free network property. Similarly, the topology of Flickr and and its growth is covered in [3]. The second group deals different aspects of contents and applications in OSNs. The authors of [4,5] characterise the usage of social network based applications. User behaviour in user generated content video systems are analysed in [6], based on the popularity of the videos. Furthermore, the structure of blog entries interaction and social connections are explored in [7], while [8] investigated information spreading in OSNs.

These studies improve understanding the characteristics of OSNs, both structurally and functionally, however the measurement of user activity, e.g. time spent online by the users, on OSNs has received little attention from research community so far. In this paper, we present a large scale measurement analysis of user behaviour in some popular OSNs. We used more than 200 PlanetLab nodes for our measurement, monitored more than 3000 users for three weeks by downloading more than 100 million profile pages. We traced members of multiple OSNs, in particular users of MySpace [9], Bebo [10], SkyRock [11], and Flixster [12], to identify common properties of online social networks and identify user groups in OSNs. We obtained our data by processing publicly accessible user profiles with a minute as sampling time over more than three weeks, we make our measurement data available to the research community.

The paper is structured as follows. We describe the goals and challenges of our measurement and the methodology for downloading and processing the social networks in Section 2. Section 3 present an in-depth statistical analysis of user activity on OSNs. In particular, after revealing high-level statistics we classify the users of OSNs into several groups. After identifying the properties of the clusters, we present a method to predict the way a user sign off from the OSN, as an illustration the wide-range applicability of our datasets. Finally, we conclude in Section 4.

2   Measurement Methodology

This section describes the goals of our measurement by identifying the main challenge of an Internet-scale measurement. In addition, we present what type of data have been obtained, how have we collected and processed them.

2.1   Measurement Goals and Challenges

In this section, we describe the non-technology related aspects of our measurement. Our research focus is the user activity on online social networks, therefore datasets that contain individual, not aggregated, online status information of OSNs' users are required. We were not able to obtain data directly from the operators of the OSNs, they only referred to the measurements of comScore [13] which contains only an average, monthly usage data, neither individual nor dynamic user activity metrics are presented. Therefore, we iteratively downloaded the public part of users' profile pages, which contain online status information, and collected real world usage datasets to discover common usage patterns and to highlight the differences of OSNs, instead of carrying out a survey by asking users of OSNs about their usage habits.

The online status of users is handled differently by OSNs: some OSNs do not display status information, some OSNs display it for authorised members (e.g. friends, group members, or logged-in users) while the others handle it publicly if this is allowed by the user. We selected four OSNs where the status information is publicly available. In order to create a statistical analysis of the user activity, the size of the sample (the monitored users) has to be selected appropriately, furthermore the sampling time of the measurement has to be selected carefully because of feasibility problems as the time of downloading and processing a single user is not negligible. Accordingly, we decided to monitor around 1000 users per OSNs on a one minute basis as a trade-off of accuracy and feasibility. The exact number of the monitored users were determined by the availability of the computers used in the measurement. If a user spends less than a minute online it might not be identified as an online user, however, we believe this is only a minor limitation of our measurement.

We tried to select users to be monitored to catch the characteristic of newly joined members of the OSNs, who spend their time on site in order to make connections. However, only MySpace and SkyRock allow to list their new members, on the other sites randomly selected users were monitored.

As several additional properties may have an effect on the activity of the users, we extracted not only the uptime, the time spent online, of the users but - if it is presented - the number of friends and their membership history. Other, non-measurable factors may have an impact on users activity, including uncertainties of human decisions, weather, or professional activities, which we do not and can not incorporate to our measurements.

Our trace do not contain information about the correlation of activities of connected members, or members of user groups, these topics should be investigated in the future. In addition, the users of OSNs may use more than one sites to connect with their friends; an ineresting future work can analyse and reveal the common parts of personal behaviour across multiple OSNs. The datasets of our measurement are available at `http://netecon_group.tmit.bme.hu/source-codes` [14] where the user identifiers are replaced for anonymisation purposes.

2.2   Measurement Setup and Tool

We now discuss the technical aspects of our measurement, including profile page downloading and processing, and we present our monitoring tool. We monitored more than 3000 users, selected randomly, of four OSNs during our measurement on a minute basis, while downloading and processing a typical profile page is around a second. The measurement was carried out between 28 January and 20 February, 2009. Based on the theorem of statistics, the size of the monitored users is large enough to draw conclusion, e.g. political polls are also usually use samples of around 1000 persons. However, we note that our measurement sample

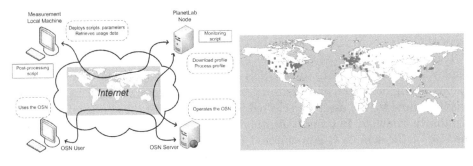

(a) Measurement setup   (b) Topology of PlanetLab nodes used

Fig. 1. Overview of the measurement

might not be a representative sample as OSNs do not publish information about the structure of their population publicly.

Accordingly, the monitoring of users can not be carried out from a single, standalone machine because of scalability reasons. Therefore, we used 212 nodes of PlanetLab, a cluster of more than 900 machines, to carry out the measurement. The machines of PlanetLab executed automated, timed scripts, implemented in Python, which fetched and processed the profile pages. As PlanetLab is a global network, each dataset contains GMT time for consistency reasons. The setup of our measurement along with the topology of the used PlanetLab nodes is presented in Figure 1. Any PlanetLab node can be out of order in any time, therefore we deployed the users to be monitored evenly between the nodes in order to minimise the damage of an unavailable node. As a consequence, we managed to monitor the vast majority of the selected users of the OSNs for more than three weeks continually. To reduce the size of the datasets, data of a user is only stored if the user is online.

3   User Activity in Online Social Networks

The members of online social networks may have different causes to use the services of the OSNs, accordingly each user has its own behaviour. In this section, we analyse our measurement results using statistical methods in order to classify the users of online social networks, furthermore we reveal the common characteristics of the members. First, we present some high-level statistics of our dataset. After that, we reveal the cluster structure of OSNs, finally we shows some interesting finding on how the users sign out from the sites.

3.1   High-Level Statistics

Our dataset contains user activity information on a minute basis, therefore high-level statistics, including average uptime, downtime, and login frequency, can be computed. Uptime, or sojourn time, describes the time period when a user is

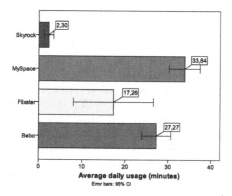

Fig. 2. Average daily usage time of the monitored users during our measurement

logged into an online social network, i.e. the time the user spent using the services of the OSN. Similarly, we use the term downtime for the time duration between two active sessions of a single user, while on login frequency we mean the number of logins of a single user during the measurement period.

The average daily usage time of the monitored users are shown in Figure 2. The users of MySpace have spent the most time on site while the members of SkyRock used their site the least. It is interesting, that data of Flixster has the highest variance. We note, that the measured average usage time depends on the way how the users leave the OSNs, Bebo has 30 minutes server time out, MySpace operates with 20-minute long sessions, while SkyRock handles a user offline after 7 minutes. However, these average sojourn times indicates that the monitored OSNs has different structure and services implying diverse user behaviours.

Detailed high-level statistics are presented in Table 1, including uptime, downtime, and the frequency of the usage. The users of MySpace have spent 11.58 minutes on site after a login in average, much less than Flixster or Bebo users. However, the duration between two log-ins is the smallest at MySpace, in average the users are only 10 hours offline then they check their OSN. Accordingly, as the number of weekly sign-ins shows, the monitored population of MySpace was the most active while the activity of SkyRock users was moderate. The different usage patterns may represent the fascination of the social networks, in terms of popular services, number of friends, because a user spends more time on a more interesting site. The implication of these findings is that it is worthy to use similar services like MySpace has on a new OSN to have more active users, as active users produce revenue for the operator of the OSN.

3.2   Identifying User Groups in Online Social Networks

In the followings, we focus on the user population of MySpace and Bebo as we characterise the different groups of the OSNs, because we were able to monitor more users in these systems due to the availability of PlanetLab nodes during

Table 1. High-level statistics of our online social network datasets

	Bebo	Flixster	MySpace	SkyRock
Number of monitored users	954	451	942	422
Average daily usage time (minutes)	27.269	17.264	33.840	2.2963
Standard deviation of daily usage	53.437	100.094	56.3072	11.654
Average uptime (minutes)	28.15	18.20	11.58	9.17
Standard deviation of uptime	27.389	44.058	15.441	13.051
Average downtime (days)	1.011	1.044	0.334	3.985
Standard deviation of downtime	2.888	3.308	1.458	6.441
Average weakly number of logins	6.385	6.2253	20.043	1.341
Standard deviation of weakly logins	17.725	28.746	33.550	5.296

Table 2. Properties of centroids of the different clusters of MySpace

	Cluster							
	1	2	3	4	5	6	7	8
Uptime (mean)	8.9721	34.7775	26.4393	17.1775	10.6759	8.7699	9.8596	5.7890
Uptime (stddev)	11.121	33.642	21.248	12.003	14.864	8.988	11.172	6.388
Uptime (median)	4.556	25.794	21.016	16.922	10.056	8.041	5.681	3.258
Uptime (sum)	2861.29	1927.47	1495.63	356.46	22.89	39.79	1018.36	153.98
Downtime (mean)	76.967	662.95	602.470	1511.56	11405.0	5519.93	247.83	1200.88
Downtime (std. dev.)	230.93	1438.79	1023.66	2056.54	8405.65	6277.05	578.51	2067.38
Downtime (median)	2.922	231.056	225.727	789.009	11714.8	3512.61	21.474	339.447
Logins	327.64	73.24	57.79	20.18	2.14	4.73	108.16	28.33
Friends	101.62	450.18	32.28	14.83	11.36	10.88	25.63	17.69
Number of users in cluster	45	17	97	160	36	86	152	227

our measurement. However, the members of Flixster and SkyRock can be also classified into several groups based on their behaviour.

The users of MySpace can be classified into eight groups based on their behaviour, we used the TwoStep clustering algorithm of the SPSS statistical software in our analysis. Each monitored user has its personal behaviour descriptors, like uptime, downtime, number of logins, for the duration of our measurement. Based on the datasets we calculate the users' individual statistics, including mean, standard deviation, median, sum, afterwards we compute the average properties which describe the user behaviour in the clusters. The detailed statistics are shown in Table 2, these values describe the centroids of the groups. The most diverse values of the properties are shown with italic characters.

In order to understand better the typical properties of the clusters, we visualize the relation between the average downtime and the uptime of the users along with the membership information in Figure 3. Figure 3(a) shows all the users while the more active user groups, in terms of shorter downtimes, are presented in Figure 3(b). Cluster 5 consists of users who are visiting their OSN very rarely, while members of Cluster 6 use MySpace a bit more frequently. Based on the average uptime, Cluster 2 consists of users who are online both for long periods

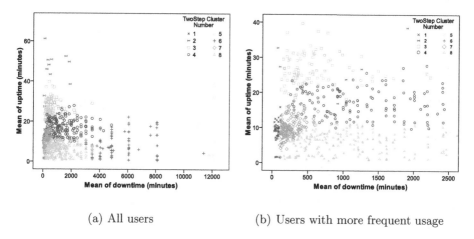

(a) All users   (b) Users with more frequent usage

Fig. 3. Members of different groups based on their average uptime and downtime periods [MySpace]

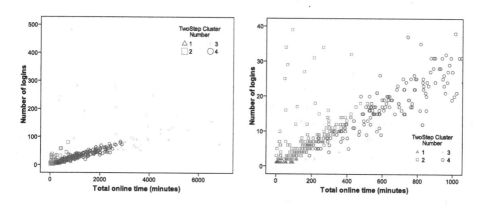

Fig. 4. Clustering users of Bebo

and frequently. In Figure 3(b), the characteristics of the remaining five groups are shown. Based on the time spent on site Cluster 3, 4, and 8 can be separated where the former is the group of most actives while the later's users are least "OSN dependent". The final two clusters (1 and 7) are separated based on their login frequencies, the users of Cluster 1 have the shortest downtime periods.

In Figure 5, five clusters out of eight are presented along with their best fitting cubic functions. Cluster 5 and 6 are distinguished based on the number of logins. These users check their pages around once a week, but if they are online they spend varying amount of time on the OSN. The deviation of uptime periods is an important factor dealing with user groups. Users with smaller deviation have used MySpace for shorter periods than users with larger deviation. These clusters have different user behaviour, therefore the members have to be treated distinctly to maximise the users' satisfaction.

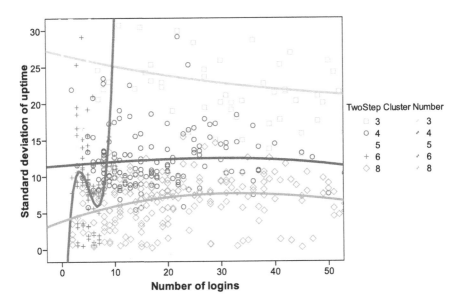

Fig. 5. Standard deviation of uptime periods based on the number of total logins

We use the same clustering algorithm to reveal user groups of Bebo. The sum of time spent online and the number of logins are presented in Figure 4 for Bebo users on two scales. Cluster 3 represents the heavy-users of Bebo, meaning they spend much more time online and/or they sign in to Bebo more frequently. These members are important for both the OSN operating company and for rival OSNs as well. On the one hand, the operator of the OSN have to pay special attention for the heavy users as these users love the services of the OSN, therefore they may persuade their friends to use that OSN. On the other hand, a rival OSN is interested in tempting these users to join their OSN, e.g. by sending special offers to the profile pages of the heavy users. These opposite interests have the same foundation as each OSN wants to earn more money by having more active users online. The members of Cluster 4 spend more time online than the users of Cluster 2, who rather check back more frequent. The last group is formed by users with little interest in Bebo services.

3.3   Sign Out Methods

The focus of our measurement method is the characterisation of user groups at different online social networks based on user activity. However, we are able to predict the way how the users left the OSN site purely based on our observations. As mentioned earlier, we have determined the length of the OSNs' time out session, i.e. the time after the site considers a user as being disconnected from the OSN. A user can left the OSN two different ways, sign out properly by

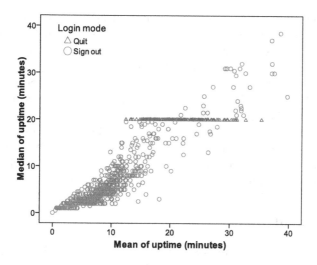

Fig. 6. Sign out methods

clicking the appropriate button or simply closing its Internet browser. In the later case, the session remains active until the time out, therefore it can cause security concerns.

MySpace notices immediately if a user signs out, however it has a 20-minute long session period. The implication of this property is strait forward, if the median of a user's uptimes is 20 minutes, than it is likely, that the user usually just closes its browser, instead of signing out properly. In this case, a short, less than a minute long online period is monitored as a 20-minute long uptime usage, because the user is treated as offline only after the server session times out. The median of the users' uptime as a function of the average uptime period is shown in Figure 6. We use median instead of mode because the uptime can have many values, therefore a value can be the mode of the sample even with only few occurrences. In this case, the median predicts better the users' behaviour. The users who close their browsers are illustrated, based on this method we argue that more than 25 percent of the users do not use the sign out button. We get almost the same ratio if we classify the users based on their modes. As a verification we look the most frequent uptimes in the dataset, the 20-minute activity is the second most frequent period (13.6%), just after the 1-minute long usage (20.7%).

4   Conclusions

In this paper, we have presented a detailed and in-depth analysis of user activity on some popular online social networks based on real world measurements. The characteristics of the activity of users on Bebo, Flixster, MySpace, and SkyRock have been analysed. We have identified several groups of OSN users, the charac- teristics of the clusters have been reviewed. Moreover, we observed that, similar to peer-to-peer systems, there exists a group of users in the OSNs, the heavy users, who use the sites really often for long periods. Our findings about different user groups with different user behaviours can be useful for OSN operators, who are willing to enhance their profit by keeping their heavy users, and also for developers of new OSNs, who can design their services incorporating solutions of popular OSNs to have lot of active users. Despite we have used only publicly accessible information in our measurement, we were able the extract personal online status information, which can be sensitive in some cases. We hope, that our work can initiate a discussion about privacy issues in OSNs, including the accessibility of online status information. Regarding future work, we plan to substantiate our measurement on more users and systems.

Acknowledgement

This paper has been partially supported by HSNLab, Budapest University of Technology and Economics, `http://www.hsnlab.hu`

References

1. PlanetLab, `http://www.planet-lab.org/`
2. Mislove, A., Marcon, M., Gummadi, K., Druschel, P., Bhattacharjee, B.: Measurement and Analysis of Online Social Networks. In: Proceedings of Internet Measurements Conference (2007)
3. Mislove, A., Koppula, H., Gummadi, K., Druschel, P., Bhattacharjee, B.: Growth of the Flickr Social Network. In: Proceedings of the First Workshop on Online Social Networks (2008)
4. Nazir, A., Raza, S., Chuah, C.: Unveiling Facebook: A Measurement Study of Social Network Based Applications. In: Proceedings of Internet Measurements Conference (2008)
5. Gjoka, M., Sirivianos, M., Markopoulou, A., Yang, X.: Poking Facebook: Characterization of OSN Applications In. In: WOSN 2008: Proceedings of the First Workshop on Online Social Networks (2008)
6. Cha, M., Kwak, H., Rodriguez, P., Ahn, Y., Moon, S.: I Tube, You Tube, Everybody Tubes: Analyzing the World's Largest User Generated Content Video System. In: Proceedings of Internet Measurements Conference (2007)
7. Chun, H., Kwak, H., Eom, Y., Ahn, Y., Moon, S., Jeong, H.: Comparison of Online Social Relations in Volume vs. Interaction: a Case Study of Cyworld. In: Proceedings of Internet Measurements Conference (2008)
8. Cha, M., Mislove, A., Adams, B., Gummadi, K.: Characterizing Social Cascades in Flickr. In: Proceedings of the First Workshop on Online Social Networks (2008)
9. MySpace, `http://www.myspace.com`
10. Bebo, `http://www.bebo.com`
11. SkyRock, `http://www.skyrock.com`
12. Flixster, `http://www.flixster.com/`
13. comScore Inc., `http://www.comscore.com/`
14. Economics of Networked Systems Group, BME, `http://netecon_group.tmit.bme.hu/`

Route Prediction on Tracking Data
to Location-Based Services

Attila István Petróczi and Csaba Gáspár-Papanek

Budapest University of Technology and Economics,
Department of Telecommunications and Media Informatics,
Magyar Tudósok Krt. 2, 1117 Budapest, Hungary
{petroczi,gaspar}@tmit.bme.hu
http://www.tmit.bme.hu/home!eng

Abstract. Wireless networks have become so widespread, it is beneficial to determine the ability of cellular networks for localization. This
property enables the development of location-based services, providing
useful information. These services can be improved by route prediction
under the condition of using simple algorithms, because of the limited
capabilities of mobile stations. This study gives alternative solutions for
this problem of route prediction based on a specific graph model. Our
models provide the opportunity to reach our destinations with less effort.

Keywords: mobility modeling, route prediction, Markov model, pattern
matching model, radio frequency identification (RFID), location-based
services (LBS).

1   Introduction

In our rushing world the modern man demands communication and information
channels, that is why they enjoy the benefits of using mobile phones and location
systems. The opportunity to use the location-based services (LBS), which are
information services accessible with mobile devices through the PLMN (public
land mobile network) and utilizing the ability to make use of the location of the
mobile device, is given by these equipments. It does not depend on the device
used. These services are based on localisation, they use GPS coordinates or
information of GSM cells. It is very useful to know where the nearest preferred
restaurant or petrol station is, but it can be even more useful to know which
one we can reach with the least effort. It means that the system offers us the
place which will be the closest to our route in the following few minutes. It is
significant in these applications that the algorithm is simple because the mobile
devices have small capacity of memory, storage and computing. Our aim is to give
such solutions that are very simple and easy to implement, to predict mobility.

Related Works

There were many research projects about route prediction in GSM and ATM
systems in the past and nowadays there are some researches dealing with the

M. Oliver and S. Sallent (Eds.): EUNICE 2009, LNCS 5733, pp. 69–77, 2009.
© Springer-Verlag Berlin Heidelberg 2009

latest technologies like satellite-based localisation networks. Their main aim is to manage the handovers and to reduce the delays caused by them in wireless networks. In the world of prediction there are two main approaches:

- the first is based on predicting the prospective movement of the mobile stations by using their previous motions (for example position, velocity)[1][2] and solving the problem of handovers by appropriate resource allocation[3]
- the supporters of the second theory believe in the methods, based on costumers' conventional behaviour patterns[4][5]. This theory was brought to the front by the Global Positioning System, and most of the applications are about prediction of vehicles' motion.

Chan et al.[2] worked out alternative methods. The first is based on the actual position to predict the next step, reminding us of the first-order Markov Model. The second algorithm is based on actual and former positions, the direction is determined by these data. We work on the generalization of this algorithm. In the third method the routes are segmented and the second algorithm is used on these segments.

Liu et al.[3] explored wireless ATM networks, where they use pattern matching algorithm to predict the next ATM cell during the route. For this reason the examination of cells' rows, measurements of signal strengths and intuitions of the cells' shape is used.

In the early 2000s the development of the mobile phone networks reached the level, when the challenges of networks' management became more complex than prediction of mobile stations' motion. As the result of their evolution the networks became as efficient as the customers and the providers required. The turning-point was that the complex, hypothetical algorithms were surpassed by the simple, algorithms exploitable in practice.

The next technical wave took place with the spreading of the positioning, mainly with the widespread availability of GPS equipments. These technical solutions require more precise prediction ability on one hand, but on the other hand they supplied more usable, precise data. In this area the most promising results were published in the [6][7]. The accuracy of these models were about 70%, but it is necessary to notice that the properties of the environment are inputs for the models. Our aim to define general prediction models, which can be implemented and used easily everywhere, so we require our models to be independent from the platform.

In the literature of the topic generally working prediction models applicable to any environment were not found. We aim to construct universally applicable models, which can collaborate with any tracking system.

2   Mobility Modelling

Our study would like to give such a general solution to predict mobility of mobile equipments and their owners that is simple and easy to implement. In our realization the basis of each single method is a graph-model, which can be generated

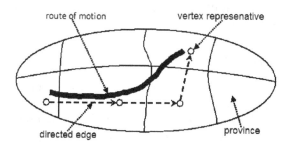

Fig. 1. A given route and its graph representative

by converting the tracking data into graphs. This means that the single directed graph representative of the tracking data is examined, that can be generated from the data according to the required accuracy. The simplest graph creation method is to divide the area into provinces. Let us map the provinces onto the vertices of the graph. We may draw the a_{ij} directed edge of the graph by examining the fixed routes. If we find a route from province i to province j, we draw a directed edge from the point p_i, to the point p_j. You can see such a directed graph representative in Fig. 1.

The methods described below give alternative solutions to predicting routes in such graph model.

3   Mobility Prediction Models

As we have already mentioned, our aim is to define and to analyse such general prediction methods, which can be applied in a wide range, and they can operate in cooperation with the infrastructure of any tracking systems. Probably they are not the most efficient ones in a special environment, but with small-scale transformations they work with any kind of systems. Our elaborated models are classified into 3 groups, such as Simple statistical model, Markov models and Pattern matching models.

Conventional Notations

Nominate with $p_i \cdot p_j$ that case, when in a given route at time t our position is the vertex p_i, at time $t+1$ the vertex p_j will be our position. In the following cases we nominate with $p_i \rightarrow p_j$ those incidences where at a given t_1 time the position is vertex p_i, then at a given $t_2 > t_1$ time the position will be vertex p_j. The models predict the next vertex based on the available information, nominate it with X.

The prediction is based on a well-known indicator confidentiality level. We count it with the following formula:

$$C(X) = \frac{the\ number\ of\ routes\ crossing\ series\ of\ vertices\ P_X}{the\ number\ of\ routes\ crossing\ series\ of\ vertices\ P_i} \qquad (1)$$

The models can give a probability on a confidentiality level, what the next station of the movement will be.

3.1   Simple Statistical Model

One of the tasks attributed to the data mining is the mining of the frequent element sets. The simple statistical model tries to use this to predict routes. The model is very simple, the accuracy of the prediction will be prospectively small. $|p_i, p_k|$ nominate the number of the set of routes, contains p_i and p_k too. At a given vertex p_i the model predict $X = p_k$ vertex for the next station of the route which satisfy in all cases the following inequality:

$$|p_i, p_k| > |p_i, p_j| \quad \forall j \neq k, \quad j = 1, 2, 3, \ldots \tag{2}$$

3.2   Markov Models

Markov models are originated with Markov chains. We assume that the system and its graph representative are given. In this case the directed graph - if there are enough given vertices and edges - behaves similar to the Markov chains. Let us map the vertices of the graph to states of the Markov chain, let us build a matrix from its edges, which can be considered the matrix of transition probabilities. These models are originated with the Markov chain. We may map them to the terminology of the graph model, so Markov models predict the vertex $X = p_{i+1}$ which has the highest confidentiality level in series $(p_{i-z} \cdot \ldots \cdot p_{i-2} \cdot p_{i-1} \cdot p_i) \cdot p_{i+1}$, where the expression in parentheses is known and $z = 0; 1; 2; \ldots$. In mathematical phrases: the model predicts that vertex $X = p_{i+1}$, with the highest corresponding $C(p_{i+1})$ value. Markov models are not capable of prediction in any situation, when there is vertex, which is not a head of any directed edges or when there are no $z - 1$ former vertices of the walk. In practice we implemented and tested the First-, the Second- and the Third-order Markov Models. The depth of the Markov models can be increased, but the demand of memory and storage monotonously rises. By analyzing the former models the following question was formulated in our minds: what kind of results can we get with easing the rigorousness of direct succession or can it help to improve the accuracy of the former models. The pattern matching models were formulated as the result of this intuition. We hope that this will be compensated in increased accuracy and efficiency compared with our former models.

3.3   Pattern Matching Models

Pattern matching models are special cases of frequent sequence mining belonging to the category of frequent sample mining. Frequent sequence mining means that we would like to define part series, which are often appearing in given series. The often expression indicates that in the case of the original task we only deal with the series if the number of the existing series among the routes is higher than a certain threshold. Unfortunately this algorithm is exponential, the frequent sequence mining demands much time and resources in large datasets. In the case of models drawn up by us, task is not entirely this. On one hand we do not demand a minimal incidence threshold from the series, on the other hand we examine only a certain long incidence of series. We expect longer running time and bigger memory claim from these algorithms, than we have experienced in Markov models. We implemented and tested four Pattern Matching Models. With the Pattern Matching Model No. 1 we ease the constraints of the First-order Markov model, instead of $(p_i) \cdot p_{i+1}$, we examine $(p_i) \rightarrow p_k$. The Pattern Matching Model No. 2 eases the constraints of the Second-order Markov model, instead of $(p_{i-1} \cdot p_i) \cdot p_{i+1}$, it examines $(p_k \rightarrow p_i) \cdot p_{i+1}$. We ease the constraints of the Third-order Markov model with Pattern Matching Model No. 1, instead of $(p_{i-2} \cdot p_{i-1} \cdot p_i) \cdot p_{i+1}$, we examine $(p_k \rightarrow p_{i-1} \cdot p_i) \cdot p_{i+1}$. Pattern Matching Model No. 4 is interpreted as the extension of the Pattern Matching Model No. 3 with another former vertex, it means we examine $(p_{k2} \rightarrow p_{k1} \rightarrow p_{i-1} \cdot p_i) \cdot p_{i+1}$. The base of the prediction is the highest corresponding $C(p_{i+1})$ value.

We can count on the fact that the running time and the memory claim of the pattern matching models will be bigger than the demand of the Markov models. We hope that this will be compensated in increased accuracy and efficiency compared with our former models.

4   Simulation

4.1   Concrete Simulation Environment and Simulation Dataset

We simulate the tracking in a shopping area like one equipped with RFID (Radio Frequency IDentification) readers and tags. It means we simulate the motion of the customers, and we store their routes in datasets. The datasets contain the identifier of the tag, the identifier of the reader and the time when the action has happened. The simulated model is two-dimensional. The readers are ideal readers, the characteristic of the readers are circles with $10\sqrt{2}$-radius. The measurements of the simulated area are 90×50, in which 45 readers watch the motions. The readers are placed in a grid, from the (5;5) to the (85;45) coordinates by 10 units. The customers move in discreet grid in the area simultaneously, one step is one unit.

A public tracking dataset of location-based services was not accessible, therefore a simulation dataset was used to demonstrate the effectiveness of our solutions. Our datasource simulates a customer of a hypermarket, where the topology of shelves, the products and their locations, the product sets bought by the costumers are based on real life. The sufficient quality of the simulated dataset is guaranteed by the complex artificial behaviour of the customer agent, which contains the following aspects:

- The customers enter the hypermarket with an explicit aim represented by a set of products, but they can buy items impulsively as well.

- When a custromer enters the hypermarket, it has rough map of the topology of the hypermarket and the positions of products, and during its movements this map is improved by new data.
- The agent has a searching strategy to find products with unknown locations, but it has a probability model to give up the searching as well.

The simulation method has an additional RFID tracking layer as well, RFID readers with overlapping effective range track the costumers shopping basket, which contains RFID tags, therefore the precise location of the agents can not be calculated by processing of the dataset of RFID readers. Our input was this simulated tracking dataset to analyse our proposed algorithms.

Divide the area into provinces according to areas seen by $n = 1, 2, 3, \ldots$ readers. In this manner the area is separeted to 121 pieces, that means we get a 121-vertex graph. The determination of the edges' number is more complicated task, but it is possible if we know the characteristic of the training set. In this situation the number of edges is 888. The complexity of the graph is evident, nevertheless we try to predict route in the graph.

During generating the simulated data we make the first filtration. We stored the stations of the routes infrequently, only when it changes province, so in the graph terminoligy when it goes across an edge or it steps to another vertex of the graph. We characterize this vertex with the identifiers of the readers seeing it. Since temporal examinations are not made, - this is the reason, why the graph representative can be used - the data is cleaned from the time moments and only the series of the provinces' identifiers are left in the stored data. From this information the routes are unambiguous definable.

After this procedure we get a tracking dataset with 14 200 routes, on which the prediction analysis of the models are done. This dataset is divided in two parts: a training set with 12 000 and a validation set with 2 200 routes. The average length of routes is 126.4 in the training set. We can consider this dataset as big enough to treat the measured accuracy as general.

If the graph is examined an interesting fact can be discovered. The outdegree of the vertices has big variation. It is thanked that, the simulated customers can go in a discrete grid, so they can step into such provinces, which is not neighbouring. The Fig. 2 shows the distribution of the vertices' outdegree. On the horizontal axis of the diagram we represent the outdegree of the vertices, and we depicted the percentile distribution of the vertices on the vertical axis.

4.2 Results

Table 1 shows the training time, the validation time, the next vertex's prediction time and the accuracy in percent of the single models. It is visible that the training time of the models are a bit long, but it is offline running time, so it can be accepted, they are needed to run rarely. Intuitive requirement is taken, that the real-time application gives result in 1 second. Our models have to satisfy this statement.

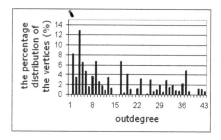

Fig. 2. The distribution of the vertices as the function of their outdegree

Table 1. Comparion of the prediction models

Model	Training Time	Validation Time	Prediction Time	Accuracy
Simple statistical model	24min	52s	0.18ms	32.4%
First-order Markov model	27min	51s	0.18ms	49.7%
Second-order Markov model	3.8h	50s	0.18ms	64.7%
Third-order Markov model	5.3h	48s	0.17ms	69.2%
Pattern matching model No. 1	8min	46s	0.16ms	6.1%
Pattern matching model No. 2	6.3h	12min	2.53ms	51.6%
Pattern matching model No. 3	12.9h	13min	2.74ms	65.2%
Pattern matching model No. 4	17.8h	12min	2.51ms	51.9%

The simulations's results of the Markov models are seen in the Fig. 3(b)-3(d). It is observable that the distribution of the models are almost the same, the diagrams are similar to each other, there are at the same place under and above the average. The variation of the distributions are almost the same, there are deviations only between the average values by the difference in elevations. The results meet our expectations, because there origin is the same first-order Markov Model. The accuracies of the models are 50, 65 and 69%. It is noticeable that completed with newer former vertices the accuracy is rising, but the degree of the improvement is falling. It means the marginal utility of a newer vertex is falling. The improvement of plus one vertex is not rewarding, because the demand of the memory and the storage is rising more.

The accuracy distributions of the pattern matching models (Fig. 3(f)-3(h)) - except for the Pattern matching model No. 1 - are very similar to each other, the variations of them are almost the same, the difference is only the average value. We can parallel them to the Markov models, the distribution of the accuracy is similar. It was expectable, because the origin of the models is the first-order Markov model. It is seen that the unstretching of the rigorousness of the direct following make the model less accurate, but on the other hand the added former vertex can improve the efficiency of the models. Nevertheless the training time

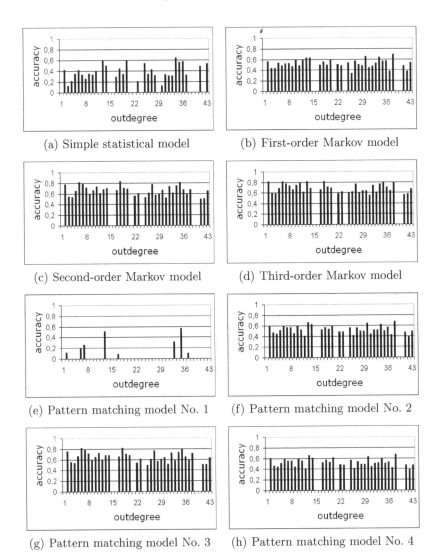

(a) Simple statistical model   (b) First-order Markov model

(c) Second-order Markov model   (d) Third-order Markov model

(e) Pattern matching model No. 1   (f) Pattern matching model No. 2

(g) Pattern matching model No. 3   (h) Pattern matching model No. 4

Fig. 3. The accuracy of the models as a function of the outdegree of the vertices

increases, and it is not worth this increase, because nearly the same accuracy can be reached with simpler models.

Analysing the Pattern matching model No. 1 (Fig. 3(e)) is very interesting, because it is very different from the others. We expect more efficiency from this model based on the success of the simple statistical model, because in that case we add the vertices, which were visited in the past. We can get the conclusion from that the examined area is closed. There are some outgoing vertices, and the customers leave the shopping area once. The pattern matching model No. 1 predict these vertices all the time. This method can predict right vertex, only if the customer is at the last but one station of his route.

By analysing the figures above we can notice another interesting fact, the accuracy of the prediction depends on the outdegree of the vertices only in small range, meaning it does not depend on the number of the potential next vertices. We can deduce that there are some typical routes in the shopping area, and there are only some individuals, who deviate from this. These individuals increase the outdegree of the vertices, but they can not affect the typical routes. In a future improvement of the model, we only add an edge to the graph, if there are more routes, across it, than a given threshold.

5 Conclusion

The success of the location-based services can be improved with mobility prediction. We gave an alternative solution for this. We defined 4 types of models, which are based on the representative graph, that can be built up by the area separated into provinces. Despite of the intuition that the simple statistical model can not be used to predict the next station of the routes, it can successfully predict that in 30% of the cases. The Markov models are originated with the Markov chains. The models use only the current and some direct former vertices for prediction. If we use these models we can reach about 70% accuracy. Many models were published in which the accuracy is about 60%, still they are used. The pattern matching models are to improve the efficiency of the Markov models. This approach can help a bit, but the offline running time increase more.

The actual published models can be improved, because the accuracy can be increased by training at specific environment. The effects the environment can be trained by the models, and it makes them more useable in the marketing world, or to in finding acquaintances in the users' neighbourhood.

References

1. Junius, M., Kennemann, O.: New Methods for Processing GSM Radio Measurement Data: Applications for locating, Handover, and Network Management. In: Vehicular Technology Conference, vol. 44(1), pp. 338–342 (1994)
2. Chan, J., et al.: A QoS Adaptive Mobility Prediction Scheme for Wireless Networks. In: Global Telecommunications Conference, vol. 3, pp. 1414–1419 (1998)
3. Liu, T., Bahl, P., Chlamtac, I.: An Optimal Self-Learning Estimator for Predicting Inter-Cell User Trajectory Wireless Radio Networks. In: Proceedings of the IEEE International Conference on Universal Personal Communications, San Diego, California, USA, pp. 438–442 (1997)
4. Schonfelder, S.: Some Notes on Space, Location and Travel Behaviour. In: 1. Swiss Transport Reseach Conference, Monte Verita, Ascona (2001)
5. Gartner, N., Messer, C.J., Rathi, A.K.: Traffic Flow Theory. A state-of-the-Art Report, http://www.tfhrc.gov/its/tft/tft.htm
6. Liao, L., Patterson, D.J., Fox, D., Kautz, H.: Building Personal Maps from GPS Data. Annals of the New York Academy of Sciences 1093, 249–265 (2006)
7. Krumm, J., Horvitz, E.: Predestination: Inferring destinations from partial trajectories. In: Dourish, P., Friday, A. (eds.) UbiComp 2006. LNCS, vol. 4206, pp. 243–260. Springer, Heidelberg (2006)

Context Aware Programmable Trackers for the Next Generation Internet

Pedro Sousa

Department of Informatics
University of Minho, Braga, Portugal
`pns@di.uminho.pt`

Abstract. This work introduces and proposes the concept of context aware programmable trackers for the next generation Internet. The proposed solution gives ground for the development of advanced applications based on the P2P paradigm and will foster collaborative efforts among several network entities (e.g. P2P applications and ISPs). The proposed concept of context aware programmable trackers allows that several peer selection strategies might be supported by a P2P tracker entity able to improve the peer selection decisions according with pre-defined objectives and external inputs provided by specific services. The flexible, adaptive and enhanced peer selection semantics that might be achieved by the proposed solution will contribute for devising novel P2P based services and business models for the future Internet.

1 Introduction

The massive use of P2P applications in the Internet is changing the traffic profile and is introducing additional problems to Internet Service Providers (ISPs). In fact, Internet usage patterns have greatly evolved in the last years mainly due to the usage of P2P overlay networks [1], where peers form self-organized network infrastructures. ISPs are now facing serious problems such as high traffic variability and distortion and excessive and unpredictable loads in critical links. Moreover, P2P applications often generate unnecessary inter-domain traffic also making difficult the use of traditional traffic engineering techniques for network optimization [7][8]. All this leads to possible disruptions in ISPs economics and foster serious coexistence problems with new Internet applications [9]. In such context, several solutions have been adopted by ISPs in order to improve network performance such as the adoption of caching devices [11] to reduce bandwidth consumption and several mechanisms to detect and control P2P traffic [12].

Internet applications following the P2P paradigm adopt a wide range of selfish strategies to improve their performance irrespectively of the side effects induced at the network level. In this context, there is a wide variety of P2P solutions [1] having distinct behaviors, objectives, adaptation strategies, routing decisions and peering solutions [13][14]. Among many distinct P2P protocols, BitTorrent [2][4] is a good example of one of the most popular solutions [5] and is now responsible for more than one third of the Internet Traffic [6]. ISPs should take

M. Oliver and S. Sallent (Eds.): EUNICE 2009, LNCS 5733, pp. 78–87, 2009.
© Springer-Verlag Berlin Heidelberg 2009

into account the possibility that in the Future Internet applications such as P2P-based ones (e.g. BitTorrent like solutions) be mainstream and common users use them to access a wide range of services. Furthermore, P2P paradigm has several advantages for fast distribution of large content when compared with the traditional client-server model also opening new opportunities in areas as content distribution, distributed file systems, games, virtual reality, software updates, etc. As consequence, ISPs should rethink how P2P traffic will be handled in the future due to the fact that ISPs offering a poor service for P2P traffic might have to face user dissatisfaction and possible economic penalties.

In this perspective, future internet applications should no longer continuously assume selfish behaviors, as ISPs will be forced to use more restrictive solutions to control (or even deny) such traffic. This leads us to the need of devising flexible solutions guiding P2P-based applications in order to: *(i)* foster the development of collaborative optimization models able to simultaneously improve both applications and ISPs performances; *(ii)* improve the differentiation capabilities of P2P services in order to support off-line agreements between service providers and network providers involving some type of preferential treatment for specific peers and *(iii)* improve (or degrade) the quality of specific peers according with their conforming or non-conforming behaviors. This proposal assumes a BitTorrent-like P2P approach and focuses on a specific component, the context aware tracker, able to achieve all the previous mentioned objectives.

The paper is organized as follows: Section 2 presents the rationale underpinning the concept of context aware programmable trackers also providing examples of distinct selection mechanisms; Section 3 illustrates a set of experiments and corresponding results; finally, Section 4 summarizes the presented work.

2   Context Aware Programmable Trackers

This section introduces the concept of context aware trackers and presents some peer selection configurations which results will be verified in Section 3.

2.1   Supporting Rationale

In order to illustrate the concept of context aware trackers lets assume the specific case of BitTorrent-like applications. Here, new peers wishing to join a specific swarm contact a tracker providing the clients with a random sample of peers. This sample is used by the peers for establishing new P2P connections with other peers in order to download a given resource[1]. In this context, the concept of context aware programmable trackers is presented by the framework of Figure 1. The several modules integrating the *Programmable P2P Tracker* internal architecture are now described in detail:

- *Peer Selection Module:* This module holds the current peer selection strategy that is being used by the context aware tracker for peer selection purposes.

---

[1] Additional details of the BitTorrent protocol can be found in [1,2,3].

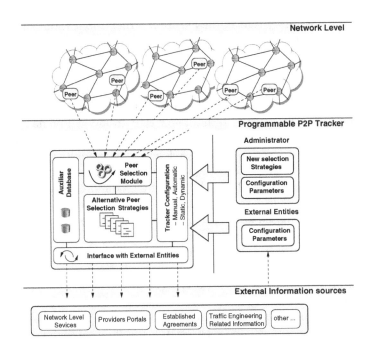

Fig. 1. Illustrative architecture for the use of Context aware Programmable Trackers

- *Alternative Peer Selection Strategies Module:* A repository with alternative selection mechanisms to be used by the tracker. These mechanisms might be programmed, uploaded and activated using appropriate configuration commands.

- *Tracker Configuration Module:* The interface for all the allowed programming and configuration procedures. This module receives commands responsible for tasks such as: selecting the active selection strategy; uploading alternative selection strategies; defining which external entities should be contacted by the tracker to gather additional information; etc. The configuration procedures may be manual or follow an automatic approach. Moreover, tracker configurations may be static or dynamic, with the later allowing the change of the peer selection strategy during the swarm lifetime.

- *Interface with External Entities:* This module is responsible for controlling all interactions with the external information sources consulted by the tracker.

- *Auxiliar Database:* This module stores several auxiliary data characterizing active peers in a given swarm. In this way, this module is responsible for storing a large part of the information required by the tracker to support peer selection procedures. This module is also responsible to temporarily hold data retrieved from external sources before new interactions occur.

Figure 1 presents some examples of external information sources that may be used in the context of the proposed solution, e.g.: network level services able to provide privileged information regarding network state data; Provider Portals (e.g. as defined in [10]); information related with established agreements with other providers; traffic engineering information, among other possibilities. All this information might be useful to support the tracker peer selection decisions.

2.2   Illustrative Configuration Examples

This section describes three illustrative peer selection strategies that were programmed in the context aware tracker. The first example describes a possible collaborative mechanism between the P2P and ISP network levels. The second and third examples describe tracker configurations able to differentiate the quality of the service provided to distinct peers of a specific P2P swarm.

Collaborative Optimization - This first example assumes a collaborative context between the application and the ISP levels. This particular selection mechanism is mainly devised for traffic engineering purposes, with the P2P tracker trying to reduce the inter-domain traffic generated by a given swarm. In this selection mechanism the tracker was programmed to gather information about the location of current peers in a specific swarm along with the location of newly arrived peers requesting the tracker services. Such information may be provided by network level entities cooperating with the P2P level. When receiving a request from a new peer, the tracker was programmed to return a random sample of peers in the swarm taking into account two distinct phases. First, if the swarm is in an initial state (or with a limited number of peers) then the default behavior is assumed, i.e. the return of a random sample of the existing peers to the newly arrived peer. The current number of peers in the swarm (or other P2P level information) might be used to assess the state of the swarm. Otherwise, if the swarm is not considered to be in an initial state then the returned sample will be mainly composed by peers belonging to the same networking domain of the requesting peer. This strategy intends to drastically reduce the intrerdomain traffic generated by P2P applications without noticeable degradation of the service quality. The first phase of this mechanism allows that diverse peering relations occur independently of peers locations. From that point on, newly arrived peers will mainly use local peers to download the network resource.

Service Differentiation *i) Penalizing Peers in a Swarm* - This example illustrates a peer selection mode that might be used as a pure penalizing mechanism able to punish non-conforming peers with some pre-defined P2P application level rules or, due to specific agreements with ISPs, punish peers which behavior is degrading the overall performance of the system. However, other scenarios may also benefit from these differentiation capabilities, such as: the need of controlling the traffic generated by a set of peers; protecting specific paths of the network from excessive P2P traffic to avoid the congestion of critical links; the need of forcing P2P connections only among a specific set of peers, among many others. This illustrative selection mechanism resorts to a tracker which is programmed in order to restrict the number of peers returned to specific clients[2]. This simple differentiation technique is expected to originate distinct levels of

---

[2] More details of this illustrative peer selection mechanism are provided in Section 3.

service quality as now low priority peers will have a reduced opportunity of discovering and connecting to other peers in the swarm. As consequence, and comparatively with peer samples having a higher dimension, such swarm elements are expected to experience lower quality service levels. Moreover, in order to prevent service starvation, these strict peer restrictions affecting low priority peers might be gradually relieved by the tracker during the swarm lifetime.

Service Differentiation *ii) Benefiting Peers in a Swarm* - A tracker operating under this programming mode is able to provide incentives to specific peers in a given swarm. In this case, such incentives are provided through a careful selection of the peers included in the samples returned by the tracker. To exemplify a selection mechanism of this type Section 3 will show the results of a tracker selection mechanism that benefits a set of peers in a given swarm by providing them privileged information regarding high upload capacity seeds that are hidden from other nodes. As consequence, such set of peers will form a kind of high priority sub-swarm that is expected to receive a better overall service from the P2P application level. This incentive based selection mechanism can be used simply to benefit specific peers in the network or with other side-effects in mind such as: divert traffic from specific links or paths of the infra-structure; avoid the generation of inter-domain traffic by providing high quality local peers in the samples; to allow the creation of enhanced sub-swarms where a restricted set of peers has access to high upload capacity seeds, among many others possibilities.

3   Experiments and Results

The ns-2 [17] simulator was used to develop and test the proposed architecture presented in Section 2, following a packet-level simulation approach. Although P2P packet-level simulations are more complex and require more computational power than flow-level approaches [15], they present more accurate results also taking into account specific cross-layer interactions which are crucial in the context of this research work. A simulation patch implementing a BitTorrent-like protocol was used for the development of the proposed solution [16]. This patch was extended in order to allow the definition of distinct peer selection techniques to be adopted by the tracker. The tracker internal structure was also modified according with the architecture proposed by Figure 1. Additional state information storage for peer selection decisions and tracker communication interfaces were also developed allowing the interactions with external entities. Several debugging and log functionalities were also integrated in the tracker.

3.1   Simulation Scenarios

Figure 2 illustrates one of the network topologies used to present some illustrative results of the proposed context aware programmable tracker concept. At the top level the network is divided in three distinct areas interconnected by inter-area links. Each area is then composed by a second level of links which configurations allow the definition of each area internal structure. In Figure 2 the concept of an

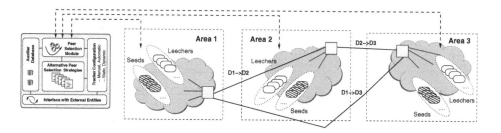

Fig. 2. Network level simulated topology for testing the programmable tracker

area may have two distinct interpretations. For instance, when testing selection mechanisms having the objective of reducing the inter-domain traffic an area will be assumed in fact as a networking domain. So, links $D1 \rightarrow D2, D1 \rightarrow D3$ and $D2 \rightarrow D3$ will be viewed as interconnections between distinct networking domains. Otherwise, for simulations disregarding domain related issues, the three areas will be interpreted as integrating an unique domain. In such cases, intra and inter area links will be viewed in fact as internal links of a domain, and their distinct capacities and propagation delays will be used to increase the heterogeneity of the domain topology. Most of the parameters controlling the BitTorrent-like protocol may be configured, including parameters such as the number of seeds and leechers per domain and their arrival processes, tracker related configurations, the use (or not) of superseeding, chunk size, file size, several timers and intervals guiding the P2P protocol, among many others. The proposed context aware P2P tracker was tested resorting to a high number of simulation experiments and each one of the individual scenarios was tested several times using distinct seeds controlling parameters such as links propagation delays, leechers arrival times to the swarm, peers distribution patterns, etc.

Due to space constraints only a set of illustrative results obtained from a specific configuration will be presented. In the selected examples most of the results were taken from a simulation scenario assuming nearly 100 leechers per area, resulting in a total number of 300 peers. The file size is 50 MB and the chunk size 256 KB. The maximum number of peer addresses requested from the tracker is 25, however depending on the selected mechanism the tracker may manipulate this value for specific peers. Most of the selected results assume the worst case scenario for file dissemination, i.e. initially only one seed and a number of leechers in the network (i.e. the flash crowd effect)[3]. Whenever possible superseeding mode was used in the simulations. At the network level the peers have, on average, an upload capacity of 1 Mbps and a download capacity which is considered to be eight timer higher than this value (i.e to simulate asymmetric access links, such as ADSL for home users). In order to improve the heterogeneity of each area, the propagation delays of the access links were randomly generated in the interval of 1-50 ms. The inter-area links were considered to be able to support a share of 10 Mbps for P2P traffic and their propagations delays are

---

[3] To assure fairness among all peers some scenarios also assume one seed per area.

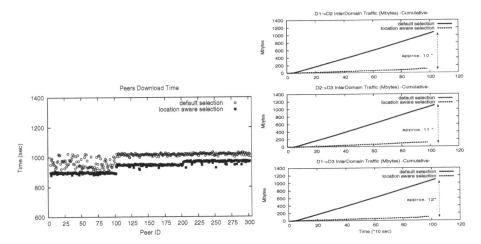

Fig. 3. Collaborative optimization: download times and inter-domain traffic (1 seed)

at least two times higher than the maximum value considered for intra-area links. The peers performance is measured taking into account the download time needed for a complete file transfer. To simplify results visualization each peer is assigned with a $peer_{id}$ identification, in this case in the interval $[1, 300]$.

3.2   Simulation Results

This section presents simulation results of the tracker configured with illustrative selection mechanisms explained and discussed in Section 2.

Collaborative Optimization - As explained, in this example the tracker was programmed to behave in a collaborative perspective, receiving peer location information from the network level with the objective of reducing the interdomain traffic generated by the P2P level. Figure 3 shows comparative results of the tracker configured in the default selection mode and when programmed with the location aware peer selection mechanism, in this case only one initial seed is considered to exist in network area one. As observed, when the tracker is programmed to perform a location aware peer selection strategy the inter-domain traffic generated is at least ten times lower than the observed in the default selection mode (see the three graphs plotting the generated interdomain traffic in the right side of Figure 3). Moreover, and even taking into account that peer selection decisions are now constrained and local peers have a higher probability of being selected, the average download times of the peers are also improved (see the peers download times in the left side of Figure 3). This means that it is possible to develop collaborative approaches effectively attending both P2P and ISP particular objectives. A second example is given by Figure 4 where one seed is considered to be present in each network area. Similar conclusions might be drawn, with an even higher decrease in the inter-domain traffic (e.g. $D1 \rightarrow D2$ inter-domain traffic is eighteen times lower comparatively with

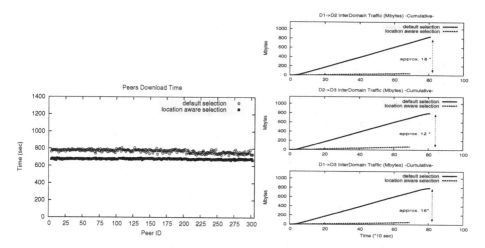

Fig. 4. Collaborative optimization: download times and inter-domain traffic (3 seeds)

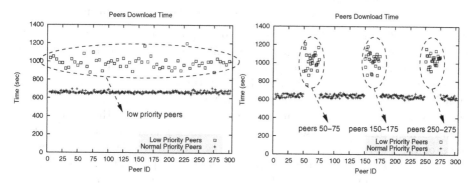

Fig. 5. Penalized peers with a) peers IDs multiple of 5 b) peers IDs in the intervals $[50, 75]$, $[150, 175]$ and $[250, 275]$

the default selection mode). In contrast with the previous case presented in Figure 3, where peers inside area one have slightly lower download times, now all the peers experience similar performances due to the fairness of seeds distribution.

Penalizing Peers in a Swarm - The results presented in Figure 5 a) and b) show two distinct scenarios with the tracker programmed to penalized specific peers in a swarm by restricting the number of peers included in the samples, as explained in Section 2.2. In this specific case, for penalized peers, the number of peers returned in the samples halves the maximum number of active connections allowed in the swarm. By this way, those low priority peers should experience a lower service quality level as they are constrained in the way they are able to establish P2P connections to get all the pieces of the original shared file. In the case of Figure 5 a) several peers in all the networking areas were penalized and, in this specific scenario, to make easier the results visualization penalized peers are those having a peer ID which is multiple of 5. In the second scenario,

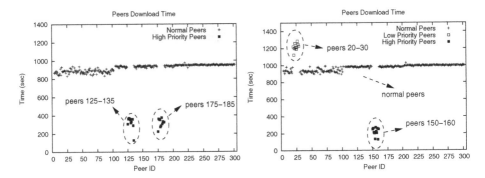

Fig. 6. a) Benefited peers in $[125, 135]$ and $[175, 185]$ b) Mixed configurations: penalized peers in $[20, 30]$ and benefited peers in $[150, 160]$

which results are plotted in Figure 5 b), specific peer groups within each network area were selected to be penalized. In this case peer IDs in the intervals $[50, 75]$, $[150, 175]$ and $[250, 275]$ were penalized. As observed, in both scenarios the tracker was able to induce the proposed differentiation semantics.

Benefiting Peers in a Swarm - Figure 6 a) shows the results obtained using a programmable tracker configured to benefit two groups of peers, in this case belonging to the intervals $[125, 135]$ and $[175, 185]$. In this case, the strategy adopted by the tracker is to include in the returned samples two high upload capacity seeds that are unaccessible to other peers in the swarm. Additionally, the tracker assures that peers in the mentioned intervals and those seeds form a kind of high priority sub-swarm, i.e. they exchange data apart from the other peers of the swarm. As consequence, and as plotted by Figure 6 a), service differentiation is effectively achieved and high priority peers effectively obtain a better service quality from the P2P level (i.e. lower download times).

Mixed Configurations - The last selected example uses the tracker configured in a hybrid differentiation mode. The results of Figure 6 b) were obtained with the tracker programmed to benefit a specific group of peers in the network area two, in this case peers in the interval $[150, 160]$, and to penalize a group of peers in the network area one, in this case peers in the interval $[20, 30]$. As observed in Figure 6 b), the results clearly show the correctness of the devised hybrid mode, showing that mixed and enhanced configurations are possible to be achieved using the proposed context aware programmable tracker architecture.

4   Summary

This paper introduced and explained the concept of context aware programmable trackers. A detailed description of an architecture devised for that purpose was firstly presented and discussed, along with illustrative examples of possible peer selection strategies which may use additional information provided by external entities. The proposed context aware tracker solution was implement resorting to simulation and, as corroborated by the presented results, enhanced collaborative behaviors and differentiation semantics are possible to be achieved at the P2P level using the proposed solution. In this way, the proposed approach will benefit the development of advanced P2P-based applications in the future internet, also underpinning the development of intelligent collaborative approaches between ISPs and the P2P applicational level. Moreover, due to the enhanced differentiation semantics that could be obtained using the proposed context-aware tracker, novel Internet services and business models based on the P2P paradigm could also take advantage of the proposed solution.

References

1. Lua, K., et al.: A survey and comparison of peer-to-peer overlay network schemes. IEEE Communications Surveys & Tutorials, pp. 72-93 (2005)
2. Choen, B.: Incentives build robustness in BitTorrent. In: Proc. 1st Workshop on Economics of Peer-to-Peer Systems, Berkeley (June 2003)
3. Legout, A., et al.: Clustering and Sharing Incentives in BitTorrent Systems. In: Proceedings of ACM SIGMETRICS 2007, San Diego, CA, USA, June 12-16 (2007)
4. Bharambe, A.R., et al.: Analyzing and Improving a BitTorrent Networks Performance Mechanisms. In: IEEE INFOCOM (2006)
5. Karagiannis, T., et al.: Is p2p dying or just hiding? Globecom, Dallas USA (November 2004)
6. Schulze, H., Mochalski, K.: Internet Study 2007: The Impact of P2P File Sharing, Voice over IP, Skype, Joost, Instant Messaging, One-Click Hosting and Media Streaming such as YouTube on the Internet, Tech. report (2007)
7. Keralapura, R., et al.: Can ISPs take the heat from overlay networks? In: Proc. of HotNets-III, San Diego, CA (November 2004)
8. Qiu, L., et al.: SelFIsh routing in Internet-like environments. In: Proc of SIGCOMM 2003, Karlsruhe, Germany (August 2003)
9. Xie, H., et al.: P4P: explicit communications for cooperative control between P2P and network providers, http://www.dcia.info/documents/P4P_Overview.pdf
10. Xie, H., et al.: P4P: Provider Portal for Applications. In: SIGCOMM 2008, Seattle, Washington, USA, August 17-22 (2008)
11. Shen, G., et al.: HPTP: Relieving the tension between ISPs and P2P. In: Proc. of IPTPS, Bellevue, WA (Feburary 2007)
12. Spognardi, A., et al.: A Methodology for P2P File-Sharing Traffic Detection. In: Proc. Second International Workshop on Hot Topics in Peer-to-Peer Systems 2005 (HOT-P2P 2005), July 2005, pp. 52–61 (2005)
13. Karagiannis, T., et al.: Should internet service providers fear peer-assisted content distribution? In: Proc. of the Internet Measurement Conf., Berkeley CA (October 2005)
14. Madhyastha, H.V., et al.: iPlane: An information plane for distributed services. In: Proc. of OSDI, Seattle, WA (2006)
15. Eger, K., et al.: Efficient Simulation of Large-Scale P2P Networks: Packet-level vs. Flow-level Simulations. In: 2nd Workshop on the Use of P2P, GRID and Agents for the Development of Content Networks, Monterey Bay, USA (2007)
16. Simulation of BitTorrent Peer-to-Peer (P2P) Networks in ns-2, http://www.tu-harburg.de/et6/research/bittorrentsim/index.html
17. ns-2 (Network Simulator). Documentation, http://www.isi.edu/nsnam/ns/
18. Odlyzko, A.: Data networks are lightly utilized, and will stay that way. Review of Network Economics 2(3), 210–237 (2003)

The Metalist Model: A Simple and Extensible Information Model for the Future Internet

Éric Renault and Djamal Zeghlache

Institut Télécom — Télécom SudParis
RS2M Department, Évry, France
{eric.renault,djamal.zeghlache}@it-sudparis.eu

Abstract. In the scope of the Future Internet, where the network is moving from a node-centric to an information-centric organization, the way to specify the metadata associated to objects becomes crucial for scalability, performance and complexity reasons. This article presents an original information model, called the metalist model, that describes metadata in a simple, efficient and extensible way. The metadata can be provided in several ways: directly from the metalist description of the object itself, embedded into the metalist via an inclusion from another metalist and automatically translated from another metadata format. These features enable gathering metadata common to many objects into common metalists to simplify updates and synchronization and smooth harmonization with other existing object formats and descriptions.

1 Introduction

The Internet has been a strategic infrastructure with a key socio-economical role for more than a decade, leading innovation, economic growth and productivity at a world-wide scale. About 1.5 billion people are connected to the Internet today and up to 4 billion people are expected to access the Internet in very few years. This will become possible mainly with the deployment of wireless technologies that will provide a fully pervasive Internet infrastructure with anywhere and any-time connectivity. In this expected evolution, users will also become producers of content, applications and services. Combined with the emergence of communicating objects this will lead to an even wider explosion. For example, billions of components like wireless terminals, RFID tags, real and virtual world objects will become accessible, moving the network to an Internet of Things, in fact an Internet of Objects and Subjects all of which will require swift and reliable networking. New usage will appear and applications available on the Internet will be significantly different. Health care, education, proximity services, energy management, etc. will directly benefit from the expected evolutions. However, this will become feasible only if the Future Internet includes new features and services like self-configuration/organization/management, computing power on-demand, resource discovery, etc. Organizations and institutions all around the world are funding research and development projects to design a new Internet that shall meet these new needs and demands.

M. Oliver and S. Sallent (Eds.): EUNICE 2009, LNCS 5733, pp. 88–97, 2009.
© Springer-Verlag Berlin Heidelberg 2009

Most of the new services related to the Future Internet are relying on the ability of the network to provide accurate information about accessible objects. With such a requirement and assumption, the description of objects becomes a crucial element for the Future Internet. Without flexible and rich object descriptions, no efficient search is possible. Many models have been developed during the past few years in order to respond to this demand through descriptions enabling and facilitating semantic search. Some important initiatives are Dublin Core [11], EXIF [7], IIM [6], OWL [10], RDF [9] and XMP [2]. Most of these solutions are focusing on a given domain, e.g. Dublin Core is dedicated to content and intellectual property, EXIF describes digital pictures, while others adopt more generic solutions such as IPTC that deals with the description of data in general. OWL, RDF and XMP are even less restrictive by allowing users to define their own schema and leading to the development of extensions. This is the case for example with OWL2 [3], OWL-L [5], OWLS-MX [8], etc.

This article presents an original information model that describes any kind of objects and allows 1) metadata to be provided directly in a very simple manner, 2) factorization of metadata to save space and increase consistency and 3) automatic translation of metadata available in any kind of format to the proposed information model. The next section of this paper introduces the different types of objects addressed by the proposed information model which is presented in Sect. 3. Section 4 gives some examples to explain the model and illustrate its use.

2 Object Definition

Our work has been developed in the scope of the 4WARD project [1] in which objects are identified and defined [4]. To link this work with prior art, a definition of the different kinds of addressed objects is provided. Note, however, that the model presented here applies to other frameworks and is not limited to this specific context.

In order to highlight the difference between the considered types of objects, the example of a web page stored in the system is used. To illustrate the applicability of the model to larger frameworks, an example related to RFID tags is also presented.

Access to information, in the Networking of Information (NetInf) paradigm of the European project 4WARD, is based on the use of three different types of objects (as shown on Fig. 1):

- at the lowest level, *Bit-level Objects* (BO) are the binary representation of the objects, i.e. they are composed of the raw data of the object; i.e. the data stored in the storage space. Regarding the storage of a web page, the BO holds the effective content of the web page.
- on top of Bit-level Objects, *Data Objects* (DO) are used to locate the BOs associated to the object. In the case of the web page, the Data Object is the URL of the web page, i.e. its location on the storage space.
- at the highest level, *Information Objects* (IO) describe the content of objects, i.e. they contain the semantics or meaning of objects. For a web page, this is

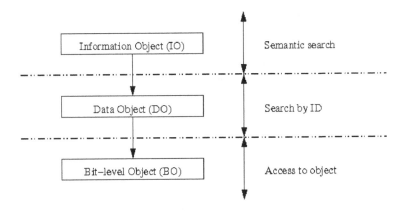

Fig. 1. Object organization in NetInf

similar to the META tag in HTML documents which are used to index web pages according to content of the pages.

Two possible search types are available. The *search by ID* is quite straightforward in the sense that it directly returns the Bit-level Object associated to the Data Object whose ID is provided. The *semantic search* relies on the information found in the metadata and gives access to the Data Objects ID. Once the object ID is obtained via this first step, a search by ID is necessary to retrieve the object.

An ID is associated to IOs and DOs, but there are no IDs for BOs. In fact, BOs are not directly accessible from outside of the NetInf architecture. BOs can only be addressed through DOs. Thus, to access an object, a user first sends a request to NetInf to get the list of objects that match a given set of keywords(those stored in the Information Objects). Associated to these information objects are Data Object IDs. After making a choice, the user sends a request to NetInf with the Data Object ID to retrieve and the Bit-level Object associated to this DO is returned to the user.

In the case of an RFID tag, the situation is very similar. In fact, the tag itself is not directly part of the Future Internet, but is accessed through a process. As a result, the running program accessing the RFID tag is the BO and any communication with the tag is performed via the process. The DO associated to this object holds the information to retrieve the location of the tag and the way to get in touch with it and the IO remains the set of meta-information that describes the characteristics, the location, the meaning, etc. of the RFID tag.

3   Information Model

As the Information Model aims at organizing Information Objects, it mainly focuses on the highest layer of Fig. 1. Several ways of providing metadata have been identified and therefore have to be taken into account:

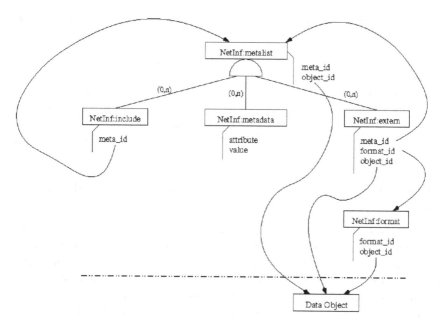

Fig. 2. Information model for the Network of Information

- the metadata can be provided directly to the Information Object and thus be embedded directly in the metalist description.
- the metadata (or part of the metadata) preexists already in another Information Object. In this case, it is better to include it using a reference rather than integrating a copy. This is useful to allow data coherence and consistency in large systems.
- the metadata preexists in another format. In this case again, it is better to include the metadata rather than inserting a copy. However, this inclusion requires a translation and this should be done automatically. Moreover, the metadata can be stored together with the object or in the object itself, or it can also be stored in a separate object. Both cases have to be taken into account.

Figure 2 presents a modeling of data that includes all three cases presented previously and described below. At the top of the diagram, the elements are related to the Information Objects while the lower part of the figure corresponds to Data Objects. Since the only requirement here is that Data Objects are all associated an ID to identify them uniquely, the rest of the paper will not provide any in depth analysis of Data Objects but instead focus on the IOs.

The name of all tags (or entity) are preceded by the "NetInf:" prefix as a reference to the *Network of Information*. This reduces name pollution and puts the focus on a single name space. The use of a prefix is especially interesting when using a modeling language like XML. Associated properties are not subject to this prefix as they are implicitly included inside the name space.

The basic element for the description of metadata is *NetInf:metadata*. It specifies metadata for an object. A NetInf:metadata is associated two properties:

- *value* is any byte stream with a semantic meaning that is helpful to describe the object. There is no real limit on what can be stored in the value. It can be as short as an empty string as this can be associated a meaning for a given attribute (see the attribute property below), and it can be as long as needed for any given use. On one hand, it can be flat or have no structure; on the other hand, it can include a hierarchy of data, e.g. with nested tags as available with XML.
- *attribute* is a string of characters that tags the value of the metadata. Attributes may be flat or organized into hierarchies. Both possibilities are offered to the user.

None of these two properties are mandatory. However, at least one of them must be specified. Typically, this means that one can specify: a value without attribute which means that the value is the metadata and it is not tagged; a value and an attribute which means that the attribute is associated the value; an attribute without value which means that the value associated to the attribute is empty. However, one cannot specify a metadata with no value and no attribute at the same time.

Metadata cannot be provided as is. They must be embedded inside a *NetInf:metalist*, i.e. a list of metadata. There are two properties associated to a NetInf:metalist:

- *meta_id* is the unique identifier of the metalist. This property is mandatory. However, its use is interesting at least for two main reasons: the first one is that it allows updating the metalist later and the second one is it allows including the list of metadata into another list (see below).
- *object_id* is the unique ID of the object the list of metadata is semantically describing. This ID is no mandatory in the metalist. If the object_id is provided, it means that the metalist describes the corresponding object. If the object_id is not provided, this means that the metalist is virtual (not associated to a specific object) and it is likely to be included into another metalist. Note that this does not mean that a metalist associated to an object via an object_id cannot be included into another metalist.

The *NetInf:include* element is used to include a list of metadata into another one. It is associated one and only one property:

- *meta_id* is the identifier of the metalist to include into the current one. This property is mandatory.

Allowing a metalist to include the list of metadata already associated to another one is a very interesting feature as it avoids redundancy and enhances coherence and consistency.

The NetInf:include element as described above allows the inclusion of metadata that are already in the metalist format. However, there may be other metadata available for an object that are described in another format. A typical example is the EXIF file for JPEG pictures taken with any modern digital camera. Almost any JPEG image includes an EXIF file that contains some extra information about the way the picture was taken (camera model, date and time, image resolution, aperture value, focal length, etc.). These metadata may be very useful for many photographers. Another typical example is the set of information associated to a file in a file system. Under the Unix file system, each file is associated a name, a size, a last modification date, a set of access rights, etc. These are also metadata that may be of interest to some users.

The *NetInf:extern* is the element that allows the inclusion of metadata provided in any other recognized format (see the description of NetInf:format below). It is associated up to three properties:

- *format_id* is a reference to the format entity (a script, a process, etc. – see below) that is able to translate the metadata from the format they are currently stored in to the metalist format. This property is mandatory.
- *object_id* is the ID of the Data Object where the metadata to translate are stored.
- *meta_id* is the ID of the Information Object which holds the ID of the Data Object where the metadata to translate are stored. Offering the possibility to access extern metadata using a meta_id is motivated by the fact that what is considered a metadata for a given object may represent or mean data for another one. With the EXIF file example, information in such a file may be data for an application (with an associated Information Object) while it can also be considered as metadata for another one (for an image typically with an Information Object associated with the image).

The last two properties are exclusive as external metadata cannot be located at two different locations. If this may occur, two extern inclusions have to be specified. If neither an object_id nor a meta_id is specified, the metadata in the original format are supposed to be located in the Data Object associated with the inner most object_id (as a NetInf:extern element may be set inside an included metalist and NetInf:include may be nested).

The last element to describe for our model is the *NetInf:format* that is used to specify the Data Object to be used to perform an automatic translation from a given metadata format to the metalist format. It is associated two properties:

- *format_id* is the unique ID associated to the format to allow future references from the metalists.
- *object_id* is the ID of the Data Object that is effectively performing the translation. This Data Object may be of any type and may be developed using any language. The only requirement is that it must conform to the specifications associated to automatic translators for the Network of Information, e.g. the Data Object containing the metadata to translate are provided on the standard input and the metadata in the metalist format provided by the automatic translator is generated on the standard output.

Note that there is no limitation on the number of NetInf:include, NetInf:metadata and NetInf:extern elements that can be provided in a NetInf:metalist and on the number of nested NetInf:include elements.

Our proposed model makes use of different identifiers and it is very important to make sure they are unique in the system. There are two possibilities to ensure their uniqueness: the first one consists in leaving the generation of IDs to the Network of Information; the second one consists in leaving the management of IDs to the users and checking the uniqueness every time an ID is provided (if not, the request is rejected). There is no real impact of the choice here on the model. At use, it may be interesting to leave the management of IDs to users with a control from NetInf as this would allow users to use more comprehensible IDs than what the Network of Information would generate automatically.

4   Some Examples

After the above formal description of the Metalist model, this section aims at providing some examples to highlight the use of the different elements. In this section, examples are presented using the XML language. This language was chosen as it is both widely used and based on a very simple hierarchical structure. However, any description language could be used.

Tag elements and properties used in the XML examples are exactly following the names presented in the formal description, especially regarding tag names that are all included inside the *NetInf* namespace.

For the first example, assume a user has gone to China and has taken pictures (s)he wants to publish on the Future Internet. The first picture to publish represents the Great Wall located close to Beijing. In order to ensure the picture is well referenced, the user sets the metadata as presented in Example 1.

```
<NetInf:metalist meta_id="mid1" object_id="oid1">
    <NetInf:metadata attribute="content">Holidays in China</NetInf:metadata>
    <NetInf:metadata attribute="content">From June 2nd to June 10th</NetInf:metadata>
    <NetInf:metadata attribute="content">The Great Wall</NetInf:metadata>
</NetInf:metalist>
```

Example 1. Simple "object description" using the Information Model

All three NetInf:metadata are provided as is inside a NetInf:metalist structure. In this example, all metadata are tagged with an attribute named *Content*. The ID associated to the metalist (*mid1*) is provided by property meta_id and the Data Object ID this Information Object is semantically describing is *oid1* provided by property object_id. The ID of the metalist (*mid1*) can then be used for later references.

It is very unlikely that visiting China the user takes only one picture. For example, (s)he may be willing to publish two pictures, the first one representing the Great Wall and the second one showing the Forbidden City. In this case, both pictures were taken during the same journey (from June 2nd to June 10th) and at the same occasion (during holiday in China). As a result, it is better to factorize this information, in order to avoid having it twice in the Network of Information.

```
<NetInf:metalist meta_id="mid1">
    <NetInf:metadata attribute="content">Holidays in China</NetInf:metadata>
    <NetInf:metadata attribute="content">From June 2nd to June 10th</NetInf:metadata>
</NetInf:metalist>

<NetInf:metalist meta_id="mid2" object_id="oid1">
    <NetInf:include meta_id="mid1" />
    <NetInf:metadata attribute="content">The Great Wall</NetInf:metadata>
</NetInf:metalist>

<NetInf:metalist meta_id="mid3" object_id="oid2">
    <NetInf:include meta_id="mid1" />
    <NetInf:metadata attribute="content">The Forbidden City</NetInf:metadata>
</NetInf:metalist>
```

Example 2. An example of inclusion

Example 2 presents a possible representation of the metadata in this case. First, common metadata are grouped into a metalist with ID equal to *mid1*. As no specific Data Object is associated to this metalist, no object_id is provided for this metalist. Then, each picture is associated a specific metalist with its specific metadata, i.e. *The Great Wall* on one hand and *The Forbidden City* on the other hand, and a reference to the common list of metadata is added using the NetInf:include element with property meta_id equal to *mid1*. Note that for both *mid2* and *mid3* metalist, an Data Object ID is provided.

The user can also be a professional photographer willing to provide his/her digital camera settings when taking the picture. These information are provided by most digital cameras and added to JPEG images using the EXIF format. As a result, data in EXIF format stored in the JPEG picture are also metadata for the picture and these are the metadata the user wants to associate to the picture.

```
<NetInf:format format_id="exif-2.2" object_id="exif-2.2tometalist" />

<NetInf:metalist meta_id="mid1" object_id="oid1">
    <NetInf:metadata attribute="content">Holidays in China</NetInf:metadata>
    <NetInf:metadata attribute="content">From June 2nd to June 10th</NetInf:metadata>
    <NetInf:metadata attribute="content">The Great Wall</NetInf:metadata>
    <NetInf:extern format_id="exif-2.2" />
</NetInf:metalist>
```

Example 3. Importing external metadata

Example 3 shows how this is made possible using the metalist model. First, the translator (the process, the script, the program, etc.) in charge of performing the translation from the EXIF version 2.2 format to the metalist format has to be declared. As long as this is public, this declaration has to be performed once in the Network of Information to be used by any user. For the sake of readability, it is assumed that the Data Object ID associated to the translator is *exif-2.2tometalist* (but this Data Object ID could also have been generated automatically by the storage system) and it is associated format_id *exif-2.2*. Then, every time a translation from the EXIF version 2.2 format has to be performed to generate a metalist, it just requires to be referenced using this format_id in the NetInf:extern tag. Note that no object_id property is provided with this tag. As a result, the inner most object_id in the set of inclusion has to be used to locate the EXIF metadata. This leads to object_id *oid1* which is the Data Object ID of the picture being semantically described. The other metadata set in this metalist are provided as a reference in order to show that NetInf:metadata and NetInf:extern can coexist in the same metalist, just like NetInf:metadata and NetInf:include do (see Example 2).

All examples presented above include very simple metadata, typically a single string of characters. However, these metadata may be far more complex. For example, the value of the metadata can be hierarchically structured using the XML language and/or using any other description language like RDF or OWL. It is then the responsibility of the user to ensure both the syntax and the semantic of the metadata is acceptable.

5   Conclusion and Future Works

This article described the Metalist model, a simple and flexible Information Model for the Future Internet. As presented above, the Metalist model includes three main features: 1) the ability to provide metadata in a simple and straight-forward way; 2) the ability to include a metalist into another one, which allows to save memory space and ensures data consistency; 3) the ability to automatically import metadata available in another format to the metalist. All these features have been illustrated with short examples along a realistic use case.

Several functions and operations on information objects can be achieved via the Metalist model, including the ability to check if the metadata provided in a metalist comply with some given schema, the development of a security in-frastructure for the management of Information Objects and Data Objects, the management of mobility, the improvement of search engines.

6   Disclaimer

This work has been supported by the IST 7th Framework Programme Integrated Project 4WARD, which is partially funded by the Commission of the European Union. The views expressed in this paper are solely those of the authors and do not necessarily represent the views of Institut Télécom (ex. GET-INT) or the respective projects and sponsors.

References

1. The FP7 4WARD Project, http://www.4ward-project.eu/
2. XMP Specification. Adobe Systems Incorporated (September 2005)
3. Cuenca Grau, B., Horrocks, I., Motik, B., Parsia, B., Patel-Schneider, P., Sattler, U.: OWL 2: the Next Step for OWL. Semantic Web Challenge 6(4), 309–322 (2008)
4. Dannewitz, C., Pentikousis, K., Rembarz, R., Renault, E., Strandberg, O., Ubillos, J.: Scenarios and Research Issues for a Network of Information. In: MobiMedia 2008, Oulu, Finland (July 2008)
5. Hsu, I.-C., Tzeng, Y.K., Huang, D.C.: OWL-L: an OWL-Based Language for Web Resources Links. Computer Standards & Interfaces 31(4), 846–855 (2009)
6. IPTC-NAA Information Interchange Model, version 4.1. International Press and Telecommunications Council (July 1999)
7. Exchangeable Image File Format for Digital Still Cameras: Exif Version 2.2. Standard of Japan Electronics and Information Technology Industries Association (April 2002)
8. Klusch, M., Fries, B., Sycara, K.: OWLS-MX: a Hybrid Semantic Web Service Matchmaker for OWL-S Services. In: Web Semantics: Science, Services and Agents on the World Wide Web. Elsevier Science Publishers, Amsterdam (2008)
9. Manola, F., Miller, E.: RDF Primer. W3C Recommendation (February 2004)
10. Dean, M., Schreiber, G.: OWL Web Ontology Language Reference. W3C Recommendation (February 2004)
11. Weibel, S., Kunze, J., Lagoze, C., Wolf, M.: Dublin Core Metadata for Resource Discovery. RFC 2413 (September 1998)

On Designing for Tussle: Future Internet in Retrospect

Costas Kalogiros[1], Alexandros Kostopoulos[1], and Alan Ford[2]

[1] Athens University of Economics and Business, Department of Informatics,
76 Patission Str., Athens 10434, Greece
`{ckalog,alexkosto}@aueb.gr`
[2] Roke Manor Research, Old Salisbury Lane, Romsey, SO51 0ZN, United Kingdom
`alan.ford@roke.co.uk`

Abstract. Over the past decades, the fundamental principles of the Internet architecture have not significantly changed. However, Internet evolution and its effects on participants' interests have triggered the need for re-defining these design principles. "Design for Tussle" is an aspiration for future network designs, which enables the involved stakeholders to express their possibly conflicting socio-economic preferences on service instances. We performed a series of case studies examining whether established technologies are compatible with this new approach. Using the knowledge gained, we provide canonical examples and help protocol and network designers better to consider how to come up to the problem of "designing for tussle" in order to realize a flexible architecture. Finally, we associate protocol success to adoption and show, using empirical evidences, that carefully embracing the "Design for Tussle" paradigm can outweigh the higher complexity in protocol design.

Keywords: Design for Tussle; Future Internet Architecture; Network Protocols; Technology Adoption; Case Studies.

1 Introduction

The Internet today is a playground of many competing forces (technical, economical and social), where different stakeholders with possibly conflicting interests interact with each other. These ongoing "tussles" may constitute a threat to the architectural integrity of the Internet. Researchers, service providers, network operators and users have recognized that the current Internet architecture is ill-suited to satisfy the demands and requirements of our modern society [8]. The fundamental design principles of the Internet architecture, designed decades ago, are currently under increasing evaluation [3].

It is suggested that the future Internet architecture should incorporate the necessary flexibility to adapt to changing economic and social stresses, the so-called "Design for Tussle" principle. This new paradigm recognizes the necessity for traditional design goals – such as protocol correctness – to be satisfied, but proposes that socio-economic ones should also be considered. Clark et al. [5] proposed an initial set of design principles that can be used to accommodate tussles, these being to "Modularize along tussle boundaries" and "Design for choice".

M. Oliver and S. Sallent (Eds.): EUNICE 2009, LNCS 5733, pp. 98–107, 2009.
© Springer-Verlag Berlin Heidelberg 2009

Meeting these two, more specific, design principles leads to a system that is able to flex under pressure and survive, even if stakeholders and the environment constantly changes. The ultimate goal of these design principles is to allow for "variation in outcome", instead of promoting a unique solution that may not be aligned with all legitimate participants' opinions. For example, protocols that are "designed for tussle" support many business models instead of a single one that the designer found to be attractive. In this way, the outcome can be determined by the interaction of all stakeholders. Of course, all legitimate participants should have the freedom to express their preferences. As an example, a provider could choose to offer a "walled garden" service if she finds it valuable. But, the designer should not bias the outcome, even if all evidence shows that this leads to a socially optimum equilibrium. History of the Internet, so far, has shown that we cannot predict the consequences when we build protocols based on assumptions for the future.

Furthermore, such an approach would set the stage for the Internet to operate more freely, without the need for regulatory intervention to battle anti-competitive tactics from powerful participants. This competitive setting is achievable if all stakeholders have the potential to exercise some sort of control, using the same or complementary protocols (for example select their provider from a list of candidates).

While Clark's paper provides the foundations for a tussle-aware architecture, it is far from obvious how such tussles can be incorporated into the Internet and how all derived principles can be applied to an architectural design. Besides, the task of protocol design in such all-encompassing platforms is already extremely complex, requiring special skills and systematic approach. Many believe that designing system components is an art rather than a science. We suggest that one should carefully balance the trade-off between traditional protocol design goals (i.e. performance) and socio-economic ones (i.e. flexibility).

We try to reduce this inherent difficulty of "designing for tussle" in two ways:

- First, we try to shed some light on the details of applying the two more specific design principles mentioned above. We do this by giving examples of functionality in established Internet protocols that, intentionally or not, meet or violate these design principles. We, also, try to give some guidance to designers by providing additional criteria that should be met.
- Furthermore, we try to justify the extra difficulty imposed on designers and standardizing organizations to embrace this new paradigm. We do this by trying to correlate the outcome over time of protocol adoption (or abandonment) to their "score" against these design principles.

In order to achieve our goal, we performed a systematic analysis of interesting case studies, from a broad commercial and strategic viewpoint. These protocols were carefully selected in order to cover functionality ranging from network to application layer. In particular, we investigated HTTP, BGP, TCP, NAT, IPv6, SIP and ENUM.

The paper is structured as follows: We give an overview of related work in Section 2. Sections 3 and 4 present a high level characterization of the above case studies with respect to the two specific design principles. In particular, Section 3 attempts to clarify how modularized protocols can be designed, and Section 4 discusses protocols which are designed for choice for example through the use of open interfaces. Section 5 correlates adoption issues of recent technology developments and proposals to their compatibility with the "design for tussle" paradigm. Finally, we conclude our work in Section 6.

2 Related Work

Saltzer et al. [11] described the fundamental design goals underlying the current Internet and the resulting design principles. These original design goals and principles have led to the current hourglass architecture, where IP provides a common layer between the transport and higher layer protocols and the disparate lower-layer communications technologies. This approach has largely contributed to the successful operation and expansion of the Internet. In particular, the "end-to-end" principle [4] was one of the central design principles of the Internet.

Over recent years, researchers have increasingly argued that the design goals and principles must be critically reviewed to ensure that the Internet continues to operate [10]. Moreover, new design principles may be needed that were not thought of for the original design of the Internet. The most notable recent principle proposed is the "design for tussle" principle, raised by Clark [5]. Later, in [6] and [13], new principles were presented for future Internet architecture; the "information exposure", the "separation of policy and mechanism", the "fuzzy end-to-end" and the "resource pooling" principle. These principles have particular focus on enabling socio-economic tussles between stakeholders.

The term "tussle" is described as an "ongoing contention among parties with conflicting interests". The Internet is increasingly used as a space where conflicts of interests arise and the different players – including users, ISPs, service providers, governments, etc. – are battling over the control for economic, social or political reasons. That tussles are not necessarily negative. Instead, they are needed to allow evolution and progress. Architects and engineers should understand the rules that define the tussles in order to shape the architecture and to ensure evolvability. In [5], more specific principles for "design for tussle" are identified. "Modularization along tussle boundaries" aims to break down the complexity of the tussle, and suggests that functions within a "tussle space" (a "place" where conflicts of a specific kind of interests occur, i.e. security) should be logically separated from functions outside of that space. It is also identified that protocols should be "designed for choice" in such a way that all the parties to an interaction have the ability to express their preferences about which other parties they interact with.

3 Tussle Isolation

The goal of *isolation of tussle* aims to ensure a separation of tussle spaces, so that tussles can occur independently of each other. According to this design principle, the function that allows a tussle to be played out should have minimal impact on other tussles, and therefore also on stakeholders that are not directly related to this tussle. This is achieved through "modularization along tussle boundaries", which is fairly simple to define, but a hard task to implement.

A useful way to think about and support modularization is to distinguish between "functional" and "stakeholder" separation. *"Functional separation"* is the creation of tussle spaces bounded according to functions, which are logically separated from functions that lie outside of this space. *"Stakeholder separation"* is separation between stakeholders, within a functional tussle space, i.e. allowing players to act with minimal dependence and keep their internal choices separate from external stakeholders. This is often closely related to functional separation, depending upon where the boundaries of the tussle spaces are defined. The following examples illustrate varying degrees of success or failure in achieving this functional and stakeholder separation.

HTTP provides a good example of a clean, simple modular design, separating functions and allowing natural protocol evolution without affecting other functions. In particular, the separation of header and data body allows extensibility without affecting the data being delivered. Responsive web applications and object-oriented services, such as those driven by AJAX, PHP and SOAP, use HTTP to deliver dynamic content, without changing the protocol.

The inter- and intra-domain routing system is a clear example of separation based on stakeholders and functions at the same time. In particular, the split between intra- and inter-domain routing allows different protocols to be used in the interior, depending on a domain's needs, while maintaining a consistent exterior presentation (in the form of BGP messages). This allows interior routing protocols (such as RIP, OSPF, etc.) to evolve, or be completely replaced, with no effect on connectivity with the rest of the Internet. As a result, each domain acts independently of the others.

However, sometimes modular design is difficult to achieve, like the case of Network Address Translators. NATs were originally developed as an administrative aid, so that networks could manage their internal hosts and addressing independently of their providers. In particular, this greatly assists in renumbering either address space (including changing provider), or adding new hosts internally without any negotiations with the upstream provider. This initial modularization was a stakeholder separation, whereby external (provider) and internal (customer) address spaces were decoupled. At the same time, the growth of the Internet was leading to potential IPv4 address exhaustion, and so NATs began to be used to slow the rate of consumption of IPv4 addresses. However, the tussle over address allocation expanded into the trust space, because NATs also protect against malicious activity initiated by external hosts. Furthermore, NATs began to have many unintended consequences on other stakeholders. NATs break end-host reachability, and thus limit innovation by restricting nodes behind a NAT to use supported protocols only, and not to operate servers. Some applications (such as Skype) with no direct impact on the original tussles of address allocation are also adversely affected. Certain workarounds, such as NAT pinholes (a.k.a. "port forwarding"), have been used to reduce the impact of this; however end users are required to be proactive in working around these issues.

IPv6 also suffers from poor functional modularization. Although its original function was also to provide an expanded address space, many other features were included as standard (such as host auto configuration, and originally mobility and security features, although these are no longer mandatory), and as such the sheer weight of the "base protocol" module makes its deployment a very expensive task. A larger amount of functional separation could have eased these issues, improved incremental deployment possibilities, and could have even facilitated backwards compatibility. For example, DHCPv6 could have been implemented as an entire modular replacement for the standard router discovery. Similarly, IPv6 suffers from poor stakeholder separation, since the use of IPv6 by one stakeholder is only of use if other stakeholders (endpoints, transit providers, software authors, etc.) also adopt it.

The design of TCP is modularized to some extent. TCP is one of the core protocols of the Internet, providing reliable end to end transmission of packets, and trying to avoid congestion occurring inside the network. Especially for the latter function, there are different implementations proposed (TCP Tahoe, Reno, Vegas, etc.) for the Additive-Increase-Multiplicative-Decrease (AIMD) scheme in order to control the transmission rate. This is functionally separated from, for example, the reliability features of TCP. These functions are, however, linked elsewhere, reducing the benefit of this separation. The occurrence of packet loss is an overloaded signal, as it is also used to detect congestion by existing TCP control mechanisms, despite the implementation of the algorithm being entirely separate. Explicit Congestion Notification (ECN) [9] and Re-feedback [2] are proposals to use the network information in the transport layer to improve congestion control, separately from the dropping of packets. In particular, Re-feedback proposes a change to the TCP/IP feedback architecture as an attempt to design for tussle for Internet congestion control. Both these mechanisms allow network elements to know the congestion on the downstream path, i.e. between the network element and the destination. Such mechanisms aim to separate congestion control from data transfer and error detection.

Finally, the design of SIP (Session Initiation Protocol) and Public ENUM (tElephone NUmbering Mapping) is modular to some degree, since they decompose the problem of calling a destination into two tasks: identifying a user, and calling the user. SIP is a signaling protocol for initiating and managing sessions such as VoIP calls, while ENUM helps the convergence of VoIP and circuit switching by providing mappings between different identifiers. This has successfully modularized these tasks, allowing alternative technologies to be used as the parties see fit (i.e. tussles to be played out), without altering the interface between the modules. In deployment terms, however, ENUM suffers from the same problem as given above for IPv6. It requires a number of stakeholders to enable it and expend time and effort configuring, deploying, and supporting it, in order for anybody to see a benefit. SIP, on the other hand, requires no additional technology beyond standard TCP/IP, and as such can be incrementally deployed by stakeholders with only limited cost before benefits can be realized.

4 Design for Choice

By modularizing the tussle boundaries we restrict the set of stakeholders that are affected by a protocol. The next step is to give each stakeholder the ability to influence the outcome of a tussle. This entails that each participant has the right to be given enough control during protocol's configuration and at "run time". Then, it should be her option whether to use this right in person, delegate it to a trusted third entity or disregard it completely. In this context, "run time" refers to the time after which the protocol or system is initially deployed, and thus differs from real-time constraints in order to meet service requirements.

During design time, the protocol designer should ensure that all major stakeholders are identified and their interests are taken into account. This task requires an open-minded view in order to include all roles that are affected by a tussle. It is important to have in mind that stakeholders may constantly change, for example new ones can enter the tussle, and this should be done with minimum spillovers.

After identifying relevant stakeholders and their interests, a protocol designer has to determine the supported actions and who can perform each one of them. These actions form the "interfaces" that allow stakeholders to interact with each other. The goal should be to allow every stakeholder to influence the tussle outcome so that collateral effects are avoided. This means that control should be distributed, even though some stakeholder instances may prefer not to exercise their right. One way to achieve this goal is to build interfaces that are open, which means standardized but at the same time flexible enough to capture unpredicted cases.

We should keep in mind that unless the interests of stakeholders are adverse, the tussle at run-time will lead to a stable outcome. This, for example, can be achieved through economics, or another reciprocative method. As Clark et al. [5] mention, if such a reciprocative method can be found then it should be implemented by following the same procedure recursively. A tussle outcome may be temporary since Internet is not a "closed" engineering system. An event triggered during run-time may tilt the tussle into a new equilibrium. This is perfectly reasonable as long as the tussle is fought out within the 'playground' defined by the tussle space boundary of the protocol.

Clark [5] mentions SMTP as a protocol that is designed for choice. During the configuration phase a user selects which provider will forward the email. However, some ISPs may not like their customers making this choice, and could undertake Deep Packet Inspection during run-time to block the well-known port in order to exert control (i.e. force the usage of their mail servers). It is clear that this is not the way in which a tussle should be played out, since they are applying a brute force method to restrict their customers' choices. We will try to clarify the notion of a protocol that is *designed for choice*, by explaining why some well-known protocols seem to be compatible to this principle, and some are not.

Perhaps, a more straightforward example is BGP. ISPs are free to devise their own routing policies, but neighbouring providers can express their preferences by using simple BGP mechanisms. In particular, these preferences can be exchanged by using attributes such as Multi-Exit Discriminator (MED) and Communities[1]. These features allow distributed control at run-time. The reason is that ISPs are not restricted to perform shortest path routing based on longest prefix; they have the ability to select routes based on a wide range of criteria.

ENUM is an example of protocols that allow for "variation of outcome". During configuration an end user becomes a subscriber (opts in) and fully controls the level of details to be inserted in the database. For example she could elect to publish all possible ways of contact along with the associated preferences-wishes, or hide her personal addresses. At run-time, the query issuer has the ability to select which contact address will be used for the session setup. In the case of a VoIP call for example, the signaling server is not restricted to follow a destination's preferences; it can apply

---

[1] Allowed expressions are described following an out-of-bound method (usually manually).

its routing strategy and select the most appropriate contact address(es) to use for any single reason or combination (lower cost, supported signaling protocol, etc). Furthermore, regulator's interests are taken into consideration so that only valid owners of a telephone number can be registered into ENUM.

Staying in the VoIP context, SIP and H.323 are examples of protocols that are designed for choice. The first versions of the H.323 protocol suite were less flexible, since a provider's signaling server (called gatekeeper) had a pivotal role in session setup. For example, a device had to request permission from a gatekeeper for any call attempt, while the latter could deny service if it sensed that network conditions did not meet customer expectations. Since H.323v4 these protocols have converged, for example gatekeepers are optional components, addresses have the same structure, and both support protocol extensions for third party applications. Nowadays, both protocols can be used in a wide range of configurations; from closed systems like IP Multimedia Subsystem (IMS) to end-user installations (i.e. OPENSIPS, OpenH323). A signaling server (of either protocol) may redirect the calling party towards the destination, may act as a proxy only for signaling, or participate in both signaling and media path in order to take advantage of MPLS networks and comply with regulator requirements (i.e. CALEA). It is important to note, however, that there is no way to influence a signaling server on the way it will handle the request. In case of a VoIP call that can either remain VoIP end-to-end or be set up through a Gateway, then the caller cannot state her preferences.

All TCP variants provide end-to-end congestion control and avoidance by relying on an AIMD scheme that is predefined. This means that unless a user has customized her Operating System kernel, she has no control over the flow's rate. Users, however, have a choice about how many connections they run at any time. This fact has been exploited by peer-to-peer (p2p) file-sharing applications and started a never-ending tussle between ISPs and p2p developers and users (since the former were seeing their links being highly utilized by "some" heavy users) [1]. Even though ISPs tried several means to mitigate their problem, p2p developers could find a counter measure and, again, this resulted in collateral damage to other types of traffic.

NAT is a technology driven by the lack of IPv4 addresses and users' desire for less administrative cost when renumbering their network. In this case control is mainly one-sided; a network administrator deploying NAT has control over the set of incoming connections that are allowed to enter. This is done by NAT pinholes that associate a specific service port to the IP address of a single local host. Care should have been taken, however, so that new protocols are not unfavourably biased. For example, most NAT devices make the assumption that TCP and UDP will be the only transport protocols and do not support newer ones (i.e. SCTP). This fact can stifle future innovation on the Internet due to increased difficulties for a new protocol / service to become widely known and, finally, trusted by users.

In general, it seems that a protocol that distributes control to a number of entities (for example to perform selection or aggregate/disaggregate information, network capacity, etc.) should also allow flexibility in policy used to exercise control, and at the same time should have open interfaces for allowing flexible interaction.

5 Protocol Adoption and Design for Tussle

Balancing traditional engineering and socio-economic goals is very difficult, especially when long-term evolution must be secured, as with the case of Internet. We believe, however, that a protocol being "Designed for Tussle" has more chances in the long-term to be deployed than a protocol that is not. In this section, we present how "designing for tussle" can affect the adoption of previously described technologies.

HTTP is a classic example of a widely adopted protocol. The simplicity, extensibility and layered approach in combination with its clean, modular design, contributed hugely to its success.

BGP is another example of protocol that is "Designed for Tussle". It has modular design and allows distribution of control at run-time in a flexible way. On the other hand, Compact Routing schemes (for example see [12]) try to deal with the problem of routing table memory scalability and provide inelastic routing algorithms. If such a routing scheme was adopted, ISPs would have no control over their routing tables; otherwise, parts of the Internet could be disconnected. This feature is crucial for ISPs and thus compact routing schemes are not expected to be deployed.

In most instances of HTTP and BGP, only two agents are involved and they have enough control to determine the session outcome. But this is not always the case. In VoIP, for example, callers, callees, and providers are only a subset of interested parties; however not all protocols distribute control adequately. Megaco embraces the master-slave paradigm, where all functionality is provided by a signaling server and thus it is not "Designed for Tussle". On the other hand, tussle-awareness and richer functionality of SIP and H.323 gave them an advantage over Megaco. But, the protocol that currently enjoys greater acceptance is SIP, which was standardized inside the IETF. Our feeling is that the main reason is their approach regarding the control distribution between the various stakeholders at their early phases. ITU-based H.323 protocol had many things in common with signaling protocols in circuit-switched networks (SS7), thus control distribution was biased in favour of providers. The better score of SIP in this design principle made it attractive to application developers' eyes who adopted it instead of H.323. Later versions of both protocols converged significantly but it doesn't seem to justify transition to H.323.

It seems that in absence of a protocol that fulfills the criteria of "Designing for Tussle", stakeholders will resort to protocols that provide the highest short-term benefit. Neither NAT nor IPv6, for example, meet the criteria mentioned before; however, the former protocol is widely adopted. The main reason is the fact that NAT is considered beneficial both for the end users and their providers, so they have the incentive to embrace it without considering the long-term consequences. On the other hand IPv6 scores low in functional separation which has a negative impact on backwards compatibility and consequently on providers' incentives to deploy it. However, if IPv6 was redesigned so that it became "tussle-aware" then the outcome could be different in the long term. Providers could gradually move to IPv6 and lessen the need for end-users to turn on NAT devices. Similarly, a "tussle-aware" NAT (for example one that does not restrict what transport protocol is in use) would not harm end-users and, as long as IPv6 is not changed, they would be willing to make a software upgrade to this version.

Another important aspect to consider is the externalities between protocols. Even though a protocol (set) exists that is "Designed for Tussle", its adoption may be delayed until protocols of complementary functionality become tussle-aware. For example TCP is not very modular and provides limited control to users with respect to their sending rate. On the other hand, some of the tussles could be played out independently of each other if users a) were free to select their sending rate, and b) were accountable for the congestion they have caused to other users (i.e. increased delay due to packet loses and consequent retransmissions) given sufficient and timely information about network conditions. This would be possible by using, for example, Re-feedback [2] and a modification of TCP that is able to adjust rate according to user preferences (for example [7]). However, the existence of tussle unaware protocols in the Internet (for example NAT) creates hurdles for the adoption of the more flexible ones, even if they perform different functionalities. As more and more protocols become tussle-aware the pressure to replace bottleneck protocols will be greater and these hurdles will ultimately disappear.

Similarly, although Public ENUM scores high in "Designed for Tussle" criteria, it has seen very limited adoption. Of course, retail VoIP services only recently started to gain significant market share, but it seems that costs and benefits are not aligned across stakeholders. User registration is optional but it assumes that the utility of being reached through the most preferred interface is higher than the registration fee. However, not all VoIP providers accept toll-free calls from other providers because they would like to be compensated for their effort. Thus callers (or their providers) see little benefit from querying ENUM. The fact that an increasing number of providers enter into closed ENUM systems, benefiting from toll-free calls between customers of peered VoIP, gives evidence that adoption of Public ENUM is a matter of supporting economic mechanisms that will align costs and benefits of stakeholders.

Of course, designing tussle-aware protocols and complementary mechanisms increase complexity. Care must be taken to balance technical objectives, such as performance, with socio-economic goals in order for the complexity to be manageable. This could be achieved by capturing the most important factors of stakeholder relationships, without following necessarily the "millions of options" approach [3]. But, we believe that long-term evolution of Internet is more important and this extra cost will be out-weighted by higher functionality and flexibility.

6   Conclusions

This paper has outlined a way forward in designing for tussle by describing a number of important design goals applicable to the architectural evolution of today's commercial Internet. The design principles proposed by Clark et al. have been analyzed using selected examples from the various case studies performed. The isolation of tussle, through both functional and stakeholder separation, and the design for choice remain fundamental design goals.

We can conclude that "designing for tussle" does exhibit benefits when designing new protocols, but it is not sufficient condition to ensure the short-term success of a certain protocol, system or technology. Some technologies – whilst designed for tussle – have not been successfully deployed and adopted immediately, while others have been very successful – despite not being designed for tussle. However, we believe that tussle-aware protocols are very important for the long-term evolution of Internet. Last but not least, care must be taken to balance technical objectives, such as performance, with socio-economic goals so that the complexity is manageable.

Acknowledgments. The authors wish to thank all participants of the Trilogy project who contributed to this work through discussion, review, and case study. In particular, the authors would like to thank Simon Schütz, K. Richardson and R. Widera for their initial contribution. C. Courcoubetis and J. Crowcroft also provided useful comments and feedback.

This research was supported by Trilogy (http://www.trilogy-project.org), a research project (ICT-216372) partially funded by the European Community under its Seventh Framework Programme. The views expressed here are those of the authors only. The European Commission is not liable for any use that may be made of the information in this document.

Costas Kalogiros was also financed by E.U.-European Social Fund (80%) and the Greek Ministry of Development-GSRT (20%).

References

1. Briscoe, B.: Flow Rate Fairness: Dismantling a Religion. ACM SIGCOMM Computer Communication Review 37(2), 63–74 (2007)
2. Briscoe, B., Jacquet, A., Di Cairano-Gilfedder, C., Salvatori, A., Soppera, A., Koyabe, M.: Policing Congestion Response in an Internetwork Using Re-feedback. In: Proc. ACM SIGCOMM 2005, CCR, vol. 35(4), pp. 277–288 (2005)
3. Clark, D.D., Sollins, K., Wroclawski, J., Faber, T.: Addressing Reality: An Architectural Response to the Real-World Demands on the Evolving Internet. In: Proc. ACM SIGCOMM Workshop on Future Directions in Network Architecture, pp. 247–257 (2003)
4. Clark, D.D.: The Design Philosophy of the Darpa Internet Protocols. In: Proc. ACM SIGCOMM, Vancouver, BC, Canada (1988)
5. Clark, D.D., Wroclawski, J., Sollins, K.R., Braden, R.: Tussle in Cyberspace: Defining Tomorrow's Internet. IEEE ACM Trans. Networking 13(3), 462–475 (2005)
6. Ford, A., Eardley, P., van Schewick, B.: New Design Principles for the Internet. In: International Workshop on the Network of the Future (to appear, 2009)
7. Ford, A., Raiciu, C., Handley, M., Barre, S.: TCP Extensions for Multipath Operation with Multiple Addresses, draft-ford-mptcp-multiaddressed-00, Internet Draft
8. Handley, M.: Why the Internet Only Just Works. BT Technology Journal 24 (2006)
9. Kunniyur, S., Srikant, R.: End-to-End Congestion Control Schemes: Utility Functions, Random Losses and ECN Marks. IEEE/ACM Transactions on Networking 11, 689–702 (2003)
10. Moors, T.: A Critical Review of End-to-End Arguments in System Design. IEEE International Conference on Communications 2, 1214–1219 (2002)
11. Saltzer, J., Reed, D., Clark, D.D.: End-to-End Arguments in System Design. In: Second International Conference on Distributed Computing Systems, pp. 509–512 (1981); ACM Transactions on Computer Systems 2(4), 277–288 (1984)
12. Thorup, M., Zwick, U.: Compact Routing Schemes. In: Proc. 30th annual ACM Symposium on Parallel Algorithms and Architectures (2001)
13. Wischik, D., Handley, M., Bagnulo Braun, M.: The Resource Pooling Principle. ACM SIGCOMM Computer Communications Review 38(5), 47–52 (2008)

NIT: A New Internet Topology Generator

Joylan Nunes Maciel[1] and Cristina Duarte Murta[2]

[1] Department of Informatics, UFPR, Brazil
[2] Department of Computing, CEFET-MG, Brazil

Abstract. Internet topology generators play an essential role in computer network research. This paper presents a new Internet autonomous system level topology generator. Synthetic topologies generated by the proposed generator are compared to real Internet topologies and to synthetic topologies generated by a well-known topology generator. The results show that, for all the considered metrics, the proposed generator is able to produce more realistic topologies. This work aims to contribute to the generation of more realistic synthetic topologies.

1   Introduction

The topology of the Internet at the autonomous systems (AS) level has evolved rapidly and its evolution pattern is changing due to network usage, development and deployment. New autonomous systems arise daily and others disappear, and the connections between these systems also change. Recent data [1] reveal that new autonomous systems arise at the rate of 10.3 per day, while the rate of disappearance is 2.87 per day. The connections (links) in this topology arise at a rate of 67.3 per day and disappear at a rate of 45.7 per day. To keep pace with this evolution, the topology must be continuously characterized, the results must be compared with the accepted patterns and reformulated if necessary.

Knowledge acquired in characterizing this evolution is important in many areas of network research including topology analysis. One of the goals of topology mapping is the implementation of topology generators for producing synthetic topologies which are used in network simulators and in laboratory tests [2,3]. The construction of synthetic graphs that represent well the real topology contributes to the effectiveness of tests and experiments of new protocols and Internet applications.

Several Internet topology generators are known, for example Inet [4], GLP [2], BRITE [5], RMAT [6] and Orbis [7]. Others, such as Tiers [8] and Transit-Stub [9], have an important historical character but don't reproduce aspects that are currently observed in the autonomous system topology. Probably the most frequently used autonomous system level topology generator at present is the Inet 3.0, which is also the first recommended on the NS2 network simulator homepage [10]. The current version of Inet (3.0) was built based on the analysis of topologies gathered in the period between November 1997 and February 2002. It has been around since its implementation in 2002.

M. Oliver and S. Sallent (Eds.): EUNICE 2009, LNCS 5733, pp. 108–117, 2009.
© Springer-Verlag Berlin Heidelberg 2009

This paper introduces NIT, a New Internet Topology generator that is able to generate synthetic topologies that resemble the autonomous systems graph. The need for a new generator is revealed by comparison of actual topologies collected recently with synthetic topologies generated by topology generators. The results indicate discrepancies in many metrics that are essential for topology characterization. The new generator proposed in this paper is capable of generating topologies more similar to real topologies than Inet is, considering the same metrics. The contributions of this paper are the proposal of a new topology generator which is based on Inet code but includes new models for the metrics, and modeling of new metrics; an analysis of the evolution of clique patterns in actual topologies, including maximal clique size and clique size distribution for topologies collected from 2004 to 2007; results of comparison of topologies generated by the new generator proposed in this paper with real topologies recently collected, and synthetic topologies generated by the Inet. The results indicate that the new generator produces topologies that better resemble the real AS-level topologies.

This paper is organized in five sections. Section 2 overviews the well-known topology generators, the topological metrics and the data collection and sources of data of Internet topology. Section 3 presents the new topology generator proposed in this study. Section 4 presents the results of comparisons of synthetic topologies generated by the new generator with real topologies and the synthetic topologies of Inet. The last section concludes the paper.

2 AS-Level Topology: Metrics, Generators, Databases

The Internet does not know its own topology, it has to be discovered. The collection and gathering of data related to the AS level topology have been the subject of a intense debate in the community [3,11,12,13,14,15]. As a consequence, more complete databases have been constructed. Furthermore, the development of the Internet infrastructure and the deployment of new services in the past five years may lead to new evolution patterns.

The topology analysis of complex networks like the Internet can be carried out through a large number of metrics [16,17,18,19]. There is no consensus in the community on the metrics that best represent the topologies of autonomous systems [20,21,14,12]. However, since the discovery that the frequency of node degrees follows a heavy-tailed distribution [22], this metric has been analyzed in several of the cited studies. Besides node degree distribution, the mostly used topological metrics are distances between nodes, distance related metrics, and metrics of graph connectivity such as clique sizes and cluster coefficients.

The discovery of high variability in the distribution of node degrees has motivated the construction of generators based on this characteristic [20,4,5]. To carry out the present study, many topology generators were analyzed with the objective of identifying those that could best reproduce characteristics of the AS-level Internet topology. Initially, we aimed to analyze and compare results from various generators. BRITE, R-MAT, Orbis, GLP and Inet 3.0 generators were considered. But at the end of the analysis, we chose Inet only. The BRITE generator was not included because it had been already compared to Inet, and Inet got better results [4,23]. Moreover, BRITE requires configuration of a large number of parameters, which amplifies the possibilities of topology generation, but makes it extremely difficult to adjust the parameters for a specific topology.

The R-MAT generator [24] recursively subdivides the adjacency matrix that represents the graph into four equal-sized partitions, and connects the partitions using randomly generated edges. Experiments carried out with R-MAT show that it generates non-connected graphs and duplicated edges and self-loops, characteristics which don't occur in the target graph of this study. This fundamental aspect of its design makes it difficult to map parameters of the target topology. Unfortunately, the source code of Orbis and GLP generators were not available at the time of our experiments. The mostly used AS-level topology generator is the Inet 3.0. Its source code is open, its configuration is simple, and it is available on the Web [25].

The AS-level topology database studied in this work was generated by the Internet Research Laboratory of UCLA and is described in [11]. This database, that we call IRL, is the result of a project that seeks to reconstruct the topology of the autonomous systems in a complete and up-to-date manner, collecting additional data from various sources, obtained by diverse methods, including BGP databases, RouteViews and RIPE projects and IRR and Looking Glass databases. The authors have designed and implemented an automatic method for collecting and updating the topology daily. Data is available starting in 2004. We have collected and analyzed eight topologies, one of each semester from 2004 to 2007.

2.1   Overview of Inet 3.0 Topology Generator

Inet relies on the distribution of node degrees as foundation for its structure. The generator's data input is the number of nodes on the graph to be generated. The algorithm is divided into four phases: generation and distribution of the degrees; construction of the connecting component; connection of nodes of degree equal to one; and finally filling edges of nodes having degrees to be completed. The connection of edges is carried out based on the preferential attachment growth model [4].

Inet models the network growth based on the number of nodes, which is related to the "age" of the topology. It begins setting up its baseline in November 1997 when the number of ASes was 3037. This is the minimum number of nodes that Inet accepts as data input. In the first phase, it estimates the number of edges according to the specified number of nodes in the topology, and assigns degrees for all nodes of the graph. The second phase goal is to make one connected component, which is accomplished by generating a spanning tree. In the third phase, the nodes of degree one are connected to the tree, assuring the construction of a single connected component. In the last phase, the lasting connections are done, and at the end all nodes will have a number of connections equal to the degree defined for each one. In Section 4 we present results of analysis of topologies generated by the Inet 3.0.

3   Description of the NIT Topology Generator

In this section we describe the NIT algorithm. The NIT algorithm has five phases: in phase 1 the node degrees are generated; in phase 2 the nodes are connected to build one large connected component of the graph; in phase 3 a number of cliques is generated in the graph; in phase 4, nodes of degree 1 are connected to the graph; and in phase 5 we set the final connections to complete the node degrees. The NIT algorithm is based on the Inet algorithm. NIT conserves the last two phases of the Inet, which are its phases 4 and 5. The first two Inet phases were remodeled in order to better capture the network topology of the present time. Phase 3 of NIT is completely new and it was designed to model the graph connectivity by the insertion of cliques in the topology.

The first task of the algorithm is to size the graph. The number of nodes is the main input but we have to estimate the number of edges based on the degree distribution. We have modeled the degree distribution with the Bounded Pareto distribution which is a heavy-tailed distribution that has minimal and maximal values as parameters. The complement of the Bounded Pareto cumulative distribution function (CCDF) is given by

$$\bar{F}(x) = \frac{j^\alpha \times \frac{1}{x^\alpha} - (\frac{j}{k})^\alpha}{1 - (\frac{j}{k})^\alpha} \tag{1}$$

in that parameter j is the minimal value (degree $= 1$) and k is the maximal value, that is obtained by modeling the highest degrees of all topologies considered. Hence, x is an integer variable from $j = 1$ to k. The α parameter models the degree variability and is obtained by the following equation:

$$E[x] = \frac{\alpha}{1 - \alpha} \times \frac{k(\frac{j}{k})^\alpha - j}{1 - (\frac{j}{k})^\alpha} \tag{2}$$

in that $E[x]$ expresses the average degree, known from the topology data, just as the j and k values. The α values calculated for all real topologies analyzed from 2004 to 2007 as well as our model for this parameter are shown in the plot on the right side of Fig. 1. It is a logarithmic adjustment with coefficient of determination $R^2 = 0,999$.

We have also modeled the evolution of the frequency of nodes of degree 1 in all topologies collected between 2004 and 2007. The model is shown in the plot on the left side of Fig. 1. It is modeled by an exponential decay equation that has $R^2 = 0,999$.

Therefore, using the models of the percentage of nodes of degree 1 and the parameters of the Bounded Pareto distribution (α, k, and j), we have calculated the distribution of the node degrees and assigned a specific degree to all nodes of the synthetic graph, finishing the first phase of the algorithm.

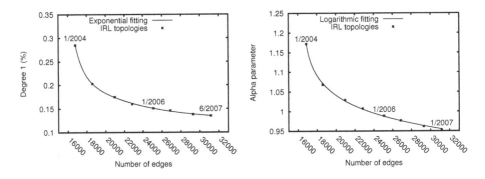

Fig. 1. Fittings for frequency of nodes of degree 1 (left side) and the α parameter (right side) of the IRL topologies

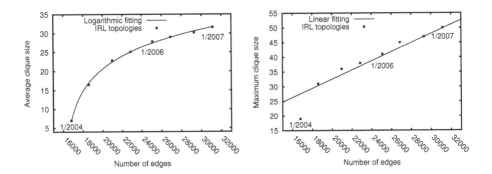

Fig. 2. Fittings for average and maximum clique size of the IRL topologies

The second phase goal is to start the graph as a connected component. This is accomplished by building a spanning tree that includes all nodes of degree three or higher. After that, the nodes of degree 2 are randomly connected. The connections are designed to avoid the large proportion of small cliques that can be found in Inet 3.0, as mentioned in the literature [4]. Small cliques do not contribute to match the clustering coefficients found in the real topology.

In the third phase, our goal is to mimic the cliques pattern founded in the real topology. We have modeled the distribution of clique sizes in the AS-level topology, which follows a Gaussian distribution. The maximum clique size and average clique size were modeled as a function of the number of nodes in the topology, resulting in a logarithmic equation ($R^2 = 0,998$) representing the average clique size and a linear equation ($R^2 = 0,938$) for representing the maximum clique size, as presented in Fig. 2.

Thus, in the third phase we estimate the average clique size and the maximum clique size as a function of the number of nodes of the required topology using these models. Nodes are chosen randomly considering their degrees to make as many cliques as indicated by the models. Modeling the clique distribution is a very important step as the cliques have considerable influence in metrics such as mean distance between nodes, node eccentricity, diameter and clustering coefficients.

Phases 4 and 5 of NIT are similar to the last two phases of Inet. In the next section we present the analysis of metrics comparing the actual topologies given by the IRL database and the synthetic topologies generated by Inet 3.0 and by the NIT algorithm.

4   Comparing Real and Synthetic Topologies

In this section we present results comparing topologies from three sources: the real AS-level topology (IRL) and the synthetic topologies generated by NIT and Inet. The baseline for comparison is the number of nodes, meaning that a comparison is made among topologies with the same number of nodes, which is a measure of the "age" of the network. The topologies are compared according to the following metrics: number of edges, distribution of distances and eccentricities, mean and maximum clique sizes, and cluster coefficients.

The growth of the number of edges in the topologies is shown in Fig. 3. We observe that NIT reproduces better the evolution of the number of edges in the real network, meaning that the Bounded Pareto distribution seems to be a good model. The number of edges generated by Inet is getting severe underestimated for large topologies, whereas NIT overestimate that value by a constant.

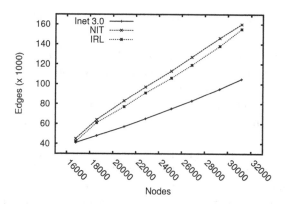

Fig. 3. Edges growth in the Inet 3.0, NIT and IRL topologies

Figure 4 shows the cumulative distribution function (CDF) and the complement of the CDF (CCDF) of vertex degrees for the most recently topology analyzed. We observe that the Bounded Pareto distribution provides a good model for the distribution of node degree. There is a divergence in the tail that includes about 0.1% of nodes but the model of the largest degree helps in the congruence.

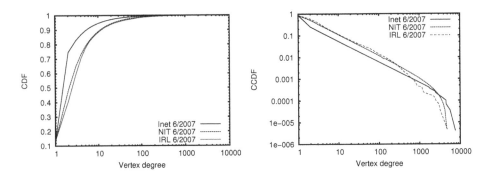

Fig. 4. Degrees Distribution of the Inet 3.0, NIT and IRL topologies

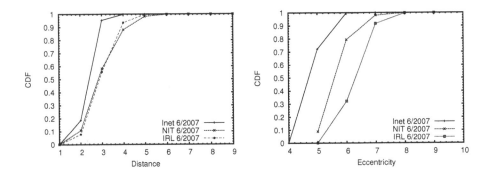

Fig. 5. Distance and Eccentricity Distributions of the Inet, NIT and IRL topologies

The distribution of distances and related metrics are structural metrics of the graph. The distance between two nodes in a graph is the number of edges in the shortest path between them. The eccentricity of a node is the distance to the farthest node. The graph diameter is the maximum eccentricity over all nodes in a graph. The graph radius is the minimum eccentricity over all nodes in a graph.

The cumulative frequency of node distances for all topologies is shown on left plot of Fig. 5. We notice a similar frequency behavior for the real topology and the topology generated by NIT. The good results obtained for the distances are due to the modeling of the number of edges (because more edges helps in graph connectivity), and the design of the clique construction phase (NIT's phase 3), that has influence in the distribution of distances.

The plot on the right of Fig. 5 shows the CDF of the vertex eccentricities in the graph. The analysis shows that the topology generated by NIT presents the same values for diameter and radius of the IRL databases, 9 and 5 respectively, although the frequencies of eccentricities diverge.

Our next analysis focuses on the distribution of clique sizes. Figure 6 shows the CCDF of clique size on the left plot and the evolution of the maximum clique size for all topologies on the right side. We observe that the Inet topology

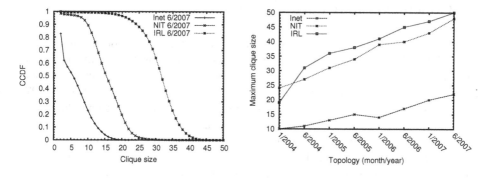

Fig. 6. Clique analysis for all topologies

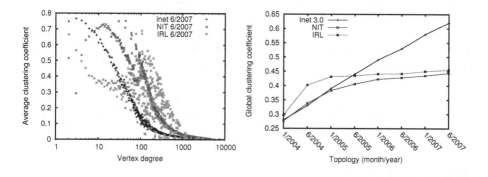

Fig. 7. Clustering coefficients of the Inet, NIT and IRL topologies

generator produces cliques of very small size compared to the real topology. The NIT generator is able to build larger cliques but in a smaller frequency than the real topology, meaning that there is room for improvement.

Our last analysis regards the clustering coefficients. These metrics express the global connectivity of the graph. We have inspected the metrics global clustering coefficient (CC_g) and the average clustering coefficient per degree (CC_m), which are presented on the right and left plots of Fig. 7, respectively. A definition of these metrics can be found in [17].

We observe the variability of CC_m in the real topology compared to the synthetic topologies. The plot on the right shows that the global clustering coefficients of the topologies generated by NIT are getting closer to the values of real topologies.

Finally, we explore the variability of topological metrics generated by different executions of the NIT generator. We generated 100 random topologies of each size (number of nodes) by specifying the first hundred prime numbers as seeds for each execution. We found that the standard deviations for the metric values were very low in all cases. The coefficient of variation, defined as the ratio of the standard deviation to the mean, is lower than 0.06 for all metrics.

5   Conclusion and Future Work

This paper presents a new Internet autonomous system level topology generator called NIT. The need for a new generator is explained by the evolution of the Internet topology in the last years. We have studied and characterized the evolution of the autonomous system level topology in the period from 2004 to 2007. The real topology is growing and getting denser, the distances are shrinking and the average and maximal clique size are becoming larger.

Our generator is based on the Inet 3.0 source code. NIT improves on Inet 3.0 in all metrics tested, introducing new models and a new phase in the algorithm. The results present evidence that the topologies produced by NIT mimics the AS level topology better than the topologies generated by Inet. The usage of topology generators, and particularly Inet, is very significant in computer network research. This work intends to contribute to the generation of more realistic synthetic topologies.

The generation of synthetic topologies that closely resemble the Internet topology is an open problem. The observation that a large number of topologies could be built from a degree distribution [26] turns the approach based on degrees insufficient to model the topology of the Internet. We believe that the association of degree distribution and metrics of distance may establish a new paradigm for the construction of synthetic topology generators, replacing the paradigm of generation based only on the node degree distribution.

Acknowledgements

This research was partially supported by the CNPq and INCT Web. We thank UCLA Internet Research Laboratory for gathering the Internet topology data and making it available on the Web. Joylan thanks LABI/UNIOESTE for supporting his work.

References

1. Oliveira, R.V., Zhang, B., Zhang, L.: Observing the Evolution of Internet AS Topology. SIGCOMM Comput. Commun. Rev., 313–324 (2007)
2. Bu, T., Towsley, D.F.: On Distinguishing between Internet Power Law Topology Generators. In: IEEE INFOCOM, pp. 638–647 (2002)
3. Alderson, D., Li, L., Willinger, W., Doyle, J.C.: Understanding Internet Topology: principles, models, and validation. In: IEEE/ACM Trans. on Networking, pp. 1205–1218 (2005)
4. Winick, J., Jamin, S.: Inet-3.0: Internet Topology Generator. Technical Report 456-02, EECS, University of Michigan (2002)
5. Medina, A., Lakhina, A., Matta, I., Byers, J.W.: BRITE: An Approach to Universal Topology Generation. In: IEEE MASCOTS, pp. 346–361 (2001)
6. Chakrabarti, D., Zhan, Y., Faloutsos, C.: R-MAT: A Recursive Model for Graph Mining. In: SIAM International Conference on Data Mining (2004)

7. Mahadevan, P., Krioukov, D., Fall, K., Vahdat, A.: Systematic Topology Analysis and Generation using degree correlations. In: ACM SIGCOMM, pp. 135–146 (2006)
8. Doar, M.B.: A Better Model for Generating Test Networks. In: IEEE GLOBECOM, pp. 86–93 (1996)
9. Zegura, E.W., Calvert, K.L., Donahoo, M.J.: A quantitative comparison of graph-based models for Internet topology. IEEE/ACM Trans. on Networking, 770–783 (1997)
10. NS2: The Network Simulator NS-2 (2008), http://www.isi.edu/nsnam/ns/
11. Zhang, B., Liu, R.A., Massey, D., Zhang, L.: Collecting the Internet AS-level Topology. In: ACM SIGCOMM Computer Communication Review, pp. 53–61 (2005)
12. Mahadevan, P., Krioukov, D., Fomenkov, M., Huffaker, B.: The Internet AS-level Topology: Three Data Sources and One Definitive Metric. In: SIGCOMM Comput. Commun. Rev., pp. 17–26 (2006)
13. Chang, H., Govindan, R., Jamin, S., Shenker, S.J., Willinger, W.: Towards Capturing Representative AS-level Internet Topologies. In: ACM SIGMETRICS, pp. 280–281 (2002)
14. Chang, H., Willinger, W.: Difficulties Measuring the Internet's AS-Level Ecosystem. Invited Paper. In: IEEE INFOCOM, pp. 1479–1483 (2006)
15. Raz, D., Cohen, R.: The Internet Dark Matter - on the Missing Links in the AS Connectivity Map. In: IEEE INFOCOM (2006)
16. Barabási, A.L., Albert, R.: Emergence of Scaling in Random Networks. Science 286, 509–512 (1999)
17. Pastor-Satorras, R., Vespignani, A.: Evolution and Structure of the Internet: A Statistical Physics Approach. Cambridge University Press, Cambridge (2004)
18. Dorogovtsev, S.N., Mendes, J.F.F.: Evolution of Networks: From Biological Nets to the Internet and WWW. Oxford University Press, Oxford (2003)
19. Magoni, D., Pansiot, J.J.: Analysis of the Autonomous System Network Topology. In: ACM SIGCOMM Comput. Commun. Rev., pp. 26–37 (2001)
20. Tangmunarunkit, H., Govindan, R., Jamin, S., Shenker, S., Willinger, W.: Network Topology Generators: degree-based vs. structural. In: ACM SIGCOMM, pp. 147–159 (2002)
21. Park, S.T., Pennock, D.M., Giles, C.L.: Comparing Static and Dynamic Measurements and Models of the Internet's AS Topology. In: IEEE INFOCOM, pp. 1616–1627 (2004)
22. Faloutsos, M., Faloutsos, P., Faloutsos, C.: On Power-law relationships of the Internet topology. In: ACM SIGCOMM, pp. 251–262 (1999)
23. Jin, C., Chen, Q., Jamin, S.: Inet: Internet Topology Generator. Technical Report 443-00, Department of EECS, University of Michigan (2000)
24. Chakrabarti, D., Faloutsos, C.: Graph mining: laws, generators, and algorithms. ACM Computing Survey 38(1) (2006)
25. Inet: Inet homepage (2008), http://topology.eecs.umich.edu/inet/
26. Li, L., Alderson, D., Willinger, W., Doyle, J.: A First-principles Approach to Understanding the Internet's router-level Topology. In: SIGCOMM Comput. Commun. Rev., pp. 3–14 (2004)

Resource Allocation in MIMO-OFDMA Wireless Systems Based on Linearly Precoded Orthogonal Space-Time Block Codes

Borja Dañobeitia, Guillem Femenias, and Felip Riera-Palou*

Mobile Communications Group, University of the Balearic Islands
Ctra. de Valldemossa, km. 7,5, 07122 Palma (Illes Balears), Spain
{borja.danobeitia,guillem.femenias,felip.riera}@uib.es

Abstract. This paper proposes and analyzes efficient rate and power allocation algorithms for MIMO-OFDMA broadcast channels based on linearly precoded orthogonal space-time block codes. The weighted sum-rate maximization problem is considered for both continuous and discrete rate allocation schemes. Since this problem is non-convex and combinatorial in nature, the Lagrange dual decomposition method is used to find an accurate near-optimal solution. The effects of using different MIMO configurations and realistic channel models with space and frequency correlation over the weighted sum-rate of the system is considered.

Keywords: Resource allocation, OFDMA, MIMO, STBC, linear precoding, Lagrange dual methods.

1 Introduction

The use of multiple-input multiple-output (MIMO) technology has shown to be a major breakthrough in providing high-rate reliable wireless communications links [1, 2, 3]. Furthermore, orthogonal frequency division multiple access (OFDMA), which decouples a broadband frequency-selective channel into multiple parallel frequency-flat fading channels through the use of the fast Fourier transform (FFT), has demonstrated to provide a high degree of flexibility in radio resource allocation, allowing the exploitation of the so-called multiuser diversity embedded in frequency-selective fading channels [4].

Over the past decade, owing to their great promises, OFDMA and MIMO have been synergistically integrated to offer the benefits of both resource allocation flexibility and high performance [5, 6] and MIMO-OFDMA systems have found their way into several standards for next-generation wireless communication networks, notably IEEE 802.16e and 3GPP-LTE (Third Generation Partnership Project-Long Term Evolution). There are different ways of exploiting

---

* This work has been supported in part by the Ministerio de Ciencia e Innovación, Spain, and FEDER, under grant TEC2008-02422 and a PhD grant from Conselleria d'Economia, Hisenda i Innovació del Govern de les Illes Balears.

M. Oliver and S. Sallent (Eds.): EUNICE 2009, LNCS 5733, pp. 118–127, 2009.
© Springer-Verlag Berlin Heidelberg 2009

multiple antennas at both ends of the MIMO-OFDMA communications link; among them, orthogonal space-time block coding (OSTBC) [7] is a simple yet very effective means of achieving transmit/receive diversity. These space-time coding schemes do not exploit channel knowledge at the transmitter. However, channel state information (CSI), if it is available, can of course be used to combine linear precoding strategies with OSTBC, exploiting in this way the joint benefits of both conventional beamforming and OSTBC [8, 9, 10].

Based on the analytical framework proposed by Seong *et al.* [11], our objective in this paper is to propose and analyze efficient rate and power allocation algorithms for MIMO-OFDMA broadcast channels based on the use of combined linear precoding and OSTBC. In particular, the weighted sum-rate maximization problem is considered. It is a non-convex combinatorial problem whose complexity increases exponentially with the number of users and subcarriers in the system [12]. However, Yu and Lui [13] showed that, even though this optimization problem is non-convex, the Lagrange dual decomposition method can be used to find an accurate suboptimal solution, as the duality gap becomes zero when the number of subcarriers goes to infinity. Motivated by this result, the downlink weighted sum-rate maximization problem for linearly precoded OSTBC-based MIMO-OFDMA wireless systems is solved in the dual domain by using Lagrange dual decomposition.

2 System Model

Let us consider the downlink of a single-cell[1] OFDMA base station equipped with N_T transmit antennas. We note that these N_T physical antennae will be transformed into M (with $M \leq N_T$) *virtual* antennas through the action of the precoder. The OFDMA system has N_{FFT} subcarriers from which N of them are used to provide service to K active mobile stations, each equipped with N_R receive antennas. Used subcarriers and active users are indexed by the sets $\mathcal{N} = \{0, \ldots, N-1\}$ and $\mathcal{K} = \{0, \ldots, K-1\}$, respectively. Let us also assume that user k has been assigned subcarrier n, and that the base station uses an OSTBC in order to achieve transmit diversity. We denote the code matrix that defines the OSTBC as $C(\boldsymbol{Z}_{k,n,\eta}) \in \mathbb{C}^{T \times M}$, which is used to distribute the ηth block of K_s symbols $\boldsymbol{Z}_{k,n,\eta} = \{z_{k,n,\eta,0}, \ldots, z_{k,n,\eta,K_s-1}\}$ among the M virtual transmit antennas and T OFDM symbol periods where, without loss of generality, symbols $\{z_{k,n,\eta,k_s}\}_{k_s=0}^{K_s-1}$ are assumed to be taken from a complex constellation $\mathcal{A}$ with average energy $\mathbb{E}\{|z_{k,n,\eta,k_s}|^2\} = 1$. Since T OFDM symbols are necessary to transmit $K_s \leq T$ symbols, the coding rate of the STBC is $R_c = K_s/T$. The elements of $C(\boldsymbol{Z}_{k,n,\eta})$ are linear combinations of the symbols $\{z_{k,n,\eta,k_s}\}_{k_s=0}^{K_s-1}$ and their conjugates. Furthermore, due to orthogonality, it holds that

$$(C(\boldsymbol{Z}_{k,n,\eta}))^H C(\boldsymbol{Z}_{k,n,\eta}) = a \left(\sum_{k_s=0}^{K_s-1} |z_{k,n,\eta,k_s}|^2\right) \boldsymbol{I}_M, \tag{1}$$

---

[1] In order to simplify the problem of resource allocation, the inter-cell interference is assumed to be either absent or simply modeled as additive white Gaussian noise.

where $(\cdot)^H$ denotes the matrix complex conjugate transpose operator, $\boldsymbol{I}_M$ is the $M \times M$ identity matrix and a is a constant that depends on the OSTBC coding matrix. For instance, $a = 1$ for the Alamouti-STBC and, taking the codes proposed by Tarokh $et\ al.$ in [7], $a = 1$ for the rate $R_c = 3/4$ OSTBCs $\mathcal{H}_3$ and $\mathcal{H}_4$, and $a = 2$ the rate $R_c = 1/2$ OSTBCs $\mathcal{G}_3$ and $\mathcal{G}_4$. Before transmission, the space-time codeword is multiplied by a precoding matrix $\boldsymbol{F}_{k,n,\eta} \in \mathbb{C}^{M \times N_T}$, satisfying the power constraint $\|\boldsymbol{F}_{k,n,\eta}^H \boldsymbol{F}_{k,n,\eta}\|_F^2 = 1$, where $\|\cdot\|_F$ denotes the matrix Frobenius norm.

At the receiver side, assuming perfect sample and symbol synchronization, and a cyclic prefix of length greater that the maximum duration of the channel impulse response, the $T \times N_R$ received signal matrix for the OSTBC block η of user k over subcarrier n is given by

$$\boldsymbol{Y}_{k,n,\eta} = \sqrt{\frac{p_{k,n,\eta}}{a\,R_c}}\,\boldsymbol{C}\left(\boldsymbol{Z}_{k,n,\eta}\right)\boldsymbol{F}_{k,n,\eta}\boldsymbol{H}_{k,n,\eta} + \boldsymbol{\nu}_{k,n,\eta}, \tag{2}$$

where $p_{k,n,\eta}$ is the power allocated to user k over subcarrier n for each OFDM symbol in OSTBC block period η and the receiver noise $\boldsymbol{\nu}_{k,n,\eta}$ is an $T \times N_R$ matrix with elements modeled as independent identically distributed (i.i.d.) zero-mean complex circular-symmetric Gaussian random variables, each with variance σ_ν^2. The matrix $\boldsymbol{H}_{k,n,\eta}$ denotes the $N_T \times N_R$ frequency domain complex channel gain matrix from all transmit antennas to all receive antennas for user k over subcarrier n and OSTBC block period η. The elements of $\boldsymbol{H}_{k,n,\eta}$ are derived from a user-dependent power delay profile [14, 15]. Assuming perfect CSI, the maximum likelihood (ML) receiver decides in favor of the block of symbols $\hat{\boldsymbol{Z}}_{k,n,\eta}$ satisfying

$$\hat{\boldsymbol{Z}}_{k,n,\eta} = \arg \min_{\hat{\boldsymbol{Z}} \in \mathcal{A}^{K_s}} \left\| \boldsymbol{Y}_{k,n,\eta} - \sqrt{\frac{p_{k,n,\eta}}{a\,R_c}}\,\boldsymbol{C}\left(\hat{\boldsymbol{Z}}\right)\boldsymbol{F}_{k,n,\eta}\boldsymbol{H}_{k,n,\eta} \right\|^2 . \tag{3}$$

Noting the column orthogonal characteristic of the space-time block coding matrix, the minimization in (3) can be decoupled into K_s parts that are only a function of z_{k,n,η,k_s}, for $k_s = 0, \ldots, K_s - 1$, respectively [7,16]. It can be shown that the ML decision rule for the k_sth symbol z_{k,n,η,k_s} is given by [16]

$$\hat{z}_{k,n,\eta,k_s} = \arg \min_{\hat{z} \in \mathcal{A}} \left| \tilde{y}_{k,n,\eta,k_s} - \sqrt{\frac{p_{k,n,\eta}}{R_c}}\,\|\boldsymbol{F}_{k,n,\eta}\boldsymbol{H}_{k,n,\eta}\|_F^2\,\hat{z} \right|^2 , \tag{4}$$

for all $k_s = 0, \ldots, K_s - 1$, with

$$\tilde{y}_{k,n,\eta,k_s} = \sqrt{\frac{p_{k,n,\eta}}{R_c}}\,\|\boldsymbol{F}_{k,n,\eta}\boldsymbol{H}_{k,n,\eta}\|_F^2\,z_{k,n,\eta,k_s} + \tilde{\nu}_{k,n,\eta,k_s}, \tag{5}$$

where $\tilde{\nu}_{k,n,\eta,k_s}$ is a noise sample modeled as a zero-mean complex circular-symmetric Gaussian random variable with variance $\sigma_\nu^2\alpha_{k,n,\eta}$. Thus, the effective instantaneous signal to noise ratio at the output of the ML detector can be expressed as

$$\gamma_{k,n,\eta} = \frac{p_{k,n,\eta}\alpha_{k,n,\eta}}{R_c\sigma_\nu^2}, \tag{6}$$

where $\alpha_{k,n,\eta} = \|\boldsymbol{F}_{k,n,\eta}\boldsymbol{H}_{k,n,\eta}\|_F^2$. The optimal precoding matrix, in the sense of maximizing the SNR, is thus obtained when $\alpha_{k,n,\eta}$ is maximized. As stated by Sanayei *et al.* in [10, Theorem 1], an optimal precoding matrix has the form[2] $\boldsymbol{F}_{k,n,\eta} = \boldsymbol{\psi}\boldsymbol{v}_{k,n,\eta}^T$, where $\boldsymbol{v} \in \mathbb{C}^{N_T \times 1}$ is the left singular vector of $\boldsymbol{H}_{k,n,\eta}$ associated with its largest singular value, denoted as $\sigma_{\max}(\boldsymbol{H}_{k,n,\eta})$, and $\boldsymbol{\psi} \in \mathbb{C}^{M \times 1}$ is an arbitrary unit norm vector. For the above choice of $\boldsymbol{F}_{k,n,\eta}$ we have that

$$
\begin{aligned}
\alpha_{k,n,\eta} &= \text{trace}\left(\boldsymbol{H}_{k,n,\eta}^H \boldsymbol{F}_{k,n,\eta}^H \boldsymbol{F}_{k,n,\eta} \boldsymbol{H}_{k,n,\eta}\right) \\
&= \text{trace}\left(\boldsymbol{H}_{k,n,\eta}^H \boldsymbol{v}_{k,n,\eta}\|\boldsymbol{\psi}\|_2^2 \boldsymbol{v}_{k,n,\eta}^T \boldsymbol{H}_{k,n,\eta}\right) = \sigma_{\max}^2(\boldsymbol{H}_{k,n,\eta}).
\end{aligned}
\tag{7}
$$

3   Optimization Variables

Power allocation: Let $\boldsymbol{p}_{n,\eta} = [p_{0,n,\eta} \cdots p_{K-1,n,\eta}]^T$ denote the vector of power allocation values for subcarrier n and STBC block η. For a given set of constraints, the allocation algorithm will be in charge of determining the power allocation vector

$$
\boldsymbol{p}_\eta = \left[(\boldsymbol{p}_{0,\eta})^T \cdots (\boldsymbol{p}_{N-1,\eta})^T\right]^T
\tag{8}
$$

optimizing the objective function. In addition to determining the power allocation values, the resource allocation algorithms should also allocate subcarriers and transmission rates. Nevertheless, as it will be shown next, the power allocation vector $\boldsymbol{p}_\eta$ can also be used to represent the allocation of all these resources, thus simplifying the formulation of the optimization problem [17].

Subcarrier allocation: As usual, it is assumed that subcarrier sharing is exclusive, that is, only one user is allowed to transmit on a given subcarrier. Hence, the subcarrier allocation constraints can be captured by constraining the power allocation vector as

$$
\boldsymbol{p}_{n,\eta} \in \boldsymbol{\mathcal{P}}_n = \left\{\boldsymbol{p}_{n,\eta} \in \mathbb{R}_+^K \; : \; p_{k,n,\eta}p_{k',n,\eta} = 0; \; \forall\, k \neq k'; \; k, k' \in \mathcal{K}\right\}.
\tag{9}
$$

Hence, the power allocation vector satisfies

$$
\boldsymbol{p}_\eta \in \boldsymbol{\mathcal{P}} = \boldsymbol{\mathcal{P}}_0 \times \cdots \times \boldsymbol{\mathcal{P}}_{N-1} \subset \mathbb{R}_+^{KN}.
\tag{10}
$$

Continuous rate allocation: The achievable capacity (ideal continuous rate) for user k over subcarrier n, measured in bits per second per Hz, can be written as

$$
\begin{aligned}
R_{k,n,\eta}\left(p_{k,n,\eta}, \alpha_{k,n,\eta}\right) &= R_c \log_2\left(1 + \gamma_{k,n,\eta}\right) \\
&= R_c \log_2\left(1 + \frac{p_{k,n,\eta}\alpha_{k,n,\eta}}{R_c\sigma_\nu^2}\right).
\end{aligned}
\tag{11}
$$

As a consequence, the transmission rate allocation is uniquely determined by the power allocation value $p_{k,n,\eta}$.

---

[2] Notice that we have defined the channel matrix as the transpose of that used in [10]. Furthermore, the objective of minimizing the error probability, as used in [10], is equivalent to our objective of maximizing the SNR.

Discrete rate allocation: Systems based on adaptive modulation and coding (AMC) can only use a discrete set $\mathcal{M} = \{0, \ldots, M - 1\}$ of modulation and coding schemes (MCS), which are characterized by a particular transmission rate r_m (in bits per second per Hertz), for all $m \in \mathcal{M}$. In this case, the set $\mathbb{R}^+$ is subdivided in M disjoint intervals, each defining the margin of effective instantaneous signal to noise ratios over which a particular MCS will be selected by the AMC scheme. Thus, the transmission rate for user k over subcarrier n and STBC block η can be expressed using the staircase function

$$R_{k,n,\eta}\left(p_{k,n,\eta}, \alpha_{k,n,\eta}\right) = \begin{cases} R_c\, r_0 & , \ 0 \leq \gamma_{k,n,\eta} < \Gamma_1 \\ R_c\, r_1 & , \ \Gamma_1 \leq \gamma_{k,n,\eta} < \Gamma_2 \\ \vdots & \quad \vdots \\ R_c\, r_{M-1} & , \ \Gamma_{M-1} \leq \gamma_{k,n,\eta} < \infty \end{cases} \tag{12}$$

where $\{\Gamma_m\}_{m=1}^{M-1}$, with $\Gamma_{m+1} \geq \Gamma_m$, are the effective instantaneous SNR boundaries defining the MCS selection intervals. Generally, these SNR boundaries are obtained by setting a target error rate P_0 and determining the margin of effective instantaneous SNR values that guarantee the target error rate when using each one of the MCSs. As in the continuous rate case, the power allocation value $p_{k,n,\eta}$ uniquely determines the transmission rate allocation.

4   Weighted Sum-Rate Maximization

Assuming the availability of perfect channel state information (CSI), the instantaneous weighted sum-rate maximization problem can be formulated as (see, for instance, [18, 11, 17])

$$\max_{p_\eta \in \mathcal{P}} \sum_{k=0}^{K-1} w_{k,\eta} \sum_{n=0}^{N-1} R_{k,n,\eta}\left(p_{k,n,\eta}, \alpha_{k,n,\eta}\right)$$
$$\text{s.t.} \ \sum_{k=0}^{K-1}\sum_{n=0}^{N-1} p_{k,n,\eta} \leq P_T, \tag{13}$$

where P_T is the maximum base station transmission power. The user weights $\{w_{k,\eta}\}_{k=0}^{K-1}$ are positive constants satisfying $\sum_{k=0}^{K-1} w_{k,\eta} = 1$ that allow the MAC layer setting priorities of different users in the system and enforcing certain notions of fairness [17]. Let us approach this optimization problem using duality principles [13]. The Lagrangian of (13) can be expressed as

$$\mathcal{L}\left(p_\eta, \lambda\right) = \sum_{k=0}^{K-1} w_{k,\eta} \sum_{n=0}^{N-1} R_{k,n,\eta}\left(p_{k,n,\eta}, \alpha_{k,n,\eta}\right) + \lambda\left(P_T - \sum_{k=0}^{K-1}\sum_{n=0}^{N-1} p_{k,n,\eta}\right).$$
$$\tag{14}$$

Using the subcarrier exclusive allocation constraint and the fact that the power variables are separable across subcarriers, the dual optimization problem can be written as

$$g(\lambda) = \min_{\lambda \geq 0} \left[\max_{\boldsymbol{p}_\eta \in \mathcal{P}} \mathcal{L}\left(\boldsymbol{p}_\eta, \lambda\right) \right]$$

$$= \min_{\lambda \geq 0} \left[\lambda P_T + \sum_{n=0}^{N-1} \max_{k \in \mathcal{K}} \left(\max_{p_{k,n,\eta} \geq 0} \left(w_{k,\eta} R_{k,n,\eta}\left(p_{k,n,\eta}, \alpha_{k,n,\eta}\right) - \lambda p_{k,n,\eta}\right) \right) \right].$$

$$(15)$$

Thus, the problem has been reduced to a per-subcarrier optimization, and since $N \gg K$, the computational complexity has been significantly reduced.

Continuous rate allocation: In case of using $R_{k,n,\eta}\left(p_{k,n,\eta}, \alpha_{k,n,\eta}\right)$ as defined in (11), the innermost maximization in (15) provides a multilevel water-filling closed-form expression for the optimal power allocation given as

$$\wp_{k,n,\eta}(\lambda) = \left[\frac{1}{\chi_{k,n,\eta}(\lambda)} - \frac{1}{\zeta_{k,n,\eta}} \right]^+, \tag{16}$$

where $[x]^+ = \max(0, x)$, $\chi_{k,n,\eta}(\lambda) = \frac{\lambda \ln 2}{w_{k,n,\eta} R_c}$ and $\zeta_{k,n,\eta} = \frac{\alpha_{k,n,\eta}}{R_c \sigma_\nu^2}$. Now, using (16) in (15) yields

$$g(\lambda) = \min_{\lambda \geq 0} \left[\lambda P_T + \sum_{n=0}^{N-1} \max_{k \in \mathcal{K}} \left(w_{k,\eta} R_{k,n,\eta}\left(\wp_{k,n,\eta}(\lambda), \alpha_{k,n,\eta}\right) - \lambda \wp_{k,n,\eta}(\lambda)\right) \right].$$

$$(17)$$

Using standard properties of dual optimization problems [13], it can be shown that the objective function for the dual problem is convex with respect to λ and thus, line search methods like, for example, Golden-section or Fibonacci, can be used to determine λ^*. Once λ^* has been found, it can be used in the optimization functions to obtain the following user and power allocation for each of the subcarriers in the system

$$k_n^* = \arg\max_{k \in \mathcal{K}} \left(w_{k,\eta} R_{k,n,\eta}\left(\wp_{k,n,\eta}(\lambda^*), \alpha_{k,n,\eta}\right) - \lambda^* \wp_{k,n,\eta}(\lambda^*)\right) \tag{18a}$$

$$p_{k,n,\eta} = \begin{cases} \wp_{k,n,\eta}(\lambda^*), & k = k_n^* \\ 0 & , \text{ otherwise.} \end{cases} \tag{18b}$$

Discrete rate allocation: In this case $R_{k,n,\eta}\left(p_{k,n,\eta}, \alpha_{k,n,\eta}\right)$ is a non-derivable discontinuous function. However, using (12) the set $\mathbb{R}^+$ can be subdivided into M segments

$$\mathcal{R}_m^+ = \left[\frac{\Gamma_m}{\zeta_{k,n,\eta}}, \frac{\Gamma_{m+1}}{\zeta_{k,n,\eta}} \right), \quad m \in \mathcal{M}, \tag{19}$$

and given that λ and $p_{k,n,\eta}$ belong to $\mathbb{R}^+$, if a power allocation $p_{k,n,\eta}$ is used such that $\Gamma_m \leq \gamma_{k,n,\eta} < \Gamma_{m+1}$ then

$$w_{k,\eta} R_{k,n,\eta}\left(p_{k,n,\eta}, \alpha_{k,n,\eta}\right) - \lambda p_{k,n,\eta}$$

$$= w_{k,\eta} R_c r_m - \lambda p_{k,n,\eta} \leq w_{k,\eta} R_c r_m - \lambda \frac{\Gamma_m}{\zeta_{k,n,\eta}}, \quad \forall \, p_{k,n,\eta} \in \mathcal{R}_m^+. \tag{20}$$

As a consequence, there only exist M candidate power allocations

$$\wp_{k,n,\eta}(\lambda) \in \left\{ \frac{\Gamma_0}{\zeta_{k,n,\eta}}, \ldots, \frac{\Gamma_{M-1}}{\zeta_{k,n,\eta}} \right\} \tag{21}$$

from which the one maximizing $w_{k,\eta} R_c r_m - \lambda \frac{\Gamma_m}{\zeta_{k,n,\eta}}$ must be selected, that is,

$$\wp_{k,n,\eta}(\lambda) = \frac{\Gamma_{m_{k,n}^*(\lambda)}}{\zeta_{n,k,\eta}}, \tag{22}$$

where

$$m_{k,n}^*(\lambda) = \arg \max_{m \in \mathcal{M}} \left(w_{k,\eta} R_c r_m - \lambda \frac{\Gamma_m}{\zeta_{k,n,\eta}} \right). \tag{23}$$

Using (22) in (15), the dual optimization problem can be rewritten as

$$g(\lambda) = \min_{\lambda \geq 0} \left[\lambda P_T + \sum_{n=0}^{N-1} \max_{k \in \mathcal{K}} \left(w_{k,\eta} R_{k,n,\eta} \left(\frac{\Gamma_{m_{k,n}^*(\lambda)}}{\zeta_{n,k,\eta}}, \alpha_{k,n,\eta} \right) - \lambda \frac{\Gamma_{m_{k,n}^*(\lambda)}}{\zeta_{n,k,\eta}} \right) \right] \tag{24}$$

and, as in the continuous rate allocation case, simple line search methods can be used to determine λ^*, that can then be substituted in the optimization functions to obtain the optimal user, rate and power allocation for each of the subcarriers of the system

$$k_n^* = \arg \max_{k \in \mathcal{K}} \left(w_{k,\eta} R_c r_{m_{k,n}^*(\lambda^*)} - \lambda^* \frac{\Gamma_{m_{k,n}^*(\lambda^*)}}{\zeta_{k,n,\eta}} \right) \tag{25a}$$

$$R_{k,n,\eta} = \begin{cases} R_c \, r_{m_{k,n}^*(\lambda^*)} \,, & k = k_n^* \\ 0 & , \text{ otherwise,} \end{cases} \qquad p_{k,n,\eta} = \begin{cases} \frac{\Gamma_{m_{k,n}^*(\lambda^*)}}{\zeta_{k,n,\eta}} \,, & k = k_n^* \\ 0 & , \text{ otherwise.} \end{cases} \tag{25b}$$

5 Numerical Results

Without loss of generality, we consider a MIMO-OFDMA system with parameters extracted from the draft specifications of IEEE 802.11n. In particular, we consider an operating setup with bandwidth $B = 20$ MHz over a carrier frequency $f_0 = 5.25$ GHz and $N_{\text{FFT}} = 64$ subcarriers from which $N = 52$ are used to transmit data. For simplicity, an uncoded Gray-mapped square 2^{r_l}-QAM with $r_l \in \{0, 2, 4, 6\}$ bits and SNR thresholds $\eta_l \in \{-\infty, 9.97, 16.96, 23.19\}$ dB has been assumed in discrete rate allocation case [17]. The use of channel coding certainly would increase the global sum-rate but would not modify the general trends and conclusions. The frequency-selective Rayleigh fading channel has been simulated using models B and E proposed by Kermoal et $al.$ in [15]. Transmit and receive antennas are configured as linear uniform arrays with antenna spacing of 1 and 1/2 wavelength, respectively. Numerical results have been obtained through a Monte-Carlo simulation using 1,000 channel realizations.

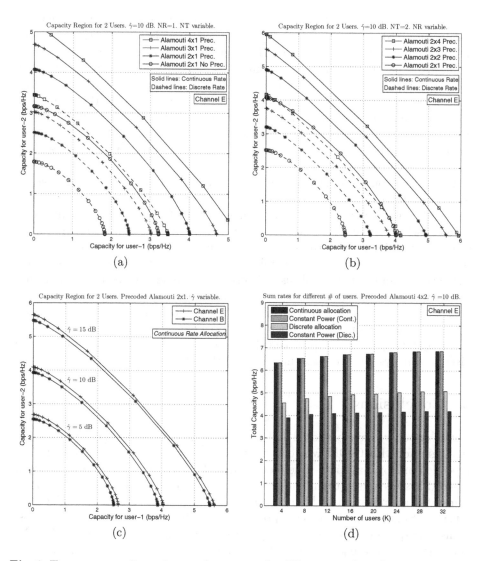

Fig. 1. Two-user capacity regions and sum rates for different number of users as a function of $N_T \times N_R$ MIMO configuration, frequency-selective channel model and resource allocation strategy

In Figs. 1(a) and 1(b), we show the capacity regions of a linearly precoded system using Alamouti STBC with 2 users and varying w_1 between 0 and 1, and setting $w_2 = 1 - w_1$. Results are presented for continuous and discrete rate allocation algorithms as a function of $N_T \times N_R$ MIMO configuration. Obviously, discrete rate allocation algorithms show a capacity loss with respect to the ideal (Shannon capacity-based) continuous rate allocation schemes. Nevertheless, as observed by Wong *et al.* in [17], the general trends are very similar to the continuous rate case. As shown in Fig. 1(a), the joint use of OSTBC and linear precoding at the transmitter side produces a substantial increase in system capacity. Fig. 1(b) shows an even more pronounced capacity increase as the number of receive antennas is incremented. However, it is important to note the diminishing capacity returns that are obtained as the number of diversity branches increases, either at the transmitter or the receiver sides. Fig. 1(c) shows the same capacity regions for different values of $\hat{\gamma} \triangleq P_T/\sigma_\nu^2$ and varying the frequency-selective Rayleigh channel model. It can be observed that, especially for lower SNRs, a higher sum rate is obtained when transmitting over channel model E. This suggests that channel selectivity (spatial and/or frequential) can be converted into *multiuser diversity*.

Fig. 1(d) depicts the sum capacity for a precoded Alamouti 4×2 system, with $\hat{\gamma} = 10$ dB, as a function of the number of users, K. Results have been obtained by generating a random set of user weights for each channel realization. Sum capacity results for a constant power allocation strategy are also shown for comparison. First of all, the effect of multiuser diversity can be observed as the sum capacity grows as the number of users increases. Second, we see that the capacity gain due to multiuser diversity is also subject to the diminishing capacity returns as the number of users increases. Finally, it is interesting to note that the capacity gain provided by the use of variable power allocation algorithms becomes negligible when using continuous rate allocation algorithms, thus suggesting that using powerful channel coding strategies in a more realistic discrete rate system can make unnecessary the use of power allocation.

6   Conclusions

In this paper we have proposed and analyzed effective rate and power allocation strategies for MIMO-OFDMA broadcast channels in systems employing linearly precoded orthogonal space-time block codes. The Lagrange dual decomposition method has been used to find an accurate near-optimal solution to the weighted sum-rate maximization problem for both continuous and discrete rate allocation schemes. Simulations have been presented for different MIMO configurations, realistic frequency-selective channel profiles and varying number of users. Results demonstrate that the joint use of OSTBC and linear precoding at the transmitter side and space diversity at receiver side produces a substantial increase in system capacity. However, diminishing capacity returns are obtained as the number of diversity branches increases, either at transmission or reception. Similarly, multiuser diversity is also affected by diminished capacity returns as the number of users grows.

References

1. Gesbert, D., Shafi, M., Shiu, D., Smith, P.J., Naguib, A.: From theory to practice: an overview of MIMO space-time coded wireless systems. IEEE JSAC 21(3), 281–302 (2003)

2. Goldsmith, A., Jafar, S.A., Jindal, N., Vishwanath, S.: Capacity limits of MIMO channels. IEEE JSAC 21(5), 684–702 (2003)
3. Paulraj, A.J., Gore, D.A., Nabar, R.U., Bolcskei, H.: An overview of MIMO communications-a key to gigabit wireless. Proc. IEEE 92(2), 198–218 (2004)
4. Wang, Z., Giannakis, G.B.: Wireless multicarrier communications. IEEE Signal Proc. Mag. 17(3), 29–48 (2000)
5. Stuber, G.L., Barry, J.R., Mclaughlin, S.W., Li, Y.G., Ingram, M.A., Pratt, T.G.: Broadband MIMO-OFDM wireless communications. Proc. IEEE 92(2), 271–294 (2004)
6. Bolcskei, H.: MIMO-OFDM wireless systems: basics, perspectives, and challenges. IEEE Wireless Communications 13(4), 31–37 (2006)
7. Tarokh, V., Jafarkhani, H., Calderbank, A.R.: Space-time block coding for wireless communications: performance results. IEEE JSAC 17(3), 451–460 (1999)
8. Skoglund, G.J.M., Ottersten, B.: Combining beamforming and orthogonal space-time block coding. IEEE Tran. Inf. Theory. 48(3), 611–627 (2002)
9. Love, D.J., Heath, J.R.W.: Limited feedback unitary precoding for orthogonal space-time block codes. IEEE Tran. Sig. Proc. 53(1), 64–73 (2005)
10. Sanayei, S., Love, D.J., Nosratinia, A.: On the design of linear precoders for orthogonal space-time block codes with limited feedback. In: Proc. IEEE WCNC, pp. 489–493 (2005)
11. Seong, K., Mohseni, M., Cioffi, J.M.: Optimal resource allocation for OFDMA downlink systems. In: Proc. International Symposium on Information Theory (ISIT), July 2006, pp. 1394–1398 (2006)
12. Hoo, L.M.C., Halder, B., Tellado, J., Cioffi, J.M.: Multiuser transmit optimization for multicarrier broadcast channels: asymptotic FDMA capacity region and algorithms. IEEE Tran. Commun. 52(6), 922–930 (2004)
13. Yu, W., Lui, R.: Dual methods for nonconvex spectrum optimization of multicarrier systems. IEEE Tran. Commun. 54(7), 1310 (2006)
14. Proakis, J.G.: Digital Communications, 4th edn. McGraw-Hill, New York (2001)
15. Kermoal, J., Schumacher, L., Pedersen, K., Mogensen, P., Frederiksen, F.: A stochastic MIMO radio channel model with experimental validation. IEEE JSAC 20(6), 1211–1226 (2002)
16. Femenias, G.: BER performance of linear STBC from orthogonal designs over MIMO correlated Nakagami-m fading channels. IEEE Tran. Veh. Technol. 53(2), 307–317 (2004)
17. Wong, I., Evans, B.: Resource allocation in multiuser multicarrier wireless systems. Springer, Heidelberg (2008)
18. Shen, Z., Andrews, J.G., Evans, B.L.: Optimal power allocation in multiuser OFDM systems. In: Proc. IEEE Global Telecommunications Conference (GLOBECOM), December 2003, pp. 337–341 (2003)

On the Influence of Packet Scheduling on the Trade-Off between System Spectral Efficiency and User Fairness in OFDMA-Based Networks

Emanuel B. Rodrigues[1], Michael L. Walker[2], and Fernando Casadevall[1]

[1] Universitat Politècnica de Catalunya (UPC),
Departament de Teoria del Senyal i Comunicacions (TSC),
Barcelona, Spain
{emanuel,ferranc}@tsc.upc.edu
[2] Università degli Studi di Padova,
Dipartimento di Ingegneria dell'Informazione,
Padova, Italy
michaellee.walker@studenti.unipd.it

Abstract. System spectral efficiency and user fairness are crucial aspects for resource allocation in multi-user OFDM-based cellular networks. This work intends to investigate the influence of the performance of packet scheduling algorithms on the trade-off between these two objectives in scenarios with non real-time and real-time services. By means of system-level simulations, we were able to create a didactic map of the relation between these two aspects and propose ways to exploit this trade-off efficiently.

Keywords: Packet Scheduling, spectral efficiency, fairness, OFDMA.

1 Introduction

The wireless shared channel in cellular networks is a medium over which many Mobile Terminals (MTs) compete for resources. In such a scenario, spectral efficiency and fairness are crucial aspects for resource allocation. From a cellular operator perspective, it is very important to use the channel efficiently because the available frequency spectrum is scarce and the revenue must be maximized. From the users' point of view, it is more important to have a fair resource allocation so that they can meet their Quality of Service (QoS) requirements and maximize their satisfaction. The time-varying nature of the wireless environment, coupled with different channel conditions for different MTs, poses significant challenges to accomplishing these goals. In general, these objectives cannot be achieved simultaneously and an efficient trade-off must be achieved. In recent years, Radio Resource Management (RRM) has been envisaged as one of the most efficient techniques to achieve a desirable trade-off among these two conflicting objectives in cellular multi-carrier systems.

Many next generation wireless systems are based on Orthogonal Frequency Division Multiple Access (OFDMA), which provides a high degree of flexibility

M. Oliver and S. Sallent (Eds.): EUNICE 2009, LNCS 5733, pp. 128–137, 2009.
© Springer-Verlag Berlin Heidelberg 2009

that can be exploited by RRM algorithms. There are different sources of diversity in an OFDMA-based system, such as time, frequency and multi-user diversities. Thus, it is possible to dynamically allocate subsets of sub-carriers for different MTs, and to adapt the Modulation and Coding Scheme (MCS) and power for each sub-carrier according to the instantaneous channel conditions. Multi-carrier Packet Scheduling (PS) is an RRM strategy that assigns the sub-carriers to the users based on priority functions that can take into account channel- and user-related information, such as channel gains, QoS metrics, buffer occupancy, etc.

Some works in the literature tried to find an efficient trade-off between system capacity and fairness in OFDMA networks based on cross-layer optimization [1,2,3], utility theory [4] or both of them [5]. The only works that have used a well defined methodology for analyzing the fairness were [1] and [4], while the others made the evaluation implicitly comparing QoS metrics. The advantage of [1] compared to the others is that it used an intuitive and easy way to assess the fairness among the users by means of a fairness index. The present paper extends the work of [1], emphasizing and explicitly showing the influence of PS algorithms on the trade-off existent between spectral efficiency and fairness on OFDMA cellular systems considering scenarios with Non-Real Time (NRT) or Real Time (RT) services.

The paper is organized as follows. Section 2 presents the system modelling. In section 3, we show the PS algorithms studied in this contribution, while section 4 depicts the simulation results. Finally, the conclusions are drawn in section 5.

2   System Model

The considered scenario is a single cell with hexagonal shape. We consider a network with one transmitter (Base Station (BS)) and J receivers (MTs). The transmitted Orthogonal Frequency Division Multiplexing (OFDM) signal is time-slotted, where in every time slot at most one user can be served over each sub-carrier.

The considered environment is Typical Urban (TU) [10] where each user experiences independent transmit conditions. The channel has a frequency-selective Rayleigh fading, with the channel coherence time such that each sub-carrier experiences only flat fading. It is assumed that the channel fading rate is slow enough so that the frequency response does not change during a Transmission Time Interval (TTI). Each user also experiences shadowing with log-normal distribution. A perfect knowledge of the Channel State Information (CSI) at the transmitter side is assumed, with no signaling overhead transmitted. The signal strength at the receiver side depends on the path-loss calculated by: $L = 128.1 + 37.6 \log_{10} d$, where d is the distance to the BS in km. It was assumed that the MTs remained stationary, hence there is no need to implement any handover scheme.

Regarding the power allocation strategy, we assume that the total BS transmission power is equally divided among all sub-carriers. The bit allocation on each sub-carrier is determined using the modified Shannon's capacity model [5]:

$c_{j,k} = \log_2\left(1 + \Gamma p_k \rho_{j,k}\right)$, where $c_{j,k}$ is the achievable throughput of user j over sub-carrier k, p_k is the transmit power allocated at sub-carrier k, $\rho_{j,k}$ is the Signal-to-Noise Ratio (SNR) of user j at sub-carrier k, and Γ is the SNR gap given by $\frac{1.5}{-\ln 5BER}$ [5] (the target Bit Error Rate (BER) was 10^{-6}). Since we used discrete modulations QPSK, 16-QAM and 64-QAM, we made an appropriate integer quantization of $c_{j,k}$. Assuming that a sub-carrier set $\mathcal{K}_j$ is assigned to user j, its transmission rate is calculated as $r_j = \sum_k r_{j,k} = \sum_k c_{j,k} \cdot \Delta f$, where Δf is the sub-carrier bandwidth and $k \in \mathcal{K}_j$.

Regarding the traffic models, all NRT users are assumed to have an infinite amount of data to transmit during the whole simulation run (full-buffer model). As an example of RT service we considered Voice over IP (VoIP). This model follows an ON-OFF pattern, where each ON and OFF period duration are exponentially distributed. During the ON period, the transmitter generates one packet with fixed size of 32 bytes every voice frame. In the case of the 3rd. Generation Partnership Project (3GPP) Adaptive Multirate (AMR) voice codec, the frame duration is 20 ms. If any packet arrives at the receiver with a delay higher than 100 ms, it is discarded. In order to simulate a scenario with only VoIP users, we would need to consider a huge amount of users so that our high capacity OFDMA system becomes loaded, which would be unfeasible in terms of computational cost. In order to solve this problem we made two assumptions: i) consider 100% of voice activity, and ii) decrease the packet inter-arrival time to 2 ms. These two assumptions can be justified if we consider that each real VoIP user has an associate cluster of C virtual users that will be responsible to generate the traffic. These virtual users are ideally located in the same position of the real user and the difference in their propagation gains is assumed negligible.

3   Packet Scheduling Algorithms

In the following, the formulation of the PS techniques studied in this paper is presented. Sections 3.1 and 3.2 present the algorithms suitable for NRT and RT services, respectively.

3.1   Non Real-Time Services

In order to study the trade-off between system capacity and user fairness in a scenario with a NRT service, we evaluated the Max-Rate (MR), Max-Min Fairness (MMF) and Proportional Fairness (PF) PS algorithms, whose mathematical formulations are presented in equations 1, 2 and 3, respectively. The MT j^* is chosen to transmit on the kth sub-carrier in TTI n if it satisfies the condition given by the corresponding equation:

$$j^* = \arg\max_j \left\{ r_{j,k}\left[n\right] \right\}, \quad \forall j \tag{1}$$

$$j^* = \arg\max_j \left\{ \frac{1}{T_j\left[n-1\right]} \right\}, \quad \forall j \tag{2}$$

$$j^* = \arg\max_j \left\{ \frac{r_{j,k}[n]}{T_j[n-1]} \right\}, \quad \forall j \tag{3}$$

where $r_{j,k}[n]$ is the achievable data rate of the jth MT on the kth sub-carrier in TTI n and $T_j[n-1]$ is the average throughput of the jth MT calculated up to TTI $n-1$. The throughput of the jth MT is averaged using a Simple Exponential Smoothing (SES) filtering, as indicated in equation 4.

$$T_j[n] = (1 - \lambda) \cdot T_j[n-1] + \lambda \cdot r_j \tag{4}$$

where r_j is the instantaneous achievable data rate of the jth MT and λ is the filtering constant.

The MR scheduling policy was firstly presented in [6]. With this strategy, a specific sub-carrier is assigned to the MT with the best channel quality (i.e. the highest achievable bit-rate) on that sub-carrier. This scheduling policy provides the maximum cell throughput at the expense of lower throughput-based fairness, since the MTs in bad fading conditions would not be chosen for transmission.

The MMF PS gives priority to the MT that has experienced the worst throughput so far [7]. In this way, in terms of throughput, it is the most fair criterion possible, since all MTs will have approximately the same throughput in the long-term. This high fairness will be achieved at the expense of low spectrum efficiency, caused by the MTs with poor channel quality. One can notice that in equation 2, the achievable bit-rate on the sub-carriers is not present. Therefore, in each TTI, all the sub-carriers will be assigned to the chosen MT j^*, giving to MMF a Time Division Multiple Access (TDMA) behavior. This fact is enforced by considering that in the model assumed in this work the NRT user always has data to transmit.

Finally, the PF strategy takes into account both the instantaneous channel conditions and the average throughput of the MTs [8]. In this way, it is a trade-off between the spectral efficiency and throughput-based fairness achieved by MR and MMF.

3.2   Real Time Services

In order to investigate the trade-off in an OFDMA system with RT service, we chose to evaluate the PF, Delay-Based First In First Out (D-FIFO) and Modified Largest Weighted Delay First (M-LWDF) PS algorithms, whose priority policies are presented in equations 5, 6 and 7, respectively. The MT j^* is chosen to transmit on sub-carrier k at TTI n if it satisfies the condition given by the corresponding equation:

$$j^* = arg\max_j \left\{ \frac{r_{j,k}[n]}{T_j[n-1]} \right\}, \quad \forall j \tag{5}$$

$$j^* = arg\max_j \left\{ D_j^{hol}[n] \right\}, \quad \forall j \tag{6}$$

$$j^* = arg\max_j \left\{ \frac{r_{j,k}[n]}{T_j[n-1]} \cdot D_j^{hol}[n] \right\}, \quad \forall j \tag{7}$$

where $D_j^{hol}[n]$ is the delay experienced by the Head Of Line (HOL) packet of user j at TTI n, while $r_{j,k}[n]$ and $T_j[n-1]$ are defined and calculated as in section 3.1.

Among the three algorithms presented in this section, PF is expected to be the most unfair in terms of delay, and the most efficient in terms of resource usage, because it is not directly influenced by the delay metric and takes into account the channel quality. PF was chosen instead of MR because the former is expected to perform better than the latter for delay-sensitive RT services.

D-FIFO gives priority to the MT with the highest HOL packet delay. In this way, in terms of delay, it is the most fair criterion possible. Like the MMF criterion, D-FIFO also does not use CSI of the sub-carriers, ignoring the frequency diversity offered by the OFDMA system. Therefore, D-FIFO assumes a TDMA behavior, giving to the user chosen for transmission at TTI n the right to transmit over all the sub-carriers. This strategy is not efficient in the resource usage, so it is expected to provide lower system throughput.

The M-LWDF algorithm [9] is a trade-off between PF and D-FIFO, since it should provide intermediate delay-based fairness and intermediate resource usage efficiency.

4   Simulation Results

Similar to [1], the present work uses a well defined methodology to evaluate the fairness among the users based on the definition of the user and system fairness indexes. This paper extends the work in [1] proposing fairness indexes suitable for RT services. Our definition of fairness is based on QoS, so the fairness indexes for NRT and RT services are based on session throughput and delay, respectively.

To calculate the fairness of the system, we first have to define the fairness indexes related to the NRT and RT users, as presented in equation 8 below.

$$\phi_j^{NRT}[n] = \frac{T_j[n-1]}{T_j^{req}}; \qquad \phi_j^{RT}[n] = \frac{D_j[n]}{D_{req}} \tag{8}$$

where T_j^{req} is the throughput requirement of the jth NRT user and D_{req} is the maximum allowable delay for the RT service. $D_j[n]$ is calculated through a SES filtering as shown in equation 9 below.

$$D_j[n] = (1-\tau) \cdot D_j[n-1] + \tau \cdot \overline{D_j^{inst}}[n] \tag{9}$$

where $\overline{D_j^{inst}}$ is the instantaneous mean delay of the packets present in the buffer of user j at TTI n.

The fairness indexes $\phi_j^{NRT}[n]$ and $\phi_j^{RT}[n]$ are calculated at each TTI and for each user depending on his type of service. The overall fairness index related to the system is defined as:

$$\Phi^{NRT}[n] = \frac{\left(\sum_{j=1}^{J} \phi_j^{NRT}[n]\right)^2}{J \cdot \sum_{j=1}^{J} \left(\phi_j^{NRT}[n]\right)^2}; \qquad \Phi^{RT}[n] = \frac{\left(\sum_{j=1}^{J} \frac{1}{\phi_j^{RT}[n]}\right)^2}{J \cdot \sum_{j=1}^{J} \left(\frac{1}{\phi_j^{RT}[n]}\right)^2} \tag{10}$$

where J is the number of MTs in the cell, and $\phi_j^{NRT}[n]$ and $\phi_j^{RT}[n]$ are calculated in equation 8. Notice that $\frac{1}{J} \leq \Phi \leq 1$. A perfect fair allocation is achieved when $\Phi = 1$, which means that the throughput or delay experienced by the MTs are equally proportional to their throughput/delay requirements (all user fairness indexes are equal). The worst allocation occurs when $\Phi = \frac{1}{J}$, which means that all sub-carriers were allocated to only one MT. In this way, the overall fairness indexes $\Phi^{NRT}[n]$ and $\Phi^{RT}[n]$ are intuitive and easy ways to assess the fairness among the users in their respective service classes.

Table 1. Simulation parameters

Parameter	Value	Unit
Number of cells	1	-
BS transmission power	5	W
Cell radius (R)	500	m
Number of sub-carriers (K)	192	-
Sub-carrier bandwidth (Δf)	15	KHz
Transmission Time Interval	0.5	ms
Shadowing standard deviation	8	dB
Noise power per sub-carrier	-123.24	dBm
BER requirement	10^{-6}	-
Modulation schemes	QPSK, 16-QAM, 64-QAM[a]	-
Throughput requirement (T_j^{req})	1.4	$Mbps$
Delay Requirement (D_{req})	100	ms
Cluster load for RT model (C)	10	-
Throughput filtering constant (λ)	0.1	-
Delay filtering constant (τ)	0.1	-
Fairness factor filtering constant	0.1	-
Simulation time span	15	s
Number of realizations for each point	10	-

[a] Only QPSK and 16-QAM were used for the simulations with RT services.

The parameters used in the simulation campaign are depicted in table 1. We divide the presentation of the results in two parts: NRT and RT in sections 4.1 and 4.2, respectively. In order to evaluate the efficiency in the resource usage, we use the total cell throughput metric. The QoS-based fairness metric presented in the graphics is the mean system fairness index: the values of the fairness indexes $\Phi^{NRT}[n]$ and $\Phi^{RT}[n]$ were calculated using equation 10, filtered with an exponential filter and averaged over the whole simulation. In order to extend the fairness analysis, we equally separate the users in two groups of same size, inner and outer users, based on path loss and shadowing. The former are the ones closest to the BS (inner zone of the cell) that experience better channel conditions, while the latter are those that are far from the BS (outer zone of the cell).

4.1   Non Real-Time Services

In Fig. 1(a), the throughput-based mean system fairness index is shown. As expected, MMF is the most fair algorithm, while MR is the most unfair. PF showed an intermediate behavior, confirming to be a trade-off. The performance of PF was closer to MMF than to MR, with a fairness index around 0.9.

Fig. 1(b) depicts the total cell throughput, which is a measure of the system spectral efficiency. As expected, MR is the algorithm with the highest performance, while MMF is not able to exploit efficiently the available resources. Again, PF presented an intermediate performance. Looking at Figs. 1(a) and 1(b), one can clearly see the conflicting objectives of capacity and fairness maximization, and how MR and MMF are able to achieve one objective in detriment of the other. PF is an exception because it is able to find a trade-off.

The mean throughput of the users classified as inner (good) and outer (bad) users is shown in Fig. 1(c). This analysis is very important to give us an insight about the distribution of fairness in the system. It is interesting to focus on the

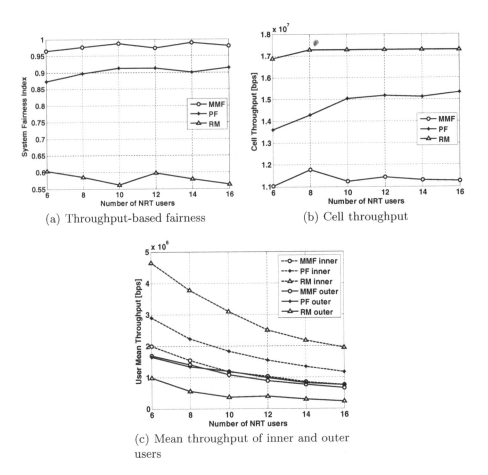

(a) Throughput-based fairness

(b) Cell throughput

(c) Mean throughput of inner and outer users

Fig. 1. Trade-off analysis for NRT services

difference between the inner and outer curves within the same algorithm in Fig. 1(c). For instance, if we consider MR, the difference between the throughput curves is the biggest. This means that MR assigns more priority to inner users than to outer users, producing a sensible decrease in fairness (see Fig. 1(a)). On the other extreme, MMF is the algorithm with the smallest difference between inner and outer curves, which proves that it is the most fair algorithm is terms of user throughput. Since PF is a trade-off, it presents an intermediate behavior.

4.2 Real Time Services

The delay-based mean system fairness index is shown in Fig. 2(a). D-FIFO is the algorithm with the highest fairness because it gives strict priority to the users with higher queuing delay. On the other hand, since PF does not take into account the delay, it presents the lowest values of the fairness index, which decreases monotonically when the number of users increases. M-LWDF takes into consideration in its scheduling policy both the channel quality and the delay, which provokes a varying behavior of the fairness in the considered range

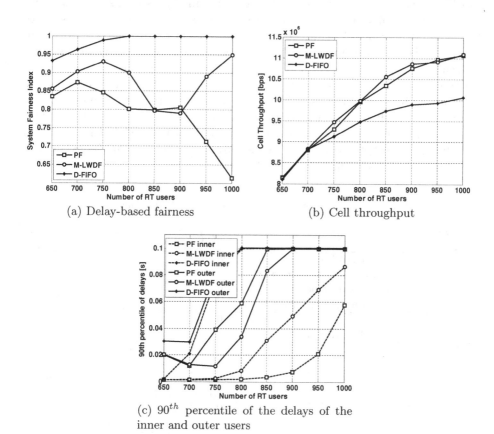

(a) Delay-based fairness

(b) Cell throughput

(c) 90th percentile of the delays of the inner and outer users

Fig. 2. Trade-off analysis for RT services

of loads. As expected, the values of the M-LWDF fairness index were inside the range of values of D-FIFO and PF.

In Fig. 2(b) the cell throughput is given. As expected, the best and worst performance were presented by PF and D-FIFO, respectively. This is explained by the fact that the former gives more importance to the channel quality, and so the resources are used more efficiently, while the latter only takes the delay information into account, which may lead to an inefficient resource allocation. A surprising result was obtained for M-LWDF, since it performs as good as PF, providing high cell throughput. Looking at Figs. 2(a) and 2(b), one can conclude that M-LWDF can achieve a good trade-off between resource efficiency and user fairness in a scenario with RT users.

Fig. 2(c) presents the 90th percentile of the packet delays of inner and outer users. Comparing Figs. 2(c) and 2(a), one can see that the difference in performance between the two groups using the same PS algorithm has an intrinsic relation with the fairness. In the case of PF, the difference between the curves is the greatest, which indicates that PF is giving considerably more priority to the inner users than it does for the outer ones, providing the lowest fairness. For D-FIFO the difference between the curves is the smallest, so the scheduler is giving almost the same priority to both groups, yielding the highest fairness. Since M-LWDF is a trade-off algorithm, it has an intermediate behavior. Although D-FIFO takes into account the delay, it is the one that presents the highest 90th percentile of the packet delays. This shows that the fact of not exploiting the OFDMA diversities is not beneficial in terms of QoS. Furthermore, when the system load increases, it causes the system to become stuck, i.e. the majority of the packets are discarded because they have a delay greater than 100 ms. This can be seen in Fig. 2(a), where the fairness index of D-FIFO is 1 for a system load higher than 800 users. This higher fairness is provided at the expense of very poor performance in terms of QoS.

Table 2. Relations between PS algorithms, spectral efficiency and fairness

	NRT services	**RT services**
RM	High spectral efficiency and low throughput-based fairness	-
MMF	Low spectral efficiency and high throughput-based fairness	-
PF	Trade-off between efficiency and fairness for NRT services	-
PF	-	High spectral efficiency and low delay-based fairness
D-FIFO	-	Low spectral efficiency and high delay-based fairness
M-LWDF	-	Trade-off between efficiency and fairness for RT services

5   Conclusions

In this work we have evaluated PS algorithms in an OFDMA-based system suitable for NRT or RT services, and investigated their influence on the trade-off between the efficient usage of the resources and the fairness among the users. Analyzing the simulation results we can draw a didactic map of the relations between the two objectives mentioned above, which can be seen in table 2.

We can conclude that there are PS algorithms that are able to find this trade-off, such as PF and M-LWDF for the cases of NRT and RT services, respectively. However, these algorithms are only able to provide a static trade-off. It would be interesting to propose PS algorithms able to provide a dynamic and controllable trade-off according to the cellular operator's objectives. This is currently being developed as the next step of this investigation.

Acknowledgments. The authors wish to acknowledge the activity of the Network of Excellence in Wireless COMmunications NEWCOM++ of the European Commission (contract n. 216715) that motivated this work. Emanuel B. Rodrigues has a Ph.D. scholarship support by the Improvement Co-ordination of Superior Level People (CAPES) - Brazil.

References

1. Rodrigues, E.B., Casadevall, F.: Adaptive Radio Resource Allocation Framework for Multi-User OFDM. In: IEEE 69th Vehicular Technology Conference - VTC Spring, Barcelona, Spain (2009)
2. Hou, H., Zhou, W., Zhou, S., Zhu, J.: Cross-Layer Resource Allocation for Heterogeneous Traffics in Multiuser OFDM Based on a New QoS Fairness Criterion. In: IEEE 66th Vehicular Technology Conference - VTC Fall, pp. 1593–1597 (2007)
3. Shuang, W., Youjun, G., Xuelin, G., Hui, T., Ping, Z.: Packet Scheduling for Multimedia Traffics in Downlink Multi-User OFDM Systems. In: International Conference on Wireless Communications, Networking and Mobile Computing - WiCOM, pp. 1–4 (2006)
4. Lei, H., Zhang, L., Zhang, X., Yang, D.: A Packet Scheduling Algorithm Using Utility Function for Mixed Services in the Downlink of OFDMA Systems. In: IEEE 66th Vehicular Technology Conference - VTC Fall, pp. 1664–1668 (2007)
5. Song, G., Li, Y.G.: Cross-Layer Optimization for OFDM Wireless Networks - Part I: Theoretical Framework and Part II: Algorithm Development. IEEE Transactions on Wireless Communications 4(2), 614–634 (2005)
6. Jang, J., Lee, K.B.: Transmit Power Adaptation for Multiuser OFDM Systems. IEEE Journal on Selected Areas in Communications 21(2), 171–178 (2003)
7. Ameigeiras, P.J.G.: Packet Scheduling and Quality of Service in HSDPA, Ph.D. dissertation, Aalborg University, Aalborg, Denmark (2003)
8. Kelly, F.: Charging and Rate Control for Elastic Traffic. European Transactions on Communications 8, 33–37 (1997)
9. Andrews, M., Kumaran, K., Ramanan, K., Stolyar, A., Whiting, P., Vijayakumar, R.: Providing Quality of Service over a Shared Wireless Link. IEEE Communications Magazine 39(2), 150–154 (2001)
10. 3GPP.: Deployment Aspects, TR. 25.943 v8.0.0 (2008)

RSSI-Based Forwarding for Multihop Wireless Sensor Networks

Azlan Awang, Xavier Lagrange, and David Ros

Institut TELECOM / TELECOM Bretagne,
Networks, Security and Multimedia dept.
2 rue de la Châtaigneraie, CS 17607,
35576 Cesson Sévigné Cedex
Université européenne de Bretagne, France
{azlan.awang,xavier.lagrange,david.ros}@telecom-bretagne.eu
http://www.telecom-bretagne.eu

Abstract. In a multihop Wireless Sensor Network (WSN), a salient point among routing protocols that do not depend on network topology and existence of neighboring nodes is the need to know sensor node's geographical location with respect to the sink node. This is obtained by some means like Global Positioning System (GPS) and localization techniques. In a prior work, we have proposed RSSI-based Forwarding (RBF) protocol that works without knowledge of node's location by using a Received Signal Strength Indicator (RSSI) level of beacon signals transmitted by the sink. Through contention, a next-hop node is determined among the forwarding candidates using a timer-based suppression scheme. We propose an improvement of the suppression scheme in which a contender closer to the sink is favored with a higher probability for being selected as a next-hop node. By means of simulation, it is shown that the performance of RBF is significantly improved using the enhanced mechanism.

Keywords: Cross-Layer Protocol; Medium Access Control; Routing; Wireless Sensor Networks.

1   Introduction

Wireless Sensor Networks (WSNs) are widely recognized as powerful means for in situ observations of events and environments over long periods of time [1]. A sensor network consists of a large number of small sensor nodes with sensing, data processing, and communication capabilities which are densely deployed in a region of interest. Each node monitors its surrounding area and gathers application specific parameters (e.g., temperature, pressure, humidity, light, and chemical activity). The sensor nodes periodically sense data, process it and organize among themselves to form a communication network. They then collaborate to deliver the observations to a monitoring node, the sink node. The sensor nodes are typically powered with non-rechargeable batteries. Due to their limited transmission power, not all nodes can communicate directly with the sink

M. Oliver and S. Sallent (Eds.): EUNICE 2009, LNCS 5733, pp. 138–147, 2009.
© Springer-Verlag Berlin Heidelberg 2009

node. Moreover, such communication would be over long distances that will drain power quickly. Multihop communication is then needed. The network must maintain the best connectivity as long as possible and it must be self-configured and self-organized in case of node failure. The possibility of node failure, wireless link failure and nodes transitioning into and out of sleep states to conserve energy introduce additional complexity to routing protocols that depend on up-to-date routing or neighborhood tables. This makes the routing state upkeep difficult. A routing solution that can deliver end-to-end traffic to a sink node without knowledge of network topology and the presence or absence of any other node is necessary, such a solution is defined as *state-free* in [2]. It offers advantages in which a sender does not need to determine a forwarding node in advance or to find a path before the actual data transmission.

Several state-free routing protocols proposed in the literature [2,3,7,8,9] assume knowledge of nodes' geographical locations for routing the sensed data toward the sink node. With the WSN's characteristics that require a large number of low-cost and energy-efficient sensor nodes, equipping a GPS on every sensor node may not be practical. Furthermore, the cost of a GPS chip is much more expensive than the sensor node itself [14]. Many location discovery protocols thus suggested to reduce or completely remove the dependence on GPS in WSNs [6,10,11,12,13].

In [5], we proposed the RBF protocol where routing and access are jointly managed, based on RSSI. In the preliminary work, RBF was tested on a topology with uniform deployment of sensor nodes. A simple propagation model was used where the path loss of a sensor node with respect to the sink was assumed as an increasing function of the distance. When nodes participate in the contention process, a suppression scheme to reduce the chance of selecting more than one node was made based on a uniform random choice of time slots within a contention window size. In this paper, we present an extension of such work by proposing an enhanced mechanism to select a next-hop node for the data forwarding task, taking into account the random effects of shadowing and testing of RBF in a random topology of sensor nodes.

The remainder of this paper is organized as follows. In section 2, we give a detailed description of the protocol. Section 3 presents some simulation results and provides an analysis of the data collected. Finally, in section 4, we conclude this paper with a summary of our findings and future work.

2 Protocol Description

2.1 Background and Assumptions

The RBF protocol is described in [5]. For the sake of clarity, we hereby remind the reader of the main features of RBF. We consider a wireless data collection network model with a large number of sensor nodes and one sink node. Each of the sensor nodes in the network is assumed to have a limited transmission power, and consequently limited transmission range. The data packets will then be relayed toward the sink using multihop communication.

We assume the sink regularly transmits a beacon packet and the transmission power of the sink is high enough to reach all nodes in the network. Furthermore, the beacon packet includes the power level used for transmitting it. For an arriving beacon packet, each node measures the received power level of the beacon signal. To cope with radio strength instability, measurements may be made on several beacon packets. Each node then estimates an RSSI level that is an average over several samples. Node's mobility does not prevent the protocol from being functioning properly since new measurements of RSSI can always be refreshed based on regularly received beacon packets. By dividing the transmitted power of the beacon packet over the RSSI level, each node i then knows the path loss L_i between itself and the sink node.

2.2   RBF Protocol Operation

RBF protocol uses the four-way Request To Send (RTS)–Clear To Send (CTS)–DATA–Acknowledgment (ACK) handshake as proposed in some schemes like XLM[4], IGF[2] and SIF[8]. Figure 1 shows the packet exchange sequence. The transmission starts with an RTS packet, which is broadcast. Nodes that receive an RTS packet check whether or not they are candidates to forward the data (see below). A CTS packet is then transmitted through a contention process. The node that wins the access is the forwarder. Finally, a normal DATA and ACK packet exchange follows between the two specific nodes. The process is repeated over multihop communications until the data is delivered to the sink.

We define a source node i as the one that originates a data packet and a node j which is within node i transmission range as a neighbor node. When node i has some data packet to transmit, it broadcasts an RTS packet to all its neighbor nodes. The RTS packet carries the path loss value of the sender (i.e. of i). Neighbor nodes that receive the RTS packet read the value and calculate the path loss ratio defined as their path loss divided by the path loss of i. If the

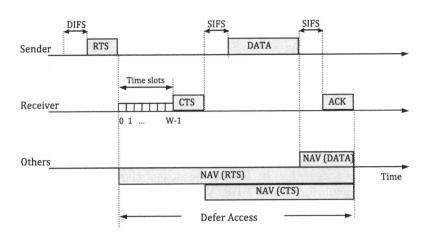

Fig. 1. Packet exchange sequence

path loss ratio of the neighbor nodes to the source node is less than one, they participate in the contention process: a window of W time slots is opened at the end of the RTS. Every candidate node randomly chooses a time slot. A node that chooses the lowest time slot wins the access. This node then responds with a CTS packet, establishing itself as the only next-hop node. Other nodes stop contending when they hear the CTS packet and adjust their network allocation vector (NAV), which indicate the amount of time that must elapse until the current transmission session is complete. Several nodes may decide to transmit a CTS packet at the same time. If there is a CTS packet collision, an RTS packet retransmission is performed.

2.3   CTS Response Time

In [5], we implemented a random backoff procedure for a node to respond with a CTS packet. A time slot is randomly chosen from a uniform distribution of time slots within a contention window size, W. Every forwarding node, therefore, has an equal probability of $\frac{1}{W}$ to select a time slot k where $k \in [0, W-1]$. This promotes fairness among the forwarding nodes but may not be optimum since any neighbor node that has a path loss ratio less than one could send a CTS packet. We refer here the amount of time elapsed before replying to an RTS packet as CTS Response Time (CRT). For our discussion to follow, we refer to the random time slot selection scheme from a uniform distribution of time slots as *Uniform CRT* and an enhanced mechanism of CRT that we are currently proposing as *Enhanced CRT*.

The basic idea of Enhanced CRT is to make sensor nodes which are closer to the sink to take the forwarding responsibility with a higher probability. We propose the routing mechanism in RBF protocol as a function of path loss that gives an indication of whether a node is closer to the sink. However, due to the random effects of shadowing, this can not be assumed. For the same transmitter and receiver separation, different levels of clutter on the propagation path can be observed. A more distant node may then have a smaller path loss than a nearby one. Nevertheless, that gives a benefit to RBF protocol since data packet is always relayed toward the sink through a series of links with lesser path loss than the sending node. Since our metric of distance is based on path loss, this helps in the routing process to search for a higher quality link with lesser path loss to route the data packet toward the sink.

Let L_i and L_j be the path loss value between the sink and source node i, and node j, respectively. When node j receives an RTS packet, L_i is read from the packet. Knowing both L_j and L_i, the path loss ratio $\frac{L_j}{L_i}$ is then used as a decision parameter for a node to participate in the contention process. We propose to choose a time slot k where $k \in [0, W-1]$ with a probability qp^k and with

$$p = b + \frac{1-b^2}{b}\left(\frac{L_j}{L_i}\right)^\alpha, \quad \text{and} \tag{1}$$

$$q = \frac{1-p}{1-p^W}. \tag{2}$$

Parameters $\alpha \in (0, 1]$ and $b \in (0, 1)$ in (1) are constants that are tunable to make a node closer to the sink to have a higher probability to send a CTS packet. It can easily be verified that $\sum_{k=0}^{W-1} qp^k = 1$.

The impact of the path loss ratio $\frac{L_j}{L_i}$, α and b parameters in (1) on the probability qp^k is described as follows. If a neighbor node j is closer to the sink with respect to the source node i, the path loss ratio $\frac{L_j}{L_i}$ will be close to zero. In this case, p is approximately equal to b and q is approximately equal to $1 - p$. The probabilities are higher near the time slot zero (see below), and therefore, we favor a forwarding node closer to the sink to respond first with a CTS packet. Other neighbor nodes with a higher path loss ratio tend to have a higher probability of choosing the last time slot of the contention window. Therefore, we can control and limit the probability of choosing the first and the last time slot.

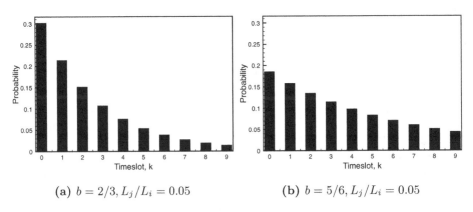

(a) $b = 2/3, L_j/L_i = 0.05$ (b) $b = 5/6, L_j/L_i = 0.05$

Fig. 2. Probability distribution when node j is closer to the sink than node i among the forwarding nodes ($L_j/L_i = 0.05$). In (b), an increase in b, decreases the probability of time slot zero but increases the probability on the last time slot.

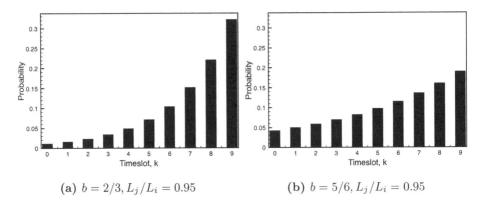

(a) $b = 2/3, L_j/L_i = 0.95$ (b) $b = 5/6, L_j/L_i = 0.95$

Fig. 3. Probability distribution when node j is closer to node i among the forwarding nodes ($L_j/L_i = 0.95$). In (b), an increase in b, increases the probability of time slot zero but decreases the probability on the last time slot.

By tuning appropriate values of α and b in (1), we could favor a node j closer to the sink to have a higher probability to respond with a CTS packet to node i. Varying the b parameter affects the CRT of a forwarding node. When b is increased, this disperses the probabilities of the time slots. For example, when $\alpha = 1$ and $b = 2/3$, the probability distribution of time slot selection from a contention window size, $W = 10$ is shown in Fig. 2a when node j is closer to the sink than node i, e.g., its path loss ratio $\frac{L_j}{L_i} = 0.05$. With the same value of α, an increase in b decreases the probability of time slot zero but increases the probability on the last time slot. This is shown in Fig. 2b for $b = 5/6$. However, when the path loss ratio is close to one, e.g., $\frac{L_j}{L_i} = 0.95$, an increase in b increases the probability of time slot zero but decreases the probability on the last time slot. The probability distributions for the path loss ratio $\frac{L_j}{L_i} = 0.95$ are shown in Fig. 3a and Fig. 3b, for $b = 2/3$ and $b = 5/6$, respectively. Optimizing the values of α and b is left for a future study.

3   Performance and Simulation Results

3.1   Simulation Model

To assess the performance of the RBF protocol, a simulation scenario was designed using OPNET® Modeler [15]. A total of 112 sensor nodes are randomly deployed in an area of radius 105 m. The sink is located in the center of the area. Table 1 shows some parameters used in the simulation. We assume the path loss of the signal varies according to the lognormal propagation model as in [16]. Equation (3) gives the path loss L at a distance d from the transmitter node where L_0 is the path loss at a reference distance d_0, γ is the path loss exponent, and X_σ is a zero-mean Gaussian distributed random variable with a standard deviation σ.

$$L = L_0 + 10\gamma \log\left(\frac{d}{d_0}\right) + X_\sigma \ . \tag{3}$$

3.2   Simulation Results and Discussion

We present simulation results where a number of sensor nodes that are most distant from the sink node generate data packets toward the sink in the center of the area. For such many-to-one communication, we evaluate the impact on the performance of RBF by varying the transmit power levels of the sensor nodes. Both simulation scenarios of *Uniform CRT* and *Enhanced CRT* mechanisms use five different transmit power levels: 3 mW (4.8 dBm), 4 mW (6 dBm), 5 mW (7 dBm), 6 mW (7.8 dBm) and 7 mW (8.5 dBm). For each transmit power level, the simulation was performed for 50 runs with 50 different random seeds.

Figure 4a shows the average number of hops for data delivery toward the sink for both Uniform CRT and Enhanced CRT mechanisms. Enhanced CRT improves the performance of RBF by favoring nodes closer to the sink to have

Table 1. Simulation Parameters

Parameter	Value
Data rate	250 kbits/s
Slot time	20 μs
SIFS time	10 μs
Sensor node transmit power	3 to 7 mW
Sink transmit power (Beacon packet)	1 W (30 dBm)
Standard deviation of shadowing, σ	5 dB
Data packet size	32 Bytes
Packet interarrival time for each node	Exponential (60 s)
Contention window size, W	64
α	1
b	0.833
Simulation time	300 s

a higher probability to send a CTS packet. This leads to a reduction of 22 to 27 percent in the average number of hops of the Uniform CRT for the same node transmit power level. As a result, the end-to-end (ETE) delay decreases. The ETE delay refers to the amount of time elapsed when a source node generates data packet and until it is delivered to the sink. Figure 4b shows the distribution of hops for data delivery toward the sink for sensor node transmit power of 4 mW. More hops are traversed by data packets using Uniform CRT since any forwarding contender with path loss ratio less than one may send a CTS packet with equal probability regardless of how far it is from the sink. With Uniform CRT, about 60 percent of data packets are routed through 6 to 10 hops to reach the sink and 40 percent are routed through 3 to 5 hops. On the other hand, with Enhanced CRT, about 89 percent of data packets are routed through 3 to 5 hops and 11 percent are routed through 6 to 7 hops. Consequently, the ETE delay is lower for the Enhanced CRT and higher for the Uniform CRT as depicted in Fig. 5a.

The ETE delay consists of propagation, transmission, processing and queuing delays. Propagation delay contributes a very small portion to the ETE delay, i.e., for a distance of 300 m, the delay is only 1 μs. Transmission and processing delay is the time spent to emit bits onto the medium, receive, decode, and retransmit packet between source and destination. Queuing delay is the time spent by a packet waiting in a queue for transmission when the channel is busy, and depends on the congestion level of the wireless channel.

A variation of transmit power level affects the contention region at the MAC layer, in which it affects set of candidate nodes for next hop selection. A higher power level results in more nodes' participation in the contention process for sending a CTS packet. At the same time, an increase in transmit power increases the transmission range of nodes which then reduces the average number of hops each route needed in the network. Thus the total transmission delay along each route decreases. A lower power level results in shorter links, which means that

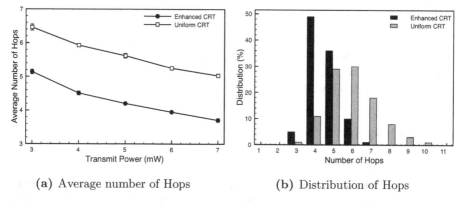

(a) Average number of Hops   (b) Distribution of Hops

Fig. 4. Number of hops for data delivery toward the sink node. (a) average number of hops versus transmit power, and (b) distribution of hops for sensor node transmit power of 4 mW.

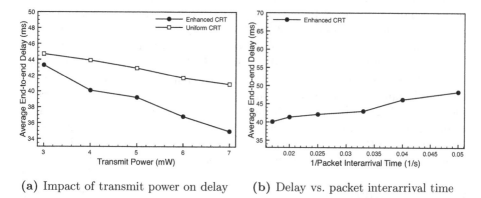

(a) Impact of transmit power on delay   (b) Delay vs. packet interarrival time

Fig. 5. Average end-to-end delay for data delivery toward the sink node. (a) for node's packet interarrival time of 60 s with different transmit powers, and (b) for sensor node transmit power of 4 mW with different node's packet interarrival times.

more hops are required per route. This results in higher ETE delay and also puts more relaying burden on the nodes in the network. In this work, a lightly loaded network is considered, thus the queuing delay is small since number of nodes contending for channel access at the same time is small. In this case, transmission and processing delay is the dominant part of the ETE delay. For such loads, the packet delivery ratio is not degraded in the proposed Enhanced CRT mechanism. Uniform CRT promotes fairness among the forwarding nodes which means that all forwarding candidates have equal probability to respond with a CTS packet but results in higher ETE delay. On the other hand, Enhanced CRT favors nodes closer to the sink which results in lower ETE delay but perhaps it may put more relaying burden on some nodes in the network. How both mechanisms affect the overall nodes' relaying burden, energy consumptions and congestion level in the network deserves further investigation in a future study.

For a transmit power of 4 mW, ETE delay with variation of nodes' packet interarrival times (60, 50, 40, 30, 25, and 20 s) is also evaluated for Enhanced CRT as depicted in Fig. 5b. With more data packets being generated by the sensor nodes, ETE delay increases.

4   Conclusion

In this paper, we have proposed an enhanced mechanism for a next hop node selection in the RBF protocol. A key component of the RBF protocol is node's path loss ratio which is used for the joint access/routing decision in the network. We have introduced probability functions in which forwarding candidates closer to the sink are favored with higher probability to take the responsibility for the data forwarding task. By varying node transmit power levels, its impact on the performance of the RBF is analyzed for both Enhanced CRT and Uniform CRT mechanisms. The RBF has been tested on a random topology of sensor nodes and with random effects of shadowing. Enhanced CRT has been shown to have an improved performance with lower average of hop counts and end-to-end delay for data delivery toward the sink. As for the future work, we would like to explore the open issues highlighted in the paper and consider energy efficiency technique such that nodes' remaining energy levels are taken into account when forwarding candidates participate in the contention process, thus balancing energy consumptions in the network. A rigorous analysis of advantages and disadvantages of the power control in the cross-layer contention-based design of the multihop WSNs could be an interesting problem to explore too.

Acknowledgments. The work of A. Awang was partially supported by Universiti Teknologi PETRONAS, Malaysia.

References

1. Akyildiz, I.F., Su, W., Sankarasubramaniam, Y., Cayirci, E.: Wireless Sensor Networks: a survey. J. Computer Networks 38(4), 393–422 (2002)
2. Blum, B.M., He, T., Son, S., Stankovic, J.A.: IGF: A State-Free Robust Communication Protocol for Wireless Sensor Networks. In: Technical Report CS-2003-11, CS Department, University of Virginia (2003)
3. Füβler, H., Widmer, J., Käsemann, M., Mauve, M., Hartenstein, H.: Contention-based forwarding for mobile ad hoc networks. J. Ad Hoc Networks 1(4) (2003)
4. Akyildiz, I.F., Vuran, M.C., Akan, O.B.: A Cross-Layer Protocol for Wireless Sensor Networks. In: Proc. Conference on Information Science and Systems (CISS 2006), Princeton, NJ, March 22-24 (2006)
5. Awang, A., Lagrange, X., Ros, D.: A Cross-Layer Medium Access Control and Routing Protocol for Wireless Sensor Networks. In: Proc. 10èmes Journées Doctorales en Informatique et Réseaux (JDIR 2009), February 2-4 (2009)

6. Liu, D., Ning, P., Du, W.: Detecting Malicious Beacon Nodes for Secure Location Discovery in Wireless Sensor Networks. In: Proc. IEEE ICDCS (2005)
7. Chen, D., Deng, J., Varshney, P.K.: On the Forwarding Area of Contention-Based Geographic Forwarding for Ad Hoc and Sensor Networks. In: Proc. IEEE SECON (2005)
8. Chen, D., Deng, J., Varshney, P.K.: A State-Free Data Delivery Protocol for Multihop Wireless Sensor Networks. In: Proc. IEEE WCNC (2005)
9. Zorzi, M., Rao, R.R.: Geographic Random Forwarding (GeRaF) for Ad Hoc and Sensor Networks: Multihop Performance. J. IEEE Trans. on Mobile Computing 2(4) (October-December 2003)
10. Bulusu, N., Heidemann, J., Estrin, D.: GPS-less Low-Cost Outdoor Localization for Very Small Devices. In: IEEE Personal Commun. Mag., pp. 28–34 (2000)
11. He, T., Huang, C., Blum, B.M., Stankovic, J.A., Abdelzaher, T.: Range-Free Localization Schemes for Large Scale Sensor Networks. In: Proc. ACM MOBICOM (2003)
12. Nasipuri, A., Li, K.: A Directionality based Location Discovery Scheme for Wireless Sensor Networks. In: Proc. ACM WSNA (2002)
13. Savvides, A., Han, C., Strivastava, M.B.: Dynamic Fine-Grained Localization in Ad-Hoc Networks of Sensors. In: Proc. ACM MOBICOM (2001)
14. Heo, J.H., Kim, J.-H., Hong, C.S.: A logical group formation and management mechanism using RSSI for wireless sensor networks. In: May, Y., Choi, D., Ata, S. (eds.) APNOMS 2008. LNCS, vol. 5297, pp. 207–216. Springer, Heidelberg (2008)
15. OPNET Technologies, Inc., http://www.opnet.com/
16. Rappaport, T.S.: Wireless Communications: Principles and Practice. Prentice Hall, New Jersey (2001)

A Pipelined IP Address Lookup Module for 100 Gbps Line Rates and beyond

Domenic Teuchert and Simon Hauger

Institute of Communication Networks and Computer Engineering (IKR)
Universität Stuttgart, Pfaffenwaldring 47
70569 Stuttgart, Germany
{dteuch,hauger}@ikr.uni-stuttgart.de

Abstract. New Internet services and technologies call for higher packet switching capacities in the core network. Thus, a performance bottleneck arises at the backbone routers, as forwarding of Internet Protocol (IP) packets requires to search the most specific entry in a forwarding table that contains up to several hundred thousand address prefixes. The Tree Bitmap algorithm provides a well-balanced solution in respect of storage needs as well as of search and update complexity. In this paper, we present a pipelined lookup module based on this algorithm, which allows for an easy adaption to diverse protocol and hardware constraints. We determined the pipelining degree required to achieve the throughput for a 100 Gbps router line card by analyzing a representative sub-unit for various configured sizes. The module supports IPv4 and IPv6 configurations providing this throughput, as we determined the performance of our design to achieve a processing rate of 178 million packets per second.

1 Introduction

The ongoing increase of the Internet traffic necessitates to upgrade the capacity of the backbone network continuously. As a consequence, 100 Gbps Ethernet will be deployed in 2010 [1] requiring core routers to perform 150 million IP address lookups per second and ingress port. For each lookup operation, the router's forwarding engine (FWE) has to determine the most suitable next-hop router by using the packet's destination IP address as a key for searching a forwarding table. This table lookup is a complex task in software as well as hardware, since it requires to find the longest matching prefix (LMP) as the most specific entry. Moreover, the forwarding table holds several hundred thousand entries and grows even further [2]. The requirements of good scalability regarding 128-bit long IPv6 addresses and of efficient table update processing lead to additional difficulties.

Facing these requirements, today's high-speed routers typically use specialized hardware to implement the FWE. Ternary Content Addressable Memories (TCAMs) can perform one table lookup per clock cycle. However, TCAMs scale unfavorably with table and key sizes, and they consume significantly more power than standard memory. Therefore, algorithmic lookup methods [3,4,5,6,7] are increasingly implemented in specialized hardware modules. Among these methods,

M. Oliver and S. Sallent (Eds.): EUNICE 2009, LNCS 5733, pp. 148–157, 2009.
© Springer-Verlag Berlin Heidelberg 2009

the Tree Bitmap algorithm [5] implemented in Cisco's CRS-1 core routers [8] offers a very smart and balanced trade-off between memory usage, lookup performance, and update complexity.

In this paper, we present the design and prototypical implementation of a flexible and fully pipelined hardware lookup module based on the Tree Bitmap algorithm. In order to investigate whether and with what effort algorithmic IP lookup modules can be realized in hardware for future line speeds of 100 Gbps and beyond, we clearly focused on maximum throughput and resource efficiency, as opposed to other published Tree Bitmap implementations [5,9]. By processing all packets in a pipeline, our design effectively performs one IP address lookup in each clock cycle. Additionally, it supports high-speed, non-blocking updates of the forwarding table. By adjusting several configuration parameters, one can also adapt the module to various requirements concerning performance, resource utilization, and memory parameters.

We tested the module's functionality on a hardware platform based on a Field Programmable Gate Array (FPGA). Due to the module's deterministic behavior, we can show that the processing logic of our design can be utilized for 100 Gbps line speeds using current FPGA devices. Additionally, we studied how many pipeline registers are needed per functional block of our lookup module, in order to achieve a desired throughput with different configurations.

In the following section, we describe a typical high-speed router architecture and give a short review of the IP address lookup problem as well as different solutions with a focus on the implemented Tree Bitmap algorithm. In Sect. 3, we detail on our hardware realization. Finally, we discuss the achieved simulation and synthesis results in Sect. 4, before we conclude this paper.

2   IP Routing

IP Routing and its underlying specifications determine the constraints for a qualified architecture and IP lookup method of a high-speed FWE. In this section, we introduce the primary factors that have directly affected our hardware design.

2.1   High-Speed Router Architecture

Routers generally perform two basic functions: (a) Exchanging topology information with other routers in order to build a routing table and (b) forwarding packets from ingress to egress ports based on this table. The former function is run on the control plane, whose timing requirements allow its implementation as part of a software-controlled processing entity, commonly termed the router's slow path. The latter function belongs to the data plane, which has to fulfill strict speed constraints. Thus, packet forwarding, as part of the router's fast path, is implemented using specialized hardware on core routers.

Typically, a decentralized architecture as shown in Fig. 1 is used to achieve high scalability in terms of the number of interfaces. Several line cards are connected to a switch fabric, each accommodating one or more physical interfaces

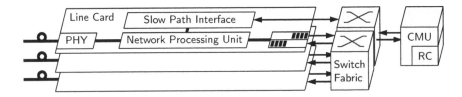

Fig. 1. Architecture of a typical core router

(PHY), packet buffers, a slow path interface, and a network processing unit (NPU). The slow path interface hands routing protocol messages over to the route controller (RC) within the control and management unit (CMU) and downloads the updated forwarding table entries from there. The NPU performs the fast path functions including packet classification, table lookup, and the associated packet modifications. The IP lookup module we present in this paper is intended to be part of such an NPU and leverages the common approach to increase the throughput by pipelining the processing tasks within the NPU.

2.2   IP Address Lookup

IP addresses consist of a prefix identifying a particular network and a host part indicating the destination within the respective network. To mitigate the increasing address shortage, Classless Inter-Domain Routing (CIDR) has been introduced, which allows prefixes to take any number of IP address bits in order to flexibly aggregate contiguous prefixes to a single entry in the forwarding table. As IP addresses are not strictly hierarchically distributed, the resulting address space fragmentation leads to exception entries—also denoted as more specifics—which account for 40–60% of the total forwarding table size in the Internet backbone [2]. It is thus necessary to find the longest matching prefix (LMP) for a precise forwarding decision. The large sizes of backbone forwarding tables in combination with CIDR make the LMP search a complex task that, moreover, has to be performed at a high frequency in core routers. Therefore, specialized hardware implementations are the method of choice.

Generally, two solutions exist: (a) TCAMs that accomplish a parallel LMP search effectively in only one clock cycle and (b) numerous algorithmic lookup methods. Although TCAMs are often applied in commercial routers, [10] shows that algorithmic solutions based on multibit tries allow to store larger tables on a given chip size. Furthermore, TCAMs have a high power dissipation per memory bit, which finally makes algorithmic lookup methods the best candidate to meet the future demand on fast IP address lookups.

Apart from hash-based methods, most algorithmic solutions are based on a binary search tree, which is referred to as *trie* in this context. Using a trie, the search space is significantly reduced in each step, but storing the trie structure causes a certain memory overhead. To address this issue, some solutions [7,3,5] propose to use a compression method to pack several trie nodes in one compacted multibit node that can be processed in a single search step. The LC-trie [7] and the Lulea algorithm [3] achieve a very good scalability of memory demand against table size but do not support incremental table updates. The Tree Bitmap algorithm, which we have implemented, uses a different compression scheme that results in short and deterministic update times while preserving the properties of fast prefix search and memory efficient table storage.

2.3   Tree Bitmap Algorithm

Like other trie-based methods, the Tree Bitmap algorithm utilizes multibit nodes that each cover, as illustrated in Fig. 2(a), a subset of the search trie according to the defined stride size t. During a lookup operation, the trie is hence traversed multibit node by multibit node. For each visited multibit node, a t-bit fragment of the destination IP address is used to check whether a more specific prefix (filled gray circle) than the currently known exists in this node, and whether a respective child node exists to continue the lookup. If no suitable child node exists, the last found prefix is the LMP.

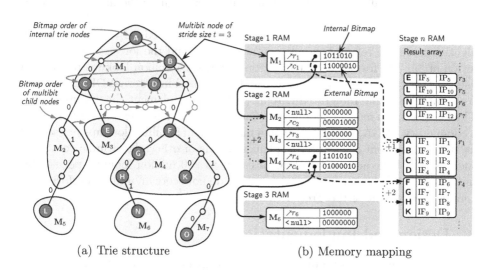

(a) Trie structure   (b) Memory mapping

Fig. 2. IP lookup table in Tree Bitmap representation

For the given example of stride size $t = 3$ in Fig. 2 and the IP address 195.·.·.· $(= 11000011_2 \ldots)$, the most specific existing prefix in the first multibit node is **B** (1*), and the suitable child node is $\mathbf{M_4}$ (going right (1), right (1), left (0)) through root node $\mathbf{M_1}$). Within multibit node $\mathbf{M_4}$, the most specific existing prefix is now **H** (= 11000*). As no further suitable child node exists (when going left (0), left (0), left (0) through $\mathbf{M_4}$), **H** is the LMP.

To store the trie structure efficiently, the Tree Bitmap algorithm uses two bitmaps and two pointers for each multibit node. The Internal Bitmap (cf. Fig. 2(b)) represents all $2^t - 1$ possible prefixes associated with the internal trie nodes of the multibit node. A set bit corresponds to an existing prefix in the forwarding table. The address of the actual next-hop entry, which is saved in a dedicated memory, is the sum of the result pointer r and an offset. This offset can be easily determined by counting the number of set bits left of the bit position that corresponds to the found prefix. In our example, **B** is the most specific existing prefix in $\mathbf{M}_1$, which is associated with the third bit from left in the Internal Bitmap. As there is only one set bit in the lower-order positions, the offset is 1. The External Bitmap similarly represents all 2^t possible child nodes. Again, a set bit corresponds to an existing child node, and an offset is computed by the number of set lower-order bits.

Beyond this basic algorithm, [5] proposed several optimizations which predominantly aim for smaller memory word widths and a higher memory utilization: One option is the use of an *Initial Array* to process some of the multibit trie's relatively small top levels in a single memory access. Besides this optimization, we also implemented *End Node* handling, which eliminates a large number of almost empty nodes by using an otherwise unused External Bitmap as an extension of the Internal Bitmap. The third optimization that has been adopted in our design is called *Split Tree Bitmap* and nearly halves the memory demand of the multibit nodes.

Previously published hardware implementations based on the Tree Bitmap algorithm are the reference implementation of [5] and the low-cost oriented solution of [9]. The former implementation achieves 25 million lookups per second using a four times replicated forwarding table stored in external DRAM and an Application-Specific Integrated Circuit (ASIC) to implement the required logic. The latter takes a more economic approach utilizing a single external SRAM and a commodity FPGA, which results in a maximum of 9 million lookups per second at 100 MHz system clock rate. Implementations of other algorithmic solutions, such as [11], have achieved lookup rates up to 250 million lookups per second but either have a higher memory demand or do not score an update performance comparable to that of the Tree Bitmap algorithm.

3   Design and Implementation

In view of the future core router requirements, we designed an IP address lookup module implementing the Tree Bitmap (TBMP) algorithm to check the suitability of trie-based lookup solutions for 100 Gbps line rates. In the following, we identify our design objectives and present details of the module structure.

3.1   Design Objectives

The key objective of our design is the capability to perform lookups with a throughput sufficient for a 100 Gbps Ethernet line card. This shall be achieved by a pipeline design that allows to process effectively one datagram per clock cycle. Thus, a minimum pipeline clock frequency of 150 MHz is required.

Secondly, the module shall support several thousand forwarding table updates per second—as needed in the Internet backbone—without interrupting the fast path.

Finally, our design aims to provide high adaptability to different hardware platforms by means of comprehensive configuration options. These do also allow for statistical research of different setups and enhancements by providing the freedom to partition the trie using arbitrarily sized strides. Easy modifiability of the multibit node encoding with respect to pointer lengths and its internal layout is therefore intended.

3.2   Overall Architecture

Our design extensively utilizes pipelining to efficiently employ the on-chip resources. By contrast, the TBMP implementation introduced by [9] uses time-division multiplexing of several TBMP automata to increase the processable lookup rate. Fig. 3 depicts the basic pipeline structure on block level. On this level, we simply segmented the search trie by assigning each trie level a separate pipeline stage with dedicated memory and processing logic. Due to the flexible module configuration, the overall pipeline structure can incorporate a variable number of these basic TBMP Lookup Stages realizing the algorithmic core functionality. Besides these, an optional Initial Array Stage, an optional Internal Node (iNode) Stage—required for the Split Tree Bitmap optimization—and the final Result Stage, holding the array of next-hop IP addresses, are part of the pipeline. The last two stages in the figure map the next-hop IP address to the corresponding layer 2 address and egress port ID (EPID), and thus avoid redundancy in the result array. The Update Interface assigns accesses of the slow path to the individual memories of the pipeline stages. To achieve a high throughput, all stages themselves are internally pipelined, too.

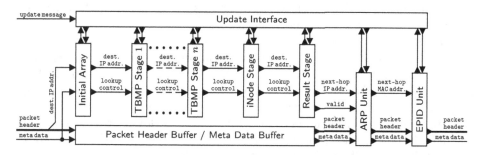

Fig. 3. Block diagram of the Tree Bitmap Lookup Module

3.3   Basic TBMP Stage

The structure of a TBMP Stage is shown in Fig. 4. Via the depicted RAM Interface Module, update and lookup operations access the on-chip memory, which holds the multibit nodes of one trie level. External memory can not be used due to the bandwidth constraints of a single RAM component and the pin count limitations of available chips. As a consequence, we accepted a limited

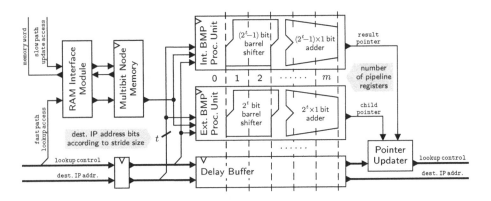

Fig. 4. Simplified block diagram of a TBMP Stage

forwarding table size of our prototype implementation, since even cutting-edge FPGAs do not offer enough memory to support on-chip table storage for core router FWEs—despite the efficient table compression of the TBMP algorithm. Besides the rather pricey option of an ASIC with larger on-chip memories, we discuss different solutions to this problem in Sect. 4.

For deterministic update access times, we have employed true dual-port RAM blocks, which allow update and lookup operations to access the node memory simultaneously. The easy realizability of dual-port RAM is a further advantage of on-chip memories. Thus, non-blocking updates are supported, making table inserts a fast operation that only depends on the slow path processing speed. Based on the formula in [5], the achievable update rate can thus be roughly estimated as $h_{\mathrm{upd}} = \frac{f_{\max}}{2^t + C}$ with $0 < C < (\frac{w}{t} + 3)$, w as the IP address length, and $f_{\max}$ as the maximum supported clock rate.

After the memory access cycle, in which a full multibit node structure is retrieved, the data is split into its node components and processed by separate units evaluating the Internal and External Bitmap. According to the TBMP algorithm, the logic of these units determines an index in the corresponding bitmap that yields the current LMP and the subsequent child node, respectively. Starting with these indexes, the units count all set bits in the lower-order positions to calculate the offsets within the memory block of the next-hop entries and accordingly within that of the multibit child nodes. The lower-order bits are extracted from the bitmap by means of a barrel shifter, and the set bits are then counted by a wide adder unit. Since the barrel shifter and the adder have to process fairly large vectors of $2^t - 1$ and 2^t bits, they take most of the combinatorics of the bitmap processing units. Therefore, we designed them in a way so that both can be mapped to an arbitrary number of pipeline registers m to adjust the length of the critical combinatorial path according to the stride size t and the desired throughput. In Sect. 4, we present the results of an empirical study investigating how many pipeline registers are required to achieve a desired performance with a given stride size.

If the optional Split Tree Bitmap optimization is employed, the Internal Bitmap unit is removed from the TBMP Stages, and a special iNode Stage is attached to the pipeline (cf. Fig. 3). With few different stride sizes, this saves combinatorics along with benefits in memory utilization and word widths. In the iNode Stage, zero, one or two simultaneous memory accesses are required for each lookup. To avoid memory duplication, such dual accesses can use both ports of the internal RAM. Possible conflicts with update accesses are resolved by an arbiter prioritizing lookups over updates. The statistical frequency of these cases, however, should not affect the update performance significantly.

4   Evaluation

The functional correctness of the TBMP Lookup Module has been validated by simulating multiple test cases. The design has been subsequently synthesized and transferred to an Altera Stratix II EP2S60 FPGA embedded in the Universal Hardware Platform (UHP) of the IKR [12]. In our test setup, a computer connected to three 1 Gbps line interfaces of the UHP has successfully shown the correct execution of lookups with different stride and optimization configurations.

For the evaluation of the potential maximum performance, we investigated a single TBMP stage. Since the throughput of the module pipeline is deterministic, a fix relationship exists between clock frequency and lookup rate. To find out the optimum pipelining degree for a given stride size t, we determined the maximum clock frequency f_{max} for different stride sizes and a varied number of registers m inside the bitmap processing unit. Fig. 5 shows the results obtained from the timing analysis of the synthesis tool used. As expected, large stride sizes require more registers to shorten the critical path so that a clock frequency of over 200 MHz is supported. Considering stride sizes in ascending order, the achievable absolute maximum performance is increasingly bounded by the growing interconnect delay between the Update Interface and the individual

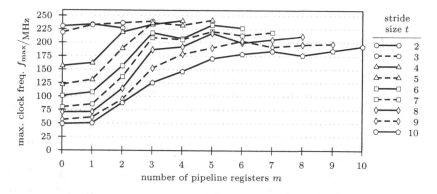

Fig. 5. TBMP Stage timing analysis results for different stride sizes with varied number of bitmap unit pipeline registers

RAM Interface Modules. Though, clock rates of more than 200 MHz have been achieved up to a stride size of 8.

If the complete lookup module is integrated on the FPGA used, performance degrades, as larger interconnect delays are unavoidable if the utilization of the on-chip resources increases. The timing analysis nevertheless resulted in 178 MHz for f_{max} in a configuration with an 8-bit wide Initial Array and three TBMP stages of stride size 8. With this frequency, the lookup module is capable to fulfill the requirements for 100 Gbps Ethernet to process more than 150 million packets per second and to handle an update rate of several ten thousand messages per second, according to the equation in Sect. 3.3.

The above mentioned implementation requires about 15,000 registers and 12,000 adaptive lookup tables, which equals to 43% logic utilization of the deployed Stratix II FPGA. Using the largest high-end FPGA of the 40-nm Stratix IV family, the processing logic of the lookup module utilizes only 4% of the available logic cells for an IPv4 implementation and 17% for an IPv6 implementation of the developed design. However, since FPGA manufacturers seek for a chip area split between logic and memory blocks that is suitable for the average application, even the above mentioned leading-edge FPGA offers not enough memory resources for a full backbone forwarding table—despite the efficient TBMP coding scheme. With 23 Mbit of embedded memory, the FPGA allows to store only about 180,000 prefixes on-chip assuming a perfectly balanced memory utilization and an average memory demand of 128 bit per prefix [5].

A solution to the memory problem could be efforts to manufacture FPGAs providing larger on-chip SRAM blocks by an adjusted logic-to-memory area split. A second approach is the use of external SRAM or DRAM components, which leads to the problem that current FPGAs offer too few IO pins to connect a dedicated memory for each trie level stage. Sharing memories between stages based on recurrent time slots does not solve the problem either, since the available memory timings do not allow to achieve the total bandwidth required for the 100 Gbps Ethernet processing performance. With today's FPGAs, only a multi-chip solution is viable. An option in a commercial scope might be an ASIC-based lookup module that can be used comparably to a TCAM device.

5   Conclusions

Increasing traffic together with the introduction of 100 Gbps Ethernet in the Internet backbone requires routers to process up to 150 million IP address lookups per second and line interface. Considering also power consumption as well as scalability with respect to growing forwarding tables and IPv6 addresses, algorithmic hardware solutions appear to be most suitable to meet these demands.

In this paper, we presented an extensively pipelined Tree Bitmap Lookup Module, which is capable to effectively process one packet per clock cycle. Additionally, it features a high-speed update interface. By offering multiple configuration parameters, one can adjust the design to different requirements. The lookup module passed several functional tests both in simulations and in a setup using our FPGA-based hardware platform. Synthesis results for an IPv4 configuration placed on an Altera Stratix II FPGA yield a maximum clock rate of 178 MHz. This allows to process up to 178 million lookups and several ten thousand updates per second being ample for 100 Gbps core router line cards. On today's high-end FPGAs, even IPv6 implementations and higher lookup rates are possible. Our prototypical lookup module utilizes the FPGA's on-chip memory, which does not suffice for large backbone forwarding tables. Thus, possible future FPGAs offering larger memories, multi-chip solutions, or ASIC-based lookup modules replacing power demanding TCAM devices are needed for commercial deployment.

References

1. D'Ambrosia, J., Law, D., Nowell, M.: 40 Gigabit Ethernet and 100 Gigabit Ethernet technology overview (November 2008)
2. Huston, G.: BGP analysis reports: IPv4 route-views statistics (March 11, 2009), http://bgp.potaroo.net/bgprpts/rva-index.html
3. Degermark, M., Brodnik, A., Carlsson, S., Pink, S.: Small forwarding tables for fast routing lookups. SIGCOMM Comp. Comm. Review 27(4), 3–14 (1997)
4. Lampson, B., Srinivasan, V., Varghese, G.: IP lookups using multiway and multi-column search. IEEE/ACM Transactions on Networking 7(3), 324–334 (1999)
5. Eatherton, W., Varghese, G., Dittia, Z.: Tree Bitmap: hardware/software IP lookups with incremental updates. SIGCOMM Comp. Comm. Review 34(2), 97–122 (2004)
6. Song, H., Turner, J., Lockwood, J.: Shape shifting tries for faster IP route lookup. In: ICNP 2005: Proc. of the 13th IEEE Int'l Conf. on Network Protocols, November 2005, pp. 358–367 (2005)
7. Nilsson, S., Karlsson, G.: IP-address lookup using LC-tries. IEEE Journal on Selected Areas in Comm. 17(6), 1083–1092 (1999)
8. Tsiang, D., Ward, D.: Advances in router architecture: The CRS-1 and IOS-XR. In: Cisco Networkers 2004 (July 2004)
9. Taylor, D.E., Lockwood, J.W., Sproull, T.S., Turner, J.S., Parlour, D.B.: Scalable IP lookup for programmable routers, vol. 2, pp. 562–571 (2002)
10. Narayan, H., Govindan, R., Varghese, G.: The impact of address allocation and routing on the structure and implementation of routing tables. In: SIGCOMM 2003: Proc. of the 2003 Conf. on Appl., Tech., Arch., and Protocols for Comp. Comm., pp. 125–136 (2003)
11. Jiang, W., Prasanna, V.K.: A memory-balanced linear pipeline architecture for trie-based IP lookup. In: HOTI 2007: Proc. of the 15th Annual IEEE Symposium on High-Performance Interconnects, pp. 83–90 (2007)
12. IKR: Universal Hardware Platform (UHP) – A hardware construction kit for rapid prototyping (March 12, 2009), http://www.ikr.uni-stuttgart.de/Content/UHP/

Comparative Study of Multicast Protection Algorithms Using Shared Links in 100GET Transport Network

Samer Sulaiman, Abdelfattah Haidine, Ralf Lehnert, and Stefan Tuerk

TU Dresden, Chair for Telecommunications
{Sulaiman,lehnert,tuerk}@ifn.et.tu-dresden.de,
Abdelfatteh.haidine@signalion.com

Abstract. In recent years new challenges have emerged in the telecommunications market resulting from the increase of network traffic and strong competition. Because of that, service providers feel constrained to replace expensive and complex IP-routers with a cheap and simple solution which guarantees the requested quality of services (QoS) with low cost. One of these solutions is to use the Ethernet technology as a switching layer, which results in using the cheap Ethernet services (E-Line, E-LAN and E-Tree) and to replace the expensive IP-routers. To achieve this migration step, new algorithms that support the available as well as the future services have to be developed. In this paper, we investigate the multicast protection issue. Three multicast protection algorithms based on the shared capacity between primary and backup solutions are proposed and evaluated. The blocking probability is used to evaluate the performance of the proposed algorithms. The sub-path algorithm resulted in a low blocking probability compared with the other algorithms.

1 Introduction

In recent years new services like IPTV, Video on Demand, Distance Learning, etc. appeared making the network traffic growths faster. Some of these services need a high bandwidth when they are unicasted to each customer. In this case, multicast technology can reduce the required bandwidth through distributing the traffic over a multicast tree rooted by the source. Basically, IP-multicast uses the UDP protocol to forward the multicast data. Because of that and because the dynamic behavior of multicast groups, it is difficult to avoid packet loss and to keep the multicast distribution tree optimum. Multicast routing protocols can be classified into two classes. On one hand, protocols use own routing information to build the distribution tree (e.g. Distance Vector Multicast Routing Protocol "DVMRP" and Multicast Open Shortest Path First "MOSPF") [RFC1075]. On the other hand, protocols use the existing unicast routing information to build the distribution tree (e.g. Protocol Independent Multicast "PIM" and Core Based Tree "CBT") [Wil02] [RFC2201] [RFC4601].

Due to the increasing cost pressure in the telecommunication market and the slump in the telecommunication services, service providers feel constrained to find a new solution which guarantees the request quality of services with low cost. Carrier-Grade Ethernet solution is proposed to replace the expensive and complex IP-router with a cheap and simple Ethernet switch. However, this replacement has to fulfill the

M. Oliver and S. Sallent (Eds.): EUNICE 2009, LNCS 5733, pp. 158–167, 2009.
© Springer-Verlag Berlin Heidelberg 2009

existing QoS and to increase the network capacity. Many investigations are done to improve the capacity of the Ethernet switch. Additionally, several approaches as well protocols are proposed to realize this migration step [AH08] [FED07] [WB08].

In view of using the Carrier Ethernet for increasing the network capacity, new challenges arise, like: 1) keeping the new technique as simple and cheap as possible comparing to the available ones, 2) developing protocols working with existing ones in different layers (IP/Eth/WDM, IP/WDM, Eth/WDM, Eth/SDH/WDM, etc.), 3) supporting the available services (IP and Ethernet, Point-to-Point "P2P" and Point-to-Multipoint "P2MP"), 4) scalability, etc. P2MP or multicast services are used to transport the same data to a group of customers simultaneously through a so-called distribution tree. Therefore, the available QoS and resilience algorithms used in unicast are not suitable for multicast. By using the unicast algorithms for multicast, the distribution tree used for forwarding the multicast data has to be subdivided into unicast paths for each receiver of the multicast group. That results in multiplying the required capacity of the shared links in the distribution tree.

Our contribution focuses on the comparison of three protection algorithms proposed to solve the multicast protection issue. Different calculation scenarios are implemented by MATLAB to evaluate the performance of the investigated algorithms.

The rest of the paper is organized as follows. An overview on the multicast protection requirements is given in section II. In section III, three protection algorithms are described. Results and comparisons between the investigated algorithms are shown in section IV.

2 Requirements for Multicast Resilience

Let us consider the use of unicast protection algorithms for the multicast case. In this case, each path of the distribution tree has to be protected with a unicast backup path. However, it is difficult to realize this idea because the multicast address is used to identify a group of unicast addresses. This results also in duplicating the packet processing and sending. Figure 1 presents an example network with 8 nodes and 15 links.

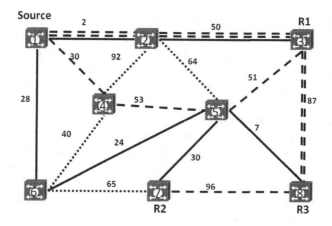

Fig. 1. Multicast resilience using unicast protection algorithm

The solid paths {(1,2,3); (1,6,5,7); (1,6,5,8)} represent the active multicast distribution tree based on source based tree algorithm, where node 1 is the source and node 3, 7 and 8 are the multicast receivers. The dashed paths {(1,4,5,3); (1,2,3,8); (1,2,3,8,7)} stand for the unicast backup paths found for each path in the distribution tree. The number above each link represents the link weight. Now we assume that a failure occurs over the link between node 2 and node 3, the unicast backup path (1,4,5,3) will be used. In this case, node 5 receives the multicast packet twice (from node 2 and node 4). The node has to process both duplicates and to send them further. Furthermore, multiple bandwidth is reserved on the links {(1,2); (2,3); (3,8)} to realize this protection process. Because of that, it is necessary to apply a multicast protection algorithm resulting in protecting the whole distribution tree and not to protect each path of this tree separately; such is the case in unicast.

3 Investigated Multicast Resilience Algorithms

The simple solution to guarantee the arrival of packets to each multicast group member is to build two separate distribution trees like using two paths in the unicast case. This solution is simple and guarantees a fast rerouting. However, it is not efficient and results in increasing the required bandwidth. Different tree protection algorithms are proposed assuming that all the network nodes are member in the tree [MBG99] [XLT03]. However, in the multicast case, the distribution tree consists of only some network nodes. Additionally, the structure of this tree can be changed dynamically according to the dynamical behavior of the multicast group. Therefore, these algorithms have to be adjusted to protect the distribution tree. Three improved algorithms based on building two distribution trees, sharing some links, will be discussed in this section. The backup tree can be activated as soon as a failure occurs in the primary tree. On the other hand, the backup tree can be used to reroute some paths or links of the primary tree. The resilience algorithms described in this section are: a) preplanned tree based, b) sub-path based and c) dual forest tree.

3.1 Preplanned Tree Based Protection

The main idea of the preplanned tree based algorithm is to find the shortest path tree from the red/blue tree constructed by the MEBG algorithm developed by Médard et al. [MBG99] [XLT03]. Let us assume that all the network nodes are member in the multicast tree. There are different algorithms used to build the distribution tree. We will here present the MEBG algorithm which guarantees fast recovery from any single link/node failure as long as the failed node is not the source node. The basic idea of this algorithm is to construct two redundant trees called blue tree and red tree. Figure 2 shows an undirected graph with 8 nodes (bridges) and 15 links. The source node is node 1. At the beginning both trees (T^B for blue tree and T^R for red tree) contain only the source node. Then we try to find a ring consisting of at least 3 nodes in which the source node is the start as well the end of this ring. Different criteria can be specified for selecting the ring depending on the design objective, such as minimizing average delay or reducing the total cost.

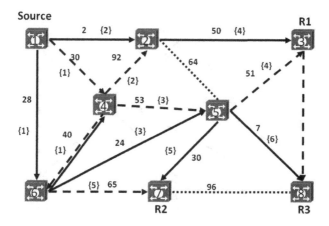

Fig. 2. Protection scheme based on preplanned tree

In this example, minimizing the average delay is used as objective to build the tree. Thus, the first found ring from Figure 2 is (1,6,4,1). All the links on this ring selected during the first iteration are labeled with label {1}. From this ring we can define two paths starting at the source node. According to the objective function the path (1,6,4), referred as solid links, has a lower cost than the path (1,4,6) with dashed links. Thus, it is added to T^B and the path (1,4,6) is added to T^R. Now we look for a new path connecting two distinct nodes (e.g. node 1 and 4) in T^B and at least one additional node not in T^B (e.g. node 2). In the same way, the link (1,2) is added to T^B and the link (4,2) to T^R. Because all links of this path are selected during the second iteration, they are labeled with {2}. The algorithm will continue until T^B and T^R span all the network nodes. In this case, two trees are constructed for the primary tree T^B and backup tree T^R. Several algorithms have been proposed to protect either each link or each path of the primary tree using the backup tree [XLT03].

As mentioned above, MEBG protects all the network nodes. This results in an unnecessary bandwidth reservation in some nodes. Since only the distribution tree nodes of a multicast group have to be protected, we improve the MEBG algorithm to build two distribution trees from T^B and T^R. The shortest path tree algorithm has been used to construct the primary as well as backup distribution tree.

3.2 Sub-path Based Protection

In this section, we propose a new protection algorithm. The basic idea of the sub-path algorithm is to divide the primary tree into sub-paths, and to find a backup path for each part. To understand the division of the primary tree, a set of protection nodes has to be defined first. It consists of all receivers and switching nodes of the primary tree. A switching node is a node which has more than one downstream in the distribution tree. Now we can define a set of sub-paths between sender and receiver, sender and switching point, receiver and receiver and switching point and receiver. To make this algorithm easy to understand, we explain it using an example. Figure 3 presents a network of 8 nodes and 13 links. Let us assume a multicast group consisting of node 1 as a sender and the nodes 2, 3, 7 and 8 as receivers. Firstly, the primary distribution

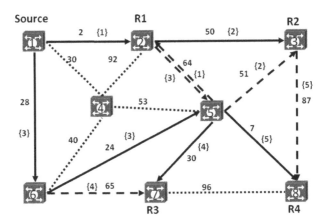

Fig. 3. Sub-path based protection

tree will be constructed as a shortest path tree (solid lines). The set of the Protection Nodes (PN) consists of the nodes 2, 3, 7, 8 and 5, where node 5 is a switching node. From this set we can define the following sub-paths: SP={(1,2); (2,3); (1,6,5); (5,7); (5,8)}. Each sub-path has to be composed of only two nodes from the set PN.

The next step is to find a backup path of each one in the set SP. To do that, we delete the sub-path from the network topology. Then, we try to find the shortest path between the start and the end node of the deleted sub-path. The link between node 1 and 2 will be firstly deleted. The shortest path from node 1 to node 2 is then the path (1,6,5,2). The shared links between the primary tree and the found backup path (1,6,5) will be deleted. This results in avoiding the duplication of the required reserved bandwidth. This sub-path and the rest of the found backup path will be labeled with {1}. This label is used to guarantee a fast recovery process from any single link/node failure as long as the failed node is not the source or a switching node. This is because the links with the same label will be immediately reactivated when information about a failure is received. The algorithm continues until all the sub-paths of the set SP are protected and labeled. In this case, we do not get a separate backup tree (dashed lines). If a link or a node of the primary tree fails, the algorithm will activate the links of the same label from the backup set.

3.3 Dual Forest Tree Algorithm

The dual forest tree algorithm starts with finding the primary tree as a shortest path tree. After that it continues finding the shortest path between the leaf nodes of this tree. A leaf node can be each node of the primary tree, which has only one connection. Figure 4 shows the primary (solid lines) as well the backup links (dashed lines) for a multicast group consisting of the node 1 as a source and the nodes 5, 7 and 8 as receivers. Because the source has only one connection in this example, it will be selected as a leaf node, too. From Figure 4, the Leaf Nodes set (LN) is composed of the nodes 1, 7 and 8. To find the shortest path between the leaf nodes, the links and the nodes of the primary tree except the leaf nodes are deleted. The shortest path between

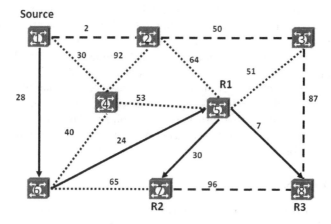

Fig. 4. Dual forest tree protection

the leaf nodes is (1,2,3,8,7). The main challenge of this algorithm is to find the shortest path between the leaf nodes without sharing any link and node of the primary tree. To solve this issue, we choose each leaf node as a root and try to find its shortest path tree. The tree with lowest cost will be then selected as a backup tree. The basic idea of this algorithm has been proposed in [FCG01] [SCM06].

4 Performance Evaluation

4.1 Reference Networks

To evaluate and compare the investigated algorithms, they are implemented in Matlab [MW08]. Primary tree cost, backup cost and blocking probability are used for comparing the performance of these algorithms. Two network topologies from the NOBEL-project [NOB08] are used for the performance evaluation. The first one is the *"German network"* with 17 nodes and 26 links and the second one is the *"European network"* with 28 nodes and 41 links.´

4.2 Evaluation Scenarios

Three scenarios are used in this work. The results of these scenarios are averaged over 100 calculation runs. The first one uses the proposed protection algorithms to find the primary tree as well the backup set for a multicast group whose size falls within the range [3, N-2], where N is the number of the network nodes. The members of these groups are randomly chosen. The first node of each group is selected as a source of this group. Because of that, a group of two members represents a unicast case. Therefore, we use at least three nodes to build a multicast group. Furthermore, a group of N members represents a broadcast case. The range [3, N-2] is chosen to evaluate the performance of the proposed algorithms in different group density (sparse and dense mode). The results of this scenario are defined as a function of multicast group size. The second scenario is similar to the first one. However, a defined number of multicast groups are randomly created for each calculation run. In this case, the link capacity will play a major role. The link capacity is 10 capacity units; however, the demand of each multicast service is one capacity unit. The results of the last scenario are defined as a function of the number of the multicast groups for each calculation run. The number of multicast groups falls within the range [1, 15]. In this scenario, each protection algorithm is used to find the primary tree and the backup set for a defined multicast group size with different number of multicast groups (within the range [1, 15]) for each calculation run. Therefore, the link capacity plays also a major role in this scenario. We have chosen this range [1, 15] to investigate the proposed algorithms with a low and a high network load.

4.3   Results Discussion

To evaluate the performance of the proposed algorithms, the blocking probability is used. The blocking probability is the number of multicast groups whose backup set cannot be found divided by the total number of created multicast groups. This criterion shows clearly the performance of the proposed algorithms. A 95% confidence interval is used to show the accuracy of the averaged value. The primary as well as backup tree cost will be discussed in this paper, too. However, their results are not presented because of the paper limit.

4.3.1   German Network with 17 Nodes and 26 Links

The results presented in Figure 5 are defined as a function of the multicast group size, while the results in Figure 6 are defined as a function of the multicast groups number. Because of using the shortest path algorithm to find the primary tree, the cost of this tree is a suboptimum compared to the minimum spanning tree. However, we get the optimum solution of the end-to-end cost in this tree. Therefore, the end-to-end cost of the primary tree constructed by the sub-path and dual forest tree algorithms is the optimum. However, the backup cost depends on the method used by the algorithms. The dual forest tree algorithm finds the shortest path tree between the leaf nodes of a primary tree. Thus, its backup cost is the lowest. On the other hand, the sub-path algorithm tries to find a backup set of defined sub-paths from a primary tree. The shared links between the primary tree and the backup set will be deleted to avoid duplicating the reserved link capacity in the same direction. This results in reducing the backup cost compared to the preplanned tree algorithm. Figure 5 shows that the dual forest tree algorithm is the worst one and the sub-path algorithm is the best one in finding the backup tree. The preplanned tree algorithm tries to find two separate trees. In the case of a large number of multicast groups and high network load, it becomes difficult to find two separate trees. However, the sub-path algorithm tries to find a set of backup paths sharing with the primary tree. This results in a network load reduction. From Figure 5(a) we can see that the blocking probability of the dual forest tree algorithm for multicast group size 14 and 15 is one. This is because the algorithm cannot find any backup set for all the investigated groups. We can infer that the sub-path algorithm is the best one in both small as well as large multicast group sizes (see Figure 6-(a) and (b)). While the dual forest tree algorithm shows the worst result in both small as well as large multicast group sizes where in large multicast group sizes, the blocking probability is almost one. This is because this algorithm tries to find the shortest path between the leaf nodes without sharing the primary links and nodes. Hence, this algorithm is not applicable for large group sizes. From Figure 6 we can see that the preplanned tree algorithm performs similarly to the sub-path algorithm for large group sizes (right diagram), while the difference becomes larger in small group sizes (left diagram). We can explain this difference by the fact that the sub-path algorithm needs less backup capacity than the preplanned tree algorithm. As mentioned above, the dual forest tree cannot find any backup tree. Furthermore, its blocking probability differs between zero and one in small multicast group size and low load. Because of that the precision of the calculated mean (Figure 5-(a) and Figure 6-(a)) becomes worse.

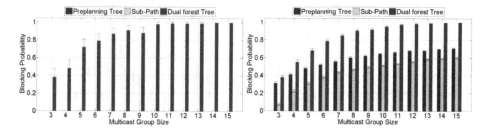

Fig. 5. Blocking probability as function of multicast group size using Germany network topology: a) Number of multicast groups = 1 (left); and b) Number of multicast groups = 15 (right)

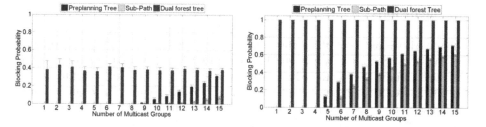

Fig. 6. Blocking probability as function of number of multicast groups using Germany network topology: a) Multicast group size = 3 (left); and b) Multicast group size = 15 (right)

4.3.2 European Network with 28 Nodes and 41 Links

We repeat the calculation process with a larger, but less meshed network topology. In the same way, we present the results in two forms: as a function of multicast group size and as a function of number of multicast groups. The results presented in Figure 7 and 8 give the same conclusions as the results presented previously. However, the performance of the investigated algorithms becomes somewhat worse, compared to the results of the fist network topology. This is because the network mesh level plays a role in finding a backup tree, when the network load and the multicast group size increase. On the contrary, the increasing of the network size can improve the performance of the investigated algorithms in the small group sizes. Form these results we can infer that the performance of the investigated algorithms depend on the network topology, network load and multicast group size.

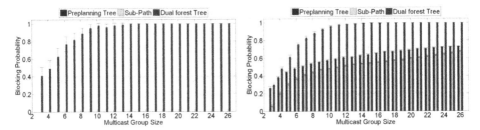

Fig. 7. Blocking probability as function of multicast group size using Europe network topology: a) Number of multicast groups = 1 (left); and b) Number of multicast groups = 15 (right)

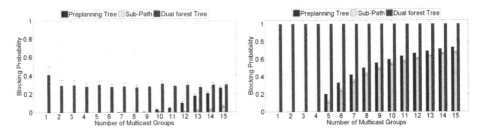

Fig. 8. Blocking probability as function of number of multicast groups using Europe network topology: a) Multicast group size = 3 (left); and b) Multicast group size = 26 (right)

5   Conclusions

In this work we proposed three algorithms used to protect the multicast distribution tree. In IP/MPLS core networks, the 1+1 unicast resilience is used to protect link as well node failures. As mentioned above using unicast algorithms to protect the multicast distribution trees is inefficient and resulting in multiplying the required bandwidth. Recently, several proposals are investigated to improve the MPLS standard to be able to protect multicast trees [WB08].

This paper focuses on the resilience issue. To reduce the required backup bandwidth, we delete the sharing links between the primary and backup tree. This results also in avoiding the double transition of the multicast data in the same link direction. Blocking probability is used to compare and evaluate the performance of the investigated algorithms. We can clearly see that the sub-path algorithm performs at the best. The preplanned tree algorithm seems to perform similar as sub-path algorithm in the large multicast group sizes. However, it becomes worse in the small group sizes with high network load. That is because the preplanned tree algorithm is based on finding two separate distribution trees that increase the reserved backup capacity. On the contrary, the performance of the dual forest tree is at the worst. Because this algorithm tries to find its backup as a shortest path between the leaf nodes of the primary tree without sharing any link and node of the primary tree, it is also not applicable for large group sizes.

It is also important to investigate the reaction time needed to reconstruct the distribution tree when a single link/node failure occurs. This time depends on the used recovery method. If we use the 1+1 class, the recovery time is smaller than in case of 1:1 class. The implementation of the 1+1 class is also simpler. However, the network load will increase. This issue will be investigated in future work.

Acknowledgment

The work presented in this paper is a result of the CELTIC project 100GET-E3, which is partially supported by Nokia Siemens Networks GmbH & Co. KG and the German Federal Ministry of Education and Research (BMBF) under grant 01BP0740.

References

[AH08]   IEEE 802.1AH Draft 4.2: Provider Backbone Bridges. IEEE 802.1 Working Group, http://www.ieee802.org/1/pages/802.1ah.html

[FCG01]   Fei, A., Cui, J., Gerla, M., Cavendish, D.: A "Dual-Tree" Scheme for Fault-Tolerant Multicast. In: ICC 2001. IEEE International Conference, vol. 3, pp. 690–694 (2001) ISBN 0-7803-7097-1

[FED07]   Fedyk, D.: Provider Link State Bridging. Nortel Networks (2007), http://www.ieee802.org/1/files/public/docs2007/aq-fedyk-plsb-present-0107.pdf

[MBG99]   Médard, M., Finn, S.G., Barry, R.A., Gallager, R.G.: Redundant trees for pre-planned recovery in arbitrary vertex-redundant or edge-redundant graphs. IEEE/ACM Trans. Networking 7, 641–652 (1999)

[MW08]   Documentation for MathWorks Products (R2007b), http://www.mathworks.com/access/helpdesk/help/helpdesk.html

[NOB08]   NOBEL 2 Project: D1.1 Architectural vision of network evolution, 01.03.2006-28.02.2008, http://www.ist-nobel.org/Nobel2/imatges/D1.1-Public%20part-final.pdf

[RFC1075] Waitzman, D., Partridge, C., Deering, S.: Distance Vector Multicast Routing Protocol. RFC1075 (1988)

[RFC2201] Ballardie, A.: Core Based Trees (CBT) Multicast Routing Architecture (1997)

[RFC4601] Fenner, B., Handley, M., Holbrook, H., Kouvelas, I.: Protocol Independent Multicast - Sparse Mode (PIM-SM): Protocol Specification, RFC4601 (2006)

[SCM06]   Saidi, M.Y., Cousin, B., Molnár, M.: Improved Dual-Forest for Multicast Protection. In: NGI 2006. 2006 2nd Conference, vol. 8, p. 378 (2006) ISBN 0-7803-9455-0

[WB08]   Ward, D., Betts, M.: MPLS Architectural Considerations for a Transport Profile. ITU-T - IETF Joint Working Team (2008), http://www.ietf.org/MPLS-TP_overview-22.pdf

[Wil02]   Williamson, B.: Cisco System: Developing IP Multicast Networks, vol. I (2002) ISBN 1-57870-077-9

[XLT03]   Xue, G., Chen, L., Thulasiraman, K.: Quality-of-Service and Quality-of-Protection Issues in Preplanned Recovery Schemes Using Redundant Trees. Selected Areas in Communications, IEEE Journal 21, 1332–1345 (2003)

Implementation and Evaluation of the Enhanced Header Compression (IPHC) for 6LoWPAN

Alessandro Ludovici, Anna Calveras, Marisa Catalan, Carles Gómez,
and Josep Paradells

Wireless Networks Group (WNG), Universitat Politècnica de Catalunya, C/Jordi Girona,
1-3, Mòdul C3 - Campus Nord. 08034 Barcelona, Spain
anna.calveras@entel.upc.edu

Abstract. 6LoWPAN defines how to carry IPv6 packets over IEEE 802.15.4 low power wireless or sensor networks. Limited bandwidth, memory and energy resources require a careful application of IPv6 in a LoWPAN. The IEEE 802.15.4 standard defines a maximum frame size of 127 bytes that decreases to 102 bytes considering the header overhead. A further reduction is due to the security, network and transport protocols header overhead that, in case of IPv6 and UDP, leave only 33 bytes for application data. A compression algorithm is necessary in order to reduce the overhead and save space in data payload. This paper describes and compares the proposed IPv6 header compression mechanisms for 6LoWPAN environments.

Keywords: 6lowpan, IPv6, header compression, sensor network, IEEE 802.15.4, blip.

1 Introduction

6LoWPAN is defined as a protocol to enable IPv6 packets to be carried on top of Low Power Wireless Personal Area Networks (LoWPANs) [1]. LoWPANs are composed of devices compatible with the IEEE 802.15.4 standard.

The aim is to develop personal networks, mainly sensor based, that can be integrated to the existing well-known network infrastructure by reusing mature and wide-used technologies. IPv6 has been chosen as network protocol because its characteristics fit to the problematic that characterizes LoWPAN environments such as the large number of nodes to address and stateless address auto-configuration.

1.1 IEEE 802.15.4

The IEEE 802.15.4 standard [2] defines protocols and interconnections of devices via radio communication in a Low Rate Wireless Personal Area Network (LR-WPAN). It follows the OSI reference model and specifies the physical and the Medium Access Control (MAC) sublayer of the data link layer. The main characteristics of these LR-WPANs include: (1) data rates of 250 kbps, 100 kbps, 40 kbps and 20 kbps; (2) IEEE 16-bit short or 64-bit extended address; (3) Low power consumption.

M. Oliver and S. Sallent (Eds.): EUNICE 2009, LNCS 5733, pp. 168–177, 2009.
© Springer-Verlag Berlin Heidelberg 2009

IEEE 802.15.4 devices are classified into Full Function Devices (FFD) and Reduced Function Devices (RFD). The FFD operates as a PAN coordinator and border router. Two important features of 802.15.4 are its self-healing and self-organizing properties. This means that nodes are able to detect the presence of other nodes and organize themselves in a network, and they can detect and recover from faults.

There exist four different frame types: (1) beacon frame, (2) data frame, (3) acknowledgment frame, (4) MAC command frame. The maximum frame size defined in IEEE 802.15.4 is fixed to 127 bytes, of which 25 bytes are reserved for frame overhead. This leaves 102 bytes for payload.

1.2 6LoWPAN Architecture

In order to transport IPv6 packets over 802.15.4 links it is required, as specified in [3], to provide an adaptation layer below the network layer (Fig.1). It is demanded in order to comply with the minimum MTU required by IPv6 that is fixed to 1280 bytes.

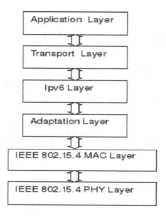

Fig. 1. 6LoWPAN protocol stack

The packet is prefixed by LoWPAN encapsulation headers that, as defined in [3], include the presence of a one byte IPv6 Dispatch header and the definition of the following header fields and their ordering constraints. The two leftmost bits are settled to 01 or 00 indicating if there is a 6LoWPAN frame or not. The remaining 6 bits can define up to 64 different dispatch header types. However, only 5 dispatch header types are defined in [3].

As mentioned before, IPv6 allows stateless address auto-configuration. This property allows hosts to generate their own address combining locally available information together with the one advertised by routers. The host generates the interface identifier

```
+----------------+----------------+----------+
| IPv6 Dispatch  | IPv6 Header    | Payload  |
+----------------+----------------+----------+
```

Fig. 2. LoWPAN encapsulated IPv6 datagram

while the router provides the subnetwork prefix associated with a link. The interface identifier is defined with a length of 64 bits [5]. Thus, there is no problem if the PAN uses 64 bits IEEE 802.15.4 extended addresses but a modification is needed when using 16 bit IEEE 802.15.4 short addresses. The modification consists of adding a 48 bits pseudo address to the 16 bits interface identifier in order to obtain the required length of 64 bits. The pseudo address is formed as follows:

PAN ID (16-bit): zero bits (16): IEEE 16-bit short address

Considering an IEEE 16-bit short address equal to "64" (hex) and PAN ID equal to "10" (hex) we obtain the following pseudo address:

00:10:00:00:00:64

2   Related Work on IPv6 Header Compression in LoWPAN

IP Header Compression can be defined as *"the process of compressing excess protocol headers before transmitting them on a link and uncompressing them to their original state on reception at the other end of the link"* [4]. Compression is possible since the information carried in the packet is redundant. The redundancy may be present because we are sending packets belonging to the same flow and so the information contained in the headers is repeated several times, or because it is already present in other protocol headers in the packet.

Traditionally, the header compression is performed over a link between two nodes called compressor and decompressor. Moreover, there is the concept of flow context,

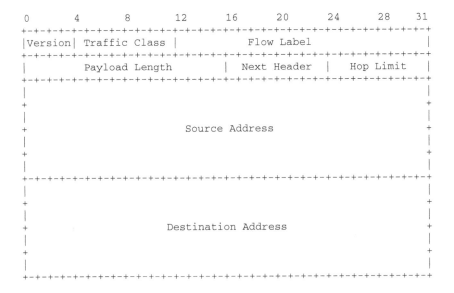

Fig. 3. 40 bytes IPv6 Header

which is a *"collection of information about field values and change patterns of field values in the packet header"* [4]. As just mentioned, IP header compression is usually a hop by hop compression. In a sensor network, this compression approach has high cost in terms of power consumption, indeed at each hop the IP header should be decompressed and re-compressed by the devices. Therefore, this approach might not fit with the constraints of 6LoWPAN networks. In addition to the increased processing operation at each node and the consequent increase of the needed power, there is also the problem of the maintenance of the context due to limited memory in sensor devices.

2.1 LOWPAN_HC1

The first specification of IPv6 header compression for LoWPAN has appeared in [3], and it is specified as LOWPAN_HC1. Considering the IPv6 header as shown in Fig.3, the common case for 6LoWPAN communications can be listed as:

- IP Version: it is 6 for all packets
- Traffic class and flow label: they are zero
- Payload length: it can be inferred from layer 2 or from the "datagram_size" field in the case we have a fragmented packet.
- Next header: it can be UDP, TCP or ICMP, so using 2 bits suffices.
- Source and Destination address: they are link-local (that is, the IPv6 interface identifier can be inferred from source and destination address present in layer 2).

All these fields can be compressed to 1 byte. As mentioned in [3], it is mandatory not to compress the hop limit field, which always needs to be carried inline. So the resulting compressed header would have a size of 2 bytes instead of the 40 bytes of the uncompressed header as seen in Fig. 4.

```
 0   1   2   3   4   5   6   7   8   9   0   1   2   3   4   5
+---+---+---+---+---+---+---+---+---+---+---+---+---+---+---+---+
|    LOWPAN_HC1 dispatch header     |  SA  |  DA  |TF |  NH  |HC2|
+---+---+---+---+---+---+---+---+---+---+---+---+---+---+---+---+
```

Fig. 4. 2 bytes encoding LOWPAN_HC1 format

LOWPAN_HC1 is only applied to link-local addresses. In consequence, it would not be possible to compress global addresses. The compression of global addresses would save 32 bytes of link-layer MTU. Moreover, a communication with global addresses would give full capabilities of the IPv6 protocol adoption to a LoWPAN, such as end-to-end communication across different LoWPANs and external IP networks.

To solve this problem, an IETF Internet draft [6], LOWPAN_HC1g, has been published, specifying a method for compressing global addresses. The LOWPAN_HC1g compression came from the fact that *"To support compression of global unicast address, LOWPAN_HC1g assumes that a PAN is assigned on compressible 64-bit global IP prefix. When either the source or destination address matches the compressible IP prefix, it can be elided*" [6]. LOWPAN_HC1g does not substitute LOWPAN_HC1, but it extends its applicability.

The compression of global addresses would be useful to gain bytes in the packet to send user data. In order to achieve this, an alternative header compression scheme has been developed under the name of LOWPAN_IPHC [7]. In this paper we focus and implement this one, which is presented in the following section.

2.2 LOWPAN_IPHC

LOWPAN_IPHC [7] is the third proposed IPv6 header compression scheme. Currently, it is at its fourth update referred as LOWPAN_IPHC-04. Hereafter, LOWPAN_IPHC refers to the fourth update. It has been thought as an improvement of LOWPAN_HC1. In particular, it extends the applicability of header compression to support communication to nodes internal and external to LoWPANs (that is global address), multicast communication and both mesh-under and route-over configurations. Global IPv6 address compression is based on shared states within contexts. In contrast with LOWPAN_HC1, in the proposed LOWPAN_IPHC it is not mandatory to carry inline the hop limit field. A mechanism is specified to compress traffic and flow label in case they are not null fields. LOWPAN_IPHC uses five of the rightmost bits of the dispatch type (bits 3 to 7 in Fig. 5) in order to specify compressed fields of IPv6 header that are not related with the address compression. The dispatch header is followed by the LOWPAN_IPHC header that defines how source and destination addresses are compressed. An additional byte is present when communicating with global address; it is called Context Identifier Extension (CID). The four leftmost bits specify the context for source address. The remaining four rightmost bits specify the context used for destination address. Using context based compression, we could compress up to 16 network prefixes and save 60 bits of payload when communicating with external 6LoWPAN networks.

As reported in [7], LOWPAN_IPHC can compress the IPv6 header down to two octets (the dispatch octet and the LOWPAN_IPHC encoding) with link-local communication as seen in Fig. 5. When routing over multiple IP hops, LOWPAN_IPHC can compress the IPv6 header down to 7 octets (2-octets dispatch/LOWPAN_IPHC, 1-octet Hop Limit, 2-octet Source Address, and 2-octet Destination Address).

```
  0   1   2   3   4   5   6   7   8   9   0   1   2   3   4   5
+---+---+---+---+---+---+---+---+---+---+---+---+---+---+---+---+
| 0 | 1 | 1 |  TF   |NH | HLIM  |CID|SAC|  SAM  | M |DAC|  DAM  |
+---+---+---+---+---+---+---+---+---+---+---+---+---+---+---+---+
```

Fig. 5. LOWPAN_IPHC Encoding

```
  0   1   2   3   4   5   6   7
+---+---+---+---+---+---+---+---+
|     SCI       |     DCI       |
+---+---+---+---+---+---+---+---+
```

Fig. 6. CID octet

3 Implementation of IPv6 Header Compression over IEEE 802.15.4 Networks

3.1 Protocol Stack

Presently there are not LOWPAN_IPHC public implementations to our best knowledge. Hence, we have developed the compression and decompression routine focusing on the integration with b6lowpan protocol stack, which is presented in the next section, and reusing functions already provided in it.

The software component has been developed on TinyOS 2.1, which is an open-source operating system designed for wireless embedded sensor networks. The implementation of 6LoWPAN functionalities have been developed and implemented by the Berkeley Wireless Embedded Systems (WEBS) [8]. It has been released as TinyOS contribution and initially named b6loWPAN. Currently it is at its fourth version and has changed the name to Berkeley IP implementation for low-power networks (*blip*). When we started implementing the header compression, b6loWPAN was at first release so we have kept working on this version. From now on we will refer to it as *blip*.

It uses LOWPAN_HC1 header compression and includes IPv6 neighbor discovery, default route selection, point-to-point routing and network programming support. Standard tools like ping6, tracert6, and nc6 can be used to interact with and troubleshoot a network of 6loWPAN devices. Pc-side code is written using the standard BSD sockets API (or any other kernel-provided networking interface).

The *blip* implementation of header compression has been substituted by our implementation of LOWPAN_IPHC IPv6 Header compression.

3.2 Hardware Platform

The hardware platform used is the Crossbow's TelosB mote. It is an open source, low-power wireless sensor module. TelosB motes have a 16-bit RISC MCU at 8 MHz and 16 registers. The platform offers 10 kB of RAM, 48kB of flash memory and 16 kB of EEPROM. Requiring at least 1.8 V, it draws 1.8 mA in the active mode and 5.1 µA in the sleep mode. The MCU has an internal voltage reference and a temperature sensor. Further sensors available on the platform are a visible light sensor (Hamamatsu S1087), a visible to IR light sensor (Hamamatsu S1087-01) and a combined humidity and temperature sensor (Sensirion SHT11).

3.3 Environment and Measurements

A performance analysis has been done taking into account sensor memory usage, sensor energy consumption, average throughput of packet transmission within the sensor network and average Round-Trip delay time. The network topology (Fig. 7) is composed by three nodes:

1. IPBaseStation: it is the "border router" and acts as a bridge between the serial and radio links; it is the destination node.
2. Relay Node: it acts as a relay node.
3. Sensor Node: it transmits UDP packets to the IPBaseStation; it is the source node.

Sensor Node   Relay Node   IPBase Station

Fig. 7. Network topology

RTT has been measured in a single-hop network topology using the ping6 command included in b6lowpan.

Power consumption analysis has been done at the "relay node" since it is where both, the decompression and compression functionalities were carried out, apart from forwarding (i.e. each time a packet reaches this node it has to decompress, compress and forward the packet). The device used for these measures is the Agilent Technologies DC Power Analyzer N6705A.

All the tests have been done on three different cases of compression: (1) LOWPAN_IPHC, (2) LOWPAN_HC1, (3) No compression.

Performance analysis has been done on communications using global addresses. In the case of LOWPAN_IPHC, the global address has been compressed down to 16 bits.

4 Results

Fig.8 shows the average throughput (in KB/sec) for the three cases listed above. The IP payload ranges from 5 to 70 bytes length. For each payload value, 10 throughput measurements have been done. The final result is the mean value of them. The compressed header reaches a size of 31 bytes for LOWPAN_IPHC, 58 for LOW-PAN_HC1 and 62 for the non-compressed headers. The non-compressed header carries all the IPv6 header fields in-line, except the payload field.

In terms of throughput, LOWPAN_IPHC outperforms the others because the bytes of MAC payload used to carry the compressed headers are halved with respect to LOWPAN_HC1. Throughput increases by 39.77% for 70 bytes of payload, which is the maximum payload admitted by LOWPAN_IPHC without the need of fragmentation. Considering the maximum data payload (44 bytes) allowed by LOWPAN_HC1 without packet fragmentation, we obtain a throughput improvement of 25% with LOWPAN_IPHC compression.

The behavior of LOWPAN_HC1 compared with the no compression case needs a brief explanation. Although the UDP header is present in the packet, it is not declared in the next header field of IPv6. Instead of it, an hop-by-hop extension header named source routing header is specified. It is a non-standard header used in *blip* for source routing. In that way we have to carry in-line 8 bits of next header field. This means that, considering the architecture of the stack, the benefit of using one or another compression algorithm depends strongly on how the address fields are compressed more than the other IPv6 fields.

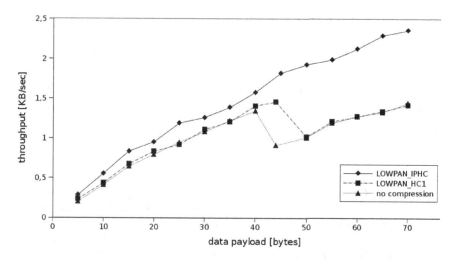

Fig. 8. Throughput obtained for LOWPAN_IPHC, LOWPAN_HC1 and no compression

In terms of energy consumption, we have focused on the effect of compressing IPv6 headers without taking into account the data application payload. Results are shown in Table 1.

Table 1. Energy Consumption

	Consumption (mA)
No compression	19.49
LOWPAN_HC1	19.41
LOWPAN_IPHC	19.27

Table 2. Memory usage

	ROM (bytes)	RAM (bytes)
LOWPAN_HC1	22020	3421
LOWPAN_IPHC	22584	3421

The sample rate has been fixed to 1 ms for a 10 minute test with the Sensor node sending a packet each second and the Base Station replying as soon as the packet arrives. LOWPAN_IPHC shows a better performance also in this case. Battery consumption is lowered 0,72 % between LOWPAN_IPHC and LOWPAN_HC1 and 1,13% between LOWPAN_IPHC and non compression case.

Table 2 compares the memory usage of the basic *blip* installed function that includes header compression LOWPAN_HC1 with the one implemented by LOW-PAN_IPHC. LOWPAN_IPHC increases by 564 bytes the occupation of ROM

Table 3. Round Trip Time (RTT) statistics

	Average RTT (ms)	Max RTT (ms)	Min RTT (ms)	Standard deviation (ms)
No compression	171.151	1311.428	87.840	88.397
LOWPAN_HC1	164.560	1192.718	81.323	68.654
LOWPAN_IPHC	79.443	1071.519	63.301	57.741

memory. This reflects the increased complexity of the compression algorithm. Mainly, the use of context based compression makes memory performance worse.

Finally, Table 3 shows the average round-trip delay time obtained from 1000 sent packets. It can be easily appreciated that LOWPAN_IPHC outperforms both no compression and LOWPAN_HC1 cases. These results reflect the throughput performance confirming that the space saved using LOWPAN_IPHC and, in particular, by compressing global addresses steps up the performance in the data transmission. LOWPAN_IPHC decreases RTT by 51.72% respect to LOWPAN_HC1. The average RTT obtained for LOWPAN_IPHC is comparable to others results found in literature [9].

5   Conclusions

In this paper we have presented the header compression mechanisms used to reduce IPv6 headers impact on the performance of 6LoWPAN environments. A first implementation and preliminary results are presented. The obtained results agree with the expected behavior of LOWPAN_IPHC and LOWPAN_HC1.

The main purpose of LOWPAN_IPHC is to offer the performance of a stateful compression in a resource-limited environment such as 6LoWPAN. As we have shown, a stateful compression approach increases the sensor memory usage. However, it outperforms all the other parameters we have taken into account. Moreover, with the refined Traffic and Flow fields compression introduced in LOWPAN_IPHC, the use of mechanisms of congestion control and QoS management on a 6LoWPAN communication would not affect dramatically the overall performance as it could happen with LOWPAN_HC1. This would benefit the application of 6LoWPAN to critical applications (i.e industrial process control, maintenance and surveillance) where there is the need to guarantee the service also in case of network congestion.

Finally, the 6LoWPAN Working Group plans to deprecate LOWPAN_HC1 header compression and push LOWPAN_IPHC [7] forward to become the new header compression standard for 6LoWPAN.

6   Future Work

As future work, the implemented LOWPAN_IPHC compression routine will be adapted to the latest *blip* version. Moreover, it would be useful to study and test possible enhancements of the header compression definition. We plan to compare the benefits of using Context based compression. This will be tested for global addresses when communication happens inside or outside the network.

Acknowledgments. This work has been supported by I2Cat Foundation, FEDER and the Spanish Government through project TEC2006-04504.

References

1. Mulligan, G.: 6LoWPAN Working Group. In: Proceedings of the 4th workshop on Embedded networked sensors, Cork, Ireland, pp. 78–82 (2007) ISBN:978-1-59593-694-3
2. IEEE Std 802.15.4TM -2006 (revision of IEEE Std 802.15.4-2003), IEEE Computer Society (September 2006)
3. Kushalnagar, N., Montenegro, G., Culler, D., Hui, J.: RFC 4944 Transmission of IPv6 Packets over IEEE 802.15.4 Networks. IETF Network Working Group (September 2007)
4. EFFNET AB, An Introduction to IPv6 Header Compression. white paper (February 2004),
   http://www.effnet.com/sites/effnet/pdf/uk/
   Whitepaper_Header_Compression.pdf
5. Hinden, R., Deering, S.: RFC 4291 - IPv6 Addressing Architecture, IETF Network Working Group (February 2006)
6. Hui, J., Culler, D.: Stateless IPv6 Header Compression for Globally Routable Packets in 6LoWPAN Subnetworks. 6LOWPAN WG draft-hui-6lowpan-hc1g-00 (June 2007)
7. Hui, J., Thubert, P.: Compression Format for IPv6 Datagrams in 6LoWPAN Networks. 6LoWPAN WG draft-ietf-6lowpan-hc-04 (December 2008)
8. Berkeley WEBS, "blip",
   http://smote.cs.berkeley.edu:8000/tracenv/wiki/blip
9. Hui, J., Culler, D.: IP is Dead, Long Live IP for Wireless Sensor Networks. In: Proceedings of the 6th ACM conference on Embedded network sensor systems. Raleigh, NC, USA, pp. 15–28 (2008) ISBN:978-1-59593-990-6

Primary Transmitter Discovery Based on Image Processing in Cognitive Radio

Liliana Bolea, Jordi Pérez-Romero, Ramón Agustí, and Oriol Sallent

Universitat Politècnica de Catalunya (UPC)
c/ Jordi Girona, 1-3, 08034, Barcelona, Spain
{lilianab,jorperez,ramon,sallent}@tsc.upc.edu

Abstract. The subject of secondary spectrum usage has been a hot research topic for some time now. Secondary users should be able to detect available primary frequency bands and use these spectrum opportunities without causing any harmful interference to primary users. The aim of this paper is to propose a new methodology, based on image processing techniques, which combines a number of sensed samples at different random geographical positions collected by secondary sensors, in order to build a map with the positions and coverage areas of the different primary transmitters. The results can be used to discover frequencies that can be used by a secondary market without causing interference to primary receivers and without any type of cooperation between primary and secondary networks.

Keywords: Sensing, Secondary Spectrum Use, Radio Environment Map, Image Processing.

1 Introduction

Recent years have witnessed the evolution of a large plethora of wireless technologies with different characteristics, as a response of the operators' and users' needs in terms of an efficient and ubiquitous delivery of advanced multimedia services. As a result, current and future wireless scenarios will be characterized by a multiplicity of Radio Access Technologies (RATs) and network operators with very different deployments (e.g. cellular, wireless local area networks, etc.). In addition to this, and with the objective of ensuring an efficient utilization of the available spectrum bands, the regulatory perspective on how the spectrum should be allocated and utilized is evolving as well [1]. New technical advances are focused on the development of strategies and policies aiming at the utmost and efficient access to shared spectrum resources. As an example, the unlicensed use of VHF and UHF TV bands by secondary users, provided no harmful interference is caused to the licensee (i.e. primary user), was targeted by the FCC in [2].

The primary-secondary spectrum sharing can take the form of cooperation or coexistence. Cooperation means there is explicit communication and coordination between primary and secondary systems, and coexistence means there is none. In the latter case,

M. Oliver and S. Sallent (Eds.): EUNICE 2009, LNCS 5733, pp. 178–187, 2009.
© Springer-Verlag Berlin Heidelberg 2009

secondary devices are essentially invisible to the primary and all of the complexity of sharing is borne by the secondary without changes required to the primary system. In this context, one of the key enabling technologies to enable secondary spectrum access is the cognitive radio, which allows the terminals determining which portions of the spectrum are available, selecting the most appropriate channel for transmission, and vacating the channel whenever a licensed user is detected [3].

In the above framework, assuming the coexistence case, knowledge about the primary transmitters' positions can be a relevant input for secondary users to determine the frequencies available for secondary use at the different points. In this respect, this paper proposes a new methodology, based on image processing techniques, aimed at combining a number of sensed samples at different geographical positions collected by secondary sensors, in order to build a map with the estimated positions and coverage areas of the different primary transmitters. The proposed methodology could be used to build databases containing the relevant aspects of radio environment characterization, such as the so-called Radio Environment Map (REM) in [4]. The REM can serve as the navigator and the vehicle of network support for Cognitive Radios. REM can also be viewed as the generalization of the available resource map proposed by Krenik for cognitive radio applications in unlicensed wide area networks [5], [6]. In [4], the authors use the REM as a database in order to compute the distance between the primary transmitter and secondary receiver. Prior work of the authors in [7] also introduced the image processing to identify the homogeneous radio-electrical regions where certain frequencies can be detected. This paper goes beyond the previous work in [7] by introducing novel object-based reconstruction techniques to enable the characterization of the scenario based on only a subset of samples.

This paper is organized as follows. Section 2 presents the problem formulation and the scenario considerations, prior to describing the proposed methodology in Section 3. Illustrative results are presented in Section 4 and conclusions are summarized in Section 5.

2 Scenario Considerations and Problem Formulation

A generic scenario such as the one depicted in Fig. 1 is considered. It is characterized by a number of primary transmitters corresponding to different RATs which operate at different frequencies and have different coverage areas (e.g. the central transmitter operating in a broadcast-like RAT with an extensive coverage area at frequency f_5, or the transmitters operating at RATs 1 and 2 with frequencies f_1, f_2, f_3 and f_4 that could correspond to some cellular-like RATs). Assuming that no cooperation between the primary and secondary networks exists, the secondary network will have to discover the positions and coverage areas of the primary transmitters to be able to decide in which places and in which frequencies secondary transmissions could be allowed. For that purpose, the secondary network can rely on the information measured by a number of sensors randomly scattered in the scenario and that could be built-in e.g. mobile terminals, and the appropriate post-processing of this information, which is the focus of this paper.

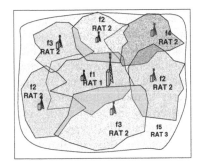

Fig. 1. Generic scenario with different RATs and frequencies

A sensor measures the received power in a number of specific frequencies in its position. It is assumed that frequency f_i is detected by the sensor at position (x,y) when the received power is above a given threshold $P_{th}(f_i)$, so that the following binary representation can be obtained for each frequency at each sensor position:

$$M\left(f_i, x, y\right) = \begin{cases} 1 & \text{if } f_i \text{ detected in} \left(x, y\right) \Leftrightarrow \text{if } P\left(f_i, x, y\right) \geq P_{th}\left(f_i\right) \\ 0 & \text{if } f_i \text{ not detected in} \left(x, y\right) \Leftrightarrow \text{if } P\left(f_i, x, y\right) < P_{th}\left(f_i\right) \end{cases} \qquad (1)$$

From this binary representation, it is possible to characterize the measurement at all frequencies given by the sensor at coordinate (x,y) by a value corresponding to the sum of the binary representations of all the N considered frequencies:

$$I\left(x, y\right) = \sum_{i=1}^{N} M\left(f_i, x, y\right) 2^{i-1} \qquad (2)$$

Each sensor would then report the value of $I(x,y)$ to a central entity in charge of combining the measurements of every sensor. The problem considered here consists then in defining a methodology to smartly combine the different measurements at random positions, which represent a partial vision of the scenario, in order to get a full vision in which the positions and coverage areas of the different primary transmitters are obtained. It is worth mentioning that this work focuses mainly on this combination of the sensing results, assuming these results are available, but both the considerations on the sensing process itself (such as errors in the process or the determination on which frequencies has to sense every sensor) and the means to report the sensing results are out of the scope of the paper and are left for future work.

3   Proposed Methodology

The proposed methodology assumes that the radio environment can be characterized by an image [7], where each pixel (i.e. a rectangular area of dimensions $\Delta x \times \Delta y$) takes the value $I(x,y)$ corresponding to the frequencies that are detected in it. Then, given that only the values $I(x,y)$ of the pixels where a sensor is located are known, these values need to be combined using image processing techniques in order to reconstruct the overall image and to discover the transmitter positions and coverage areas, as it is illustrated in Fig. 2. It is assumed that a pixel can only have the result of one sensor.

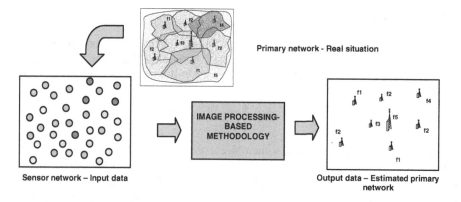

Fig. 2. Inputs and outputs of the considered problem

Assuming that the coverage area of a transmitter to be discovered will be approximately circular, which would be valid according to the distance-dependent path loss whenever omnidirectional antennas are used, the proposed methodology aims at identifying in the image the existing circular regions. For that purpose, starting from the sensed pixel values, which will be affected by propagation and shadowing effects, an object-based reconstruction technique will be developed to identify those "objects" (i.e. an object is a region where a certain frequency f_i is detected) that can be assimilated as circular areas and correspondingly as transmitter coverage areas. For that purpose, the steps of the proposed methodology are illustrated in Fig. 3 and explained in the following.

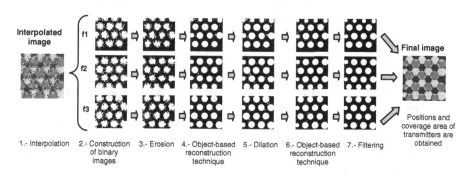

Fig. 3. Steps of the proposed methodology

3.1 Interpolation

Interpolation is the first step of this methodology. From the results of the sensors we build an image by interpolating the intermediate pixels for those positions where no sensor was available. We do that by attributing to each unknown pixel the value of the nearest known pixel.

3.2 Construction of Binary Images

From the interpolated image, we build a set of binary images, each one corresponding to a given frequency f_i. Each pixel of a binary image takes the value 1 if frequency f_i is detected and 0 otherwise. These binary images will be used as the basis to identify the different objects.

3.3 Erosion

It is possible that in some cases, some objects are not properly detected in the binary images, because they are not clearly separated from each other. This can occur due to e.g. shadowing effects in the propagation. In order to eliminate this drawback, before the object-based reconstruction technique, we apply an image processing technique called *erosion* to the binary images resulting from the interpolated image. In the erosion, the value of the output pixel is the minimum value of all the pixels in the input pixel's neighborhood. We assume that a pixel's neighborhood is defined by a circular area of radius 5 pixels. In image processing terminology, this corresponds to making the erosion with a circular structuring element [8]. Note that in the particular case of a binary image, if any of the pixels of the neighborhood is set to the value 0, the output pixel after the erosion will be set to 0, which will tend to decrease the size of the objects and thus to separate them.

3.4 Object-Based Reconstruction Technique

Object-based reconstruction technique tries to regenerate the image based on object properties, in particular assuming that the coverage area of a transmitter will be approximately circular. For each binary image (i.e. for each frequency f_i), we:

- Detect the objects (i.e. regions where frequency f_i is detected), following the so-called *connected-component labelling* technique [9] that consists in scanning the image and making groups of adjacent pixels having the same value (4-connected pixels are assumed, meaning that pixels are adjacent if one of their four edge - sharing neighbours touch). Each group of pixels will be then an "object".
- Measure objects properties (centroid and diameter of the object, which correspond to the centre and diameter of a circle with equivalent area than the object). Note that the centroid of every object represents the estimate position of primary transmitter;
- Regenerate a new image replacing each object by a circle with the corresponding diameter (see Fig. 3).

3.5 Dilation

Because of the prior erosion process, the resulting object area after object-based reconstruction technique has become smaller than in the binary images, which would lead to more reduced coverage areas than in the real situation. To compensate this effect, we apply the *dilation* technique to the binary images resulting from the object-based reconstruction technique. The dilation is the image processing technique opposite to the erosion process, and in this case the value of the output pixel is the maximum value of all the pixels in the input pixel's neighborhood [8]. In particular, in a binary image, if any of the pixels of the neighborhood is set to the value 1, the output pixel is set to 1, which will tend to increase the size of the objects. The same neighborhood shape (i.e. circular structuring element) as in the erosion is considered.

3.6 Object-Based Reconstruction Technique

After the dilation process, it may occur that some small circles intersect with other bigger circles. For that purpose, we execute again the *object-based reconstruction technique* to clearly regenerate the circular areas.

3.7 Filtering

Due to the shadowing effects in the propagation, after the reconstruction process, it may happen that certain objects are detected with an area significantly smaller than that of the rest of objects, so they cannot be considered as transmitters. To cope with this, in the last step, we *filter* the resulting images by eliminating those objects that have an area 30 times smaller than the average area of all the detected objects.

Finally, after the filtering, we combine the binary images to obtain a new image including information of all the frequencies. This image includes the positions, coverage areas and frequencies of the different primary transmitters.

4 Results

In order to illustrate the capabilities of the proposed methodology, it is evaluated in a cellular scenario with cell radius 1km, hexagonal layout and with a 3 frequency reuse pattern (f_1, f_2, f_3). The total scenario size is 10km x 10km, and the pixel size is $\Delta x = \Delta y = 10m$. The transmitter power is 30dBm, propagation losses as a function of distance d(km) are given by $L = 128.1 + 37.6 * \log_{10}(d)$ and the shadowing standard deviation is 3dB. Power threshold $P_{th}(f_i)$ is set at -99.6dBm for all frequencies. In Fig. 4 we can see the original image corresponding to the digitalization (i.e. the image if all the pixels were known). Having just $N = 3$ frequencies, pixels are encoded according to equation (2) with $8 = 2^N$ different intensity levels (i.e. colours) where the value 7=111 corresponds to the areas where three cells are overlapped, the values 3=011, 5=101 and 6=110 corresponds to the areas where two cells overlap and finally the values 1=001, 2=010 and 4=100 correspond to the central areas of each cell.

We sense the original image with a random sensor distribution with average density D sensors/km^2 and apply the proposed methodology. In Fig. 5 we can see the difference between the original image with shadowing effects, the sensed and interpolated image and the reconstructed image, in case that density of sensors D=100sensors/km^2. Visually we can remark that we obtain an important improvement of the original image as the shadowing effects are no longer included in the reconstructed image, so that the positions and coverage areas of the different transmitters can be more clearly identified.

Fig. 4. Image corresponding to the cellular scenario with 3dB standard deviation shadowing. In the right part, the colour scale corresponding to each pixel intensity between 0 and 7 is plot.

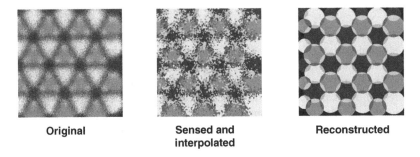

| Original | Sensed and interpolated | Reconstructed |

Fig. 5. Comparison between the original image, the sensed and interpolated image, and the reconstructed image for the case D=100 sensors/km^2

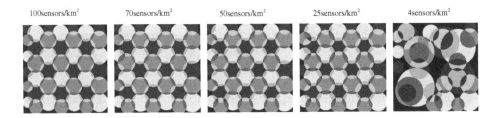

Fig. 6. Images resulted after proposed methodology for different sensor densities

In Fig. 6, we observe the resulting images for different values of the sensor density D. Note that if we have a low density of sensors such as D=4sensors/km^2, we can not properly identify the transmitters.

Every centroid of the detected objects represents the estimation of the position of each transmitter. In order to measure the accuracy in this estimation, we compute the relative error in the position estimation as the difference between the real transmitter position and the detected position, divided by the transmitter coverage radius. For this computation, we do not account for the transmitters that are located in the borders of the image, since they do not form a complete circle in the original image and consequently they lead to larger errors due to border effects.

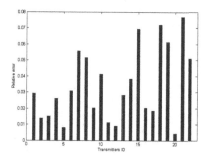

Fig. 7. Relative error in the transmitter positions for D=100sensors/km^2

Fig. 7 represents the relative error for each transmitter in the considered scenario in case that density of sensors D=100sensors/km^2. It can be observed that, in all the cases, the values of the relative errors are below 8%.

The mean error and the standard deviation for different density of sensors are shown in Fig. 8. In addition, Fig. 9 plots the rate of transmitter detection representing the ratio between the number of transmitters properly detected and the exact number of transmitters. In case that density of sensors D=4 sensors/km^2, only a 40% of the transmitters are detected, and the mean error is high, as well as the standard deviation. As the density of sensors grows, the rate of detection is 100%, and the mean error is smaller. Gathering more than about 25 sensors per km^2 (i.e. on average 1 sensor every 200×200 m^2 or equivalently about 80 sensors per transmitter coverage area) leads to minor marginal gains to the mean error of about 5% (or 50 meters in the base station position) and to a detection probability of 100% in the analysis performed.

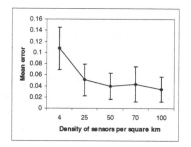

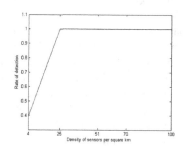

Fig. 8. Mean error and standard deviation, represented as vertical lines

Fig. 9. Rate of transmitter detection

Fig. 10 and Fig. 11 plot the obtained results for different values of cell radius. As we expect, in case that the cell radius is small (e.g. 500m), we have fewer sensors inside the cell coverage area, the errors are bigger, and the rate of detection smaller. Instead, if the cell radius is large (e.g. 1500m), the number of sensors inside the cell coverage area is also larger, the errors are smaller and the rate of detection is higher.

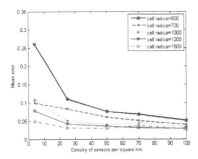
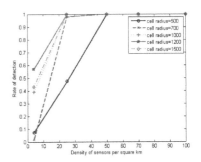

Fig. 10. Mean error for different values of cell radius

Fig. 11. Rate of transmitter detection for different values of cell radius

Table 1. Minimum density of sensors necessary for different cell radius

	cell radius 500 m	cell radius 700 m	cell radius 1000 m	cell radius 1200 m	cell radius 1500 m
density of sensors per km^2	110	73	28	22	10

Accepting an error below 5% and a rate of transmitter detection above 95%, we can obtain from the results the minimum density of sensors necessary in order to make a proper estimation of the position of the transmitters. This is indicated in Table 1.

5 Conclusions

This paper has presented a new methodology, based on image processing techniques that combine a number of sensed samples at different geographical positions collected by sensors, in order to discover the positions and coverage areas of the different primary transmitters. Utilization of these databases in a secondary spectrum usage permits the secondary network to discover the presence of primary network transmitters and to use spectrum opportunities without disturbing the primaries. The results obtained reveal the utility and efficacy of the proposed methodology, with relative errors below 5% in the transmitter position.

Acknowledgments. This work has been supported by the Spanish Research Council and FEDER funds under COGNOS grant (ref. TEC 2007-60985).

References

1. Cave, M.: Essentials of modern spectrum management. Cambridge University Press, Cambridge (2007)
2. Federal Communications Commission (FCC): Notice of Proposed Rule Making, ET Docket no. 04-113, May 25 (2004)

3. Akyildiz, I.F., Lee, W.-Y., Vuran, M.C., Mohanty, S.: Next generation/dynamic spectrum access/cognitive radio wireless networks: a survey. Computer Networks 50(13), 2127–2159 (2006)
4. Zhao, Y., Raymond, D., da Silva, C.R.C.M., Reed, J.H., Midkiff, S.F.: Performance evaluation of radio environment map-enabled cognitive spectrum-sharing networks. In: Proc. IEEE Military Comm. Conf., Orlando, FL, pp. 1–7 (2007)
5. Krenik, W., Batra, A.: Cognitive Radio Techniques for Wide Area Networks. In: Proc. Conference on Design Automation, pp. 409–412 (2005)
6. Krenik, W., Panasik, C.: The Potential for Unlicensed Wide Area Networks. Wireless Advanced Architectures Group, Texas Instruments White Paper (November 2004)
7. Pérez-Romero, J., Sallent, O., Agustí, R.: On the Applicability of Image Processing Techniques in the Radio Environment Characterisation. In: 69th IEEE Vehicular Technology Conference: VTC 2009 Spring, Barcelona, Spain (2009)
8. "Morphological operations", Image Processing Toolbox, The Mathworks,
http://www.mathworks.com/access/helpdesk/help/toolbox/images/index.html
9. Fisher, R., Perkins, S., Walker, A., Wolfart, E.: Connected Component Labeling (2003),
http://homepages.inf.ed.ac.uk/rbf/HIPR2/label.htm#1

A Flexible Framework for Complete Session Mobility and Its Implementation

Marc Barisch, Jochen Kögel, and Sebastian Meier

Institute of Communication Networks and Computer Engineering
Universität Stuttgart
Pfaffenwaldring 47, 70569 Stuttgart, Germany
{marc.barisch,jochen.koegel,smeier}@ikr.uni-stuttgart.de

Abstract. Users with several devices need a convenient mechanism to transfer running service sessions from one device to another device. This paper proposes a framework that allows session mobility without modifications on the communication partner's system from application layer down to network layer. That means we can transfer ongoing sessions with minor interruptions of the communication and thus call it complete session mobility. Due to the framework's flexibility we support a multitude of technologies across all layers. The architecture has been verified by a prototype that has been implemented on a Linux system.

1 Introduction

Nowadays a user owns several devices that are connected to the Internet and that can be used to consume services. Currently, these devices are independent of each other, which decreases the usability from the user's point of view. In particular, a user cannot easily transfer ongoing service sessions from one of his devices to another one. For example, a user wants to exploit the diverse capabilities of his devices and transfer a running video session from the TV at home to the mobile phone when he leaves the house. Moreover, the limited battery power of mobile devices motivates the need to transfer service sessions between devices. If one device runs out of power the service session can be transferred to another user device and the user can continue to use the service.

In order to accomplish the transfer of ongoing service sessions between devices of a user, we have to design a suitable framework. Such a solution should also take the following requirements into account:

High degree of flexibility: The solution has to cover a wide range of different applications. We target to support multimedia sessions, like voice, and video calls, web sessions and online games.

No involvement of communication partner: Existing solutions, e.g. based on SIP [1] require the exchange of signaling messages with the communication partner, i.e. the service provider, to transfer a service session between devices. This requires that the communication partner supports such session transfers. In addition, the communication partner is explicitly informed about the session transfer, which can be critical for privacy-aware users.

M. Oliver and S. Sallent (Eds.): EUNICE 2009, LNCS 5733, pp. 188–198, 2009.
© Springer-Verlag Berlin Heidelberg 2009

We propose a flexible and pluggable framework that allows session mobility. This framework takes into account that a service session consists of application state and communication state, which need to be transferred between devices. Since application state is very specific we demand that a service supports well-defined interfaces for state export and import. Regarding the communication state, which exists between the user's device and a communication partner, we need to redirect the traffic and to re-establish the corresponding states on the destination device. For redirecting the traffic we employ mobility techniques on the network layer. The re-establishment of the network state requires the extraction of information from the operating system's (OS) network stack of the network layer as well as of the transport layer.

The remainder of this paper is structured as follows. Section 2 provides an overview on the terminology used throughout this paper. Afterwards Section 3 presents the related work for the architecture proposed in Section 4. The partial implementation of the architecture is elaborated in Section 5. Finally, we discuss the open issues of our architecture in Section 6.

2 Terminology

Since we propose a layered session mobility framework based on mobility techniques on the network layer, we introduce the relevant terminology first. Based on a well-established mobility terminology introduced in Section 2.1, we elaborate on our cross-layer session concept in Section 2.2.

2.1 Mobility Terminology

The term mobility is widely used in communication networks with different meanings. In our understanding, mobility is "the ability to use services, irrespective of changes of the location and technical equipment" [2]. For its realization, suitable mechanisms have to be in place to support service usage despite of changes of network connections or change of terminals.

Specifically, we can distinguish three fundamental types of mobility according to the moving object: terminal mobility, personal mobility, and session mobility. Terminal mobility allows to maintain the network connection if the terminal is moving, i.e. keep the network address if the terminal changes its location. With user mobility, a user can consume services in the same way independently of the chosen terminal. E.g., a user can change the terminal and is still reachable with the same identifier. With session mobility, a user can continue to use an application session, even if he changes the terminal.

Orthogonal to the mobility types we classify mobility approaches according to the extent of continuity: services or sessions are either stopped before and continued after movements (discontinuity), or continue to be active during the movement (continuity). In the latter case, the movement can either lead to noticeable impact (non-seamless handover) or unnoticeable impact (seamless handover).

Our solution aims at session mobility in conjunction with user mobility. This means that we want to keep network connections with its identifiers persistent and move running application sessions from one device to another. Depending on the application and network or device performance, the continuity will go as far as enabling seamless handover. We call this complete session mobility.

2.2 Session Terminology

In order to transfer a session between two user devices we need to define a session concept. Fig. 1 shows that a service session consists of one application session at least. In case of non-communicating services, e.g. applications running on a user device without interaction across the network, or services that only communicate temporarily, there is no need for a communication session.

An application session is made up of at least one application state part. Several application state parts can exist to distinguish for example between control and media flows in case of VoIP communication. An application state part in turn can have associations to communication flows that make up the communication session. A communication flow needs to be identified, e.g. by the so called 5-tuple that consists of source and destination IP address, source and destination port and transport protocol. For example in case of TCP also a flow state exists. Moreover it might have an associated security context, e.g. to reflect a TLS [3] association. Communication flows of different communication sessions might depend on each other. For example in case of a security association on the network layer between two end systems all flows depend on each other.

The introduced model shows that we need solutions to transfer the application state and the state contained in the transport and network layer. Therefore, Section 3 introduces relevant proposals that have influenced the design of our framework.

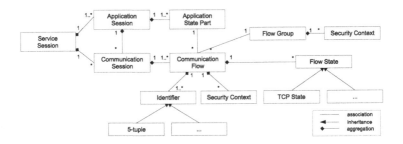

Fig. 1. Session Model

3   Related Work

For the transfer of service sessions we have investigated relevant technologies on the network layer that allow the redirection of traffic (c.f. Section 3.1), transport layer concepts (c.f. Section 3.2) and concepts that support session mobility on the application layer (c.f. Section 3.3). Moreover, we discuss several integrated approaches in Section 3.4.

3.1 Network Layer Mobility

At the design time of IP, hosts were static and IP address changes were rather seldom. Therefore, IP addresses are used to identify a host as well as its location in the network. With the advent of mobile devices, there is a need for solutions that allow the seamless change of IP addresses, and thus the redirection of the traffic to a different topological location, during a running communication session. A common approach on the network layer is to decouple the duality of the IP address and to introduce separate identifiers for hosts and their location in the network. Akyildiz et al. [4] provide an overview on mobility solutions on the network layer.

Basically we can distinguish two different approaches to support mobility: Tunnels and Signaling. Tunnel approaches [5] use a fixed anchor point in the network which redirects the traffic to the current IP address of the mobile device. With Signaling approaches [6,7] an explicit end-to-end signaling protocol is used to inform the the communication partner of the IP address change.

In Mobile IP (MIP) [5] without route optimization all traffic sent from the communication partner is forwarded via a tunnel by the home agent to the mobile node. Thus, the home agent serves as a fixed anchor point for the mobile node and maintains the mapping to the current IP address. Moreover, MIP supports an explicit signaling between the mobile node and the correspondent to overcome the drawbacks of triangular routing.

Approaches based on end-to-end signaling are Shim6 [6] and the Host Identity Protocol (HIP) [7]. Both approaches introduce some kind of additional layer between the transport and the network layer to eliminate the dual-use of IP addresses. This allows changing the IP address based on the exchange of signaling messages without interrupting an ongoing communication session. Both solutions have in common that the communication partner has to support the protocol. In contrast to Shim6, which solely operates on existing IP addresses, HIP introduces additional host identifiers to identify hosts.

All introduced approaches fit in our framework in order to redirect network traffic from one user device to another. In case of Mobile IP we need to update the binding of the home address, whereas in case of HIP and Shim6 we need to signal the update of the IP address and to transfer the corresponding state.

3.2 Mobility on the Transport Layer

Two mobility approaches can be identified on the transport layer: multihoming and device transition. Multihoming provides persistent transport connections despite changing IP addresses. Various techniques for supporting explicit handoff signaling in transport protocols are presented in [8]. In most cases such solutions are based on protocol extensions that need to be supported by the communication partner. Instead of extending the transport layer protocol [9,10] introduce an additional session layer between the application and the transport layer. Such solutions require the introduction of additional addressing concepts.

Beyond IP address changes, device transition enables the migration of transport connections between devices. We can differentiate solutions that extend existing protocols, e.g. TCP [11], and solutions without any involvement of the communication partner. This is done by extracting, manipulating and transferring OS internal transport protocol state information. Several sample implementations for Linux exist, such as SockMi [12] and tcpcp [13] that allow the transfer of TCP sockets. Since our framework is intended to support device transition, we focused on the latter approach for transport layer mobility.

3.3   Application Layer Mobility

Session mobility on the application layer has been thoroughly considered by different research communities. The SIP community has addressed the need to transfer a multimedia session from on device to another device based on the existing SIP protocol [1].

For the OS community it has been important to migrate complete processes [14] between different devices. This includes the transfer of the complete code and stack of the running process. We restrict ourself to the extraction of the application state via well-defined interfaces. This allows to support heterogeneous applications complying with a defined interface standard.

3.4   Integrated Approaches

Abeille proposed the Virtual Terminal concept [15] that supports session mobility with mobility solutions on the network layer in order to redirect traffic between different devices. In contrast to our architecture, the concept does neither consider the transfer of the application state nor the consequences on the transport layer. Similar to [15] is the approach proposed by [16] that is based on HIP. They have focused on extensions for HIP to transfer an HIP association between different hosts and claim that the framework can be extended to complete session mobility.

4   Architecture

4.1   Overview

Fig. 2 shows the architecture of our pluggable framework for session mobility. It consists of one central component per device, the Relocation Manager (RM), which coordinates the session transfer between two devices. In order to transfer a session it extracts all the required session state from so called adapter components via a generic interface A. Available adapter components register with the RM. Basically, three different kinds of adapter components can be distinguished

- **Network Adapters:** The network adapters turn commands via the A interface into technology specific actions in order to redirect the network traffic from one device to the other device. For example in case of HIP, a HIP network adapter it is required to transfer the corresponding security association from one device to the other device and to trigger an update of the IP address to redirect the traffic.

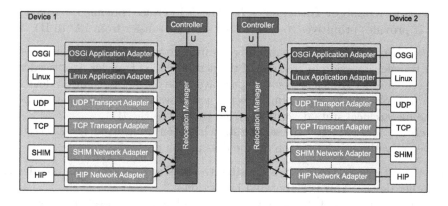

Fig. 2. Overview on the architecture

- **Transport Adapters:** The transport adapters extract transport layer specific information from the OS. In case of the TCP transport adapter all necessary state information is extracted from the OS in order to re-establish the socket on the other device.
- **Application Adapters:** On the application layer, the application adapters take care of the state extraction from the applications. An application needs to provide an application adapter specific interface for state export and import.

A session transfer is initiated and controlled via the Controller component that connects to the RM via the U interface.

4.2   Definition of Interfaces

Adapter Interface - A. The generic interface A between the adapters and the RM is used to import and export state from the network, transport and application layer. In our architecture, A provides the following primitives.

- *Suspend*: Freezes layer dependent state information which is going to be transferred from the exporting device (ED) to the importing device (ID).
- *Resume*: Unfreezes state information. An ID may resume work when called. Furthermore, an ED may resume work in case of session migration failures.
- *Shutdown*: Instructs an adapter to free all resources upon successful session migration.
- *Get Resources*: Queries for resources used by a network stack component.
- *Reserve Resources*: Checks and reserves resources for further use.
- *Get State*: Exports internal state information.
- *Set State*: Imports internal state information.
- *Do Presignaling*: Triggers signaling between ID or ED and peer device before transferring the session.
- *Do Postsignaling*: Triggers signaling between ID or ED and peer device after successful session migration.

Relocation Manager Interface - R. The R interface is defined between two RMs. It provides primitives to control the session transfer from ED to ID.

- *Check Preconditions*: This primitive is used to verify whether it is possible to transfer a session in advance of the actual session transfer. It is needed to check whether sufficient resources are available on the destination device.
- *Initiate Session Transfer*: Initiates the actual session transfer and transports the hierarchical state description from the ED to the ID.
- *Activate Session*: After the session state has been transferred, the ED triggers the activation of the session on the destination device.

With these three primitives it is possible to transfer a session from one device to another device. This is elaborated in Section 4.3.

For the description of the state we defined an hierarchical exchange format as illustrated in Fig. 3. It reflects the session model shown in Fig. 1. We distinguish the transfer of the application state, which is assumed to be a binary large object (BLOB), the transport state that reflects in most cases serialized structures out of the OS kernel, and the network state. Thus, the complete state description looks like this:

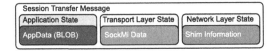

Fig. 3. Exchange format for session transfer

All message exchanges via the R interface are security critical, because they might contain sensitive information. Before the transfer of a session between devices can take place, devices need to mutually authenticate each other. Moreover, the messages exchanged need to be encrypted to prevent eavesdropping.

Controller Interface - U. The controller interface provides the corresponding controller component with information on the availabe sessions and allows for the initiation of session transfers. The primitives of this interface are subject to further study. Currently a user has to trigger the corresponding transfer manually.

4.3 Message Flow

For the transfer of sessions between user devices, two message flows are essential. First, a mechanism is required to discover user devices that are available for session transfer, which is discussed subsequently. Second, the message flow for the actual session transfer is elaborated.

Device Discovery. In order to know which devices are available for session transfer we assume for simplicity a centralized approach: All user devices register themselves with a central repository and update the registration periodically. The central repository serves as anchor point and must always be available. It allows a device to retrieve a list of all currently available devices and present it towards the user, who then triggers the session transfer. This mechanism could be enhanced based on service discovery protocols like Service Location Protocol [17]. Additional improvements could use beacon mechanisms or exploit geographic information in order to propose only close-by devices for session transfer.

Session Migration. Fig. 4 illustrates the message flow to transfer a session between the ED and the ID. For simplicity only one adapter is depicted. When the RM of the ED receives the *Export* command for a session, e.g. $S1$, it first sends a *Suspend* message to the adapter to freeze its internal state before obtaining information on the required resources. Afterwards the RM of the IM is contacted to check whether it has sufficient resources to take over the session. If the check is positive, the resources are reserved and confirmed. The *Do Presignaling* primitive provides the flexibility for additional steps that have to take place before the actual state can be extracted with *Get State*.

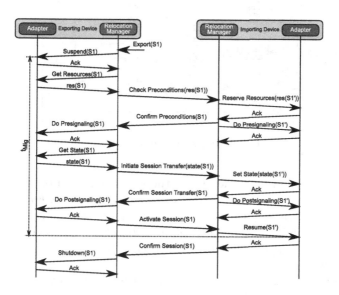

Fig. 4. Session migration message flow

Afterwards, the complete session state is transferred from ED to ID, which subsequently imports the state into the corresponding adapters. If *Set State* is successful, both RMs have the possibility to trigger additional steps with *Do Postsignaling*. Finally, the EM's RM activates the session and releases the remaining resources with *Shutdown*. The in Fig. 4 depicted session migration delay t_{Mig} has to be short in order to minimize the packet loss.

5 Implementation

We implemented the above introduced architecture on a Linux system running kernel 2.6.24. The implementation consists of three different adapters and the RM. Since we have not considered complex logic that triggers session transfers, user action to manually trigger session transfers is needed. On the application layer, a Linux application adapter allows the transfer of special adapted Linux applications. Such applications have to provide an interface that allows the import and export of the application state. For demonstration purposes we have implemented a simple echo server that provides the needed interfaces.

If the application has open TCP sockets, we are in the position to transfer the corresponding TCP transport layer state by using the SockMi [12] implementation in the TCP adapter. The transfer of open TCP sockets also requires the redirection of the corresponding traffic stream. We achieve this by exploiting the SHIM protocol and extended its implementation LinShim [18] to manipulate locator pairs.

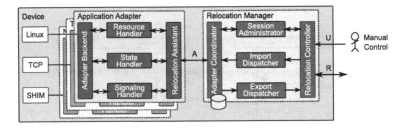

Fig. 5. Implemented architecture

Fig. 5 provides additional details on the implementation of the RM and the generic adapter design. The RM consists of an *Adapter Coordinator* that manages and communicates with the registered adapters based on the coordination by the *Session Administrator*. Data obtained from the adapters is (de-)serialized by the *Export* and *Import Dispatcher* in order to transport it by the R interface across the network.

The modular design of the adapters consists of functional blocks that are responsible for managing the resources required, the import and export of state, and the explicit signaling that needs to be triggered with the adapter backend. All activities are coordinated by the *Relocation Assistant*.

6 Summary and Conclusion

Our approach for complete session mobility moves running applications between devices while maintaining network connections. This includes transferring all state of open connections (e.g. TCP) between devices, so that the application can continue to use the connections as on the old device, as well as switching network identifiers between devices (e.g. with MIP, HIP).

We proposed a framework that collects state from applications and the network stack, moves it to a different device, and reestablishes the state required to continue the session there. The framework is kept flexible with generic interfaces for pluggable adapters to the specific mobility protocol or applications. We proofed the applicability of this approach by implementing a prototype with adapters for SHIM6 and TCP on Linux.

While our first tests are promising, some issues still have to be solved. First, switching IP addresses in active TCP connections is uncommon in today's IP networks. Thus, devices in the network that track the connection state (firewalls, NAT) cannot associate address switched TCP packets with connections and will block traffic. This could be resolved with appropriate signaling. Second, we considered transfer of TCP state with Linux only, while transferring TCP state between operating systems with different stack implementation demands for suitable transformation of state information in order to work correctly. Moreover, we need to conduct thorough performance measurements on the prototype and elaborate on security issues regarding the transfer of sessions between devices.

Acknowledgments

This work was supported in part by the European Union under the FP7 programme (SWIFT project).

References

1. Schulzrinne, H., Wedlund, E.: Application-Layer Mobility Using SIP. Mobile Comp. Comm. Rev. 4, 47–57 (2000)
2. ITU-T: ITU-T Recommendation Q.1706/Y.2801 (2006)
3. Dierks, T., et al.: The Transport Layer Security (TLS) Protocol Version 1.1. RFC 4346 (April 2006)
4. Akyildiz, I., et al.: A Survey of Mobility Management in Next-Generation All-IP-based Wireless Systems. IEEE Wireless Communications 11(4) (August 2004)
5. Johnson, D., et al.: Mobility Support in IPv6. RFC 3775 (June 2004)
6. Nordmark, E., Bagnulo, M.: Shim6: Level 3 Multihoming Shim Protocol for IPv6, draft-ietf-shim6-proto-12.txt. IETF Internet draft (February 2009)
7. Moskowitz, R., Nikander, P., Jokela, P., Henderson, T.: Host Identity Protocol. RFC 5201 (April 2008)
8. Atiquzzaman, M., et al.: Survey and Classification of Transport Layer Mobility Management Schemes. In: IEEE PIMRC 2005, September 2005, vol. 4. IEEE, Los Alamitos (2005)
9. Suri, N.: et al.: Mockets: A Comprehensive Application-level Communications Library. In: Proc. IEEE Military Communications Conference MILCOM 2005, October 17–20, 2005, pp. 970–976 (2005)
10. B., Landfeldt, et al.: SLM, A Framework for Session Layer Mobility Management. In: Proc. Eight International Conference on Computer Communications and Networks, October 11–13, 1999, pp. 452–456 (1999)

11. Sultan, F., et al.: Migratory TCP: Connection Migration for Service Continuity in the Internet. In: Proc. 22nd International Conference on Distributed Computing Systems, pp. 469–470 (2002)
12. Bernaschi, M., et al.: SockMi: A Solution for Migrating TCP/IP Connections. In: Proc. 15th EUROMICRO PDP 2007 (2007)
13. Almesberger, W.: Tcp connection passing. In: Proceedings of the Ottawa Linux Symposium 2004 (2004)
14. Milojičić, D.S., et al.: Process Migration. ACM Comput. Surv. 32(3) (2000)
15. Abeille, J., et al.: MobiSplit in a Virtualized, Multi-Device Environment. In: IEEE ICC 2007, Glasgow, Scotland (2007)
16. Koponen, T., et al.: Application Layer Mobility with HIP. In: ICT 2005 (2005)
17. Guttman, E., et al.: Service Location Protocol, Version 2. RFC 2608 (June 1999)
18. Barré, S.: LinShim6 - Implementation of the Shim6 Protocol. Technical report, Université Catholique de Louvain (2008)

A Model-Driven Approach for Telecommunications Network Services Definition

Vanea Chiprianov[1,3], Yvon Kermarrec[1,3], and Patrick D. Alff[2]

[1] Institut Telecom, Telecom Bretagne, UMR CNRS 3192 Lab-STICC
Technopole Brest Iroise, CS 83818 29238 Brest Cedes 3, France
{vanea.chiprianov,yvon.kermarrec}@telecom-bretagne.eu
[2] BT-North America
2160 E. Grand Ave, El Segundo, CA 90245, United States
[3] Universite europenne de Bretagne, France

Abstract. Present day Telecommunications market imposes a short concept-to-market time for service providers. To reduce it, we propose a computer-aided, model-driven, service-specific tool, with support for collaborative work and for checking properties on models. We started by defining a prototype of the Meta-model (MM) of the service domain. Using this prototype, we defined a simple graphical modeling language specific for service designers. We are currently enlarging the MM of the domain using model transformations from Network Abstractions Layers (NALs). In the future, we will investigate approaches to ensure the support for collaborative work and for checking properties on models.

1 Introduction

Present day Telecommunications customer-centric market, with its high demand rate and fierce competition, imposes a fast pace to service providers. To shorten the concept-to-market time, the service providers need to make their service definition more efficient by designing the product right-the-first-time. The current service definition process is largely based on trays of documents being exchanged between service designers and programmers. We contend that capturing the service definition knowledge into a computer-aided, model-driven (Sect. 2) design tool shortens this process and enables capitalization on previous experience.

Capturing domain specific knowledge may be done by iteratively constructing a Domain Definition Meta-model (DDMM), as presented in Sect. 3 and represented by the central entity in Fig. 1 (in this figure we represent with filled ellipses what we have already done; in parentheses we indicate the toolkit we used). Starting from the DDMM, we can define one or several Domain Specific Languages (DSLs) (Sect. 4) which increase the performance of service designers. The approach of defining several DSLs and semi-automatically generating tools (editors, checkers) for them from an information model has been previously proposed for policy-based management systems [1].

Defining a telecom service is a collaborative work which involves several designers. They need specific support for team work and especially a solution to

M. Oliver and S. Sallent (Eds.): EUNICE 2009, LNCS 5733, pp. 199–207, 2009.
© Springer-Verlag Berlin Heidelberg 2009

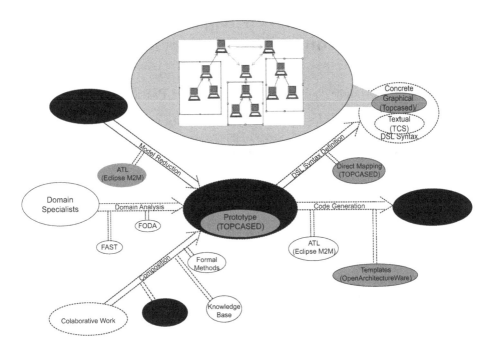

Fig. 1. Telecommunications-specific Modeling

put together their individual work into a composed definition of the service. We
discuss this aspect in Sect. 5, together with the need to verify and validate the
definition of a service. The DDMM can support the service designers in their
collaborative work when defining a new service and can also be used for verifying properties on models that were defined using the aforementioned DSLs.
Therefore, as highlighted by [2] also, the DDMM is central to our approach.

2   Model Driven Engineering

Model Driven Engineering (MDE) is a software engineering approach concerned
with bridging the conceptual gap between the problem and implementation domains by using as primary artifacts of development abstract models that describe
the system from multiple viewpoints and by providing automated support for
analyzing models and transforming them to concrete implementations. The basic
principle of MDE is *"everything is a model"* [3].

"A model represents reality for the given purpose; the model is an **abstraction**
*of reality in the sense that it cannot represent all aspects of reality. This allows us
to deal with the world in a* **simplified** *manner, avoiding the complexity, danger
and irreversibility of reality"* [4].

MDE main challenges have been recently surveyed by [5]:

1. Modeling language: how can one create and use problem-level abstractions in modeling languages;
2. Separation of concerns: how can one use multiple, possibly overlapping models of the same system described from several viewpoints, possibly in heterogeneous languages;
3. Model manipulation and management challenges: define, analyze and use model transformations, maintain traceability links among model elements, maintain consistency among viewpoints and use models during runtime.

In our approach of modeling services, we meet the same challenges. To address them, we propose:

1. A DSML, presented in Sect. 4, defined using a model-based approach.
2. An approach based on collaborative work, as presented in Sect. 5.
3. Using model transformations extensively, starting from constructing the DDMM from an NAL, as presented in Sect. 3, to connecting to tools that use formalisms that enable checking properties on models 5.

3   Elaborating the Domain Definition Meta-Model

We approached the definition of the DDMM with an iterative method in mind. We started with the definition of a simple MM, for prototype purposes. This prototype is aimed at defining a simple virtual private network (see Fig. 4). The prototype consists of a *Network*, which may contain several inner networks and several *Nodes*. The nodes are either *Computers*, *Internet* or *Routers*; they are connected by links which constitute outlinks for the source nodes, and inlinks for the target nodes. The routers can be either customer edge routers (*CE*) or provider edge routers (*PE*). Each PE and CE has an *Interface*, which contains a virtual routing and forwarding (*VRF*) table containing the VrfRouteTargets and information about the neighboring PEs (*BgpIpv4AddressFamilyNeighbors*). PEs use the Border Gateway Protocol (*BgpRoutingProtocol*) to communicate with each other. We also enriched the DDMM with validation rules [6], thus enabling domain level validation. As tool we chose TOPCASED [7], a strongly model oriented system engineering toolkit for critical and embedded applications.

We are currently working on enlarging the DDMM. For this, we start from existing NALs which are specified in UML and simplify them to suit the needs of service designers (see top left ellipses in Fig. 1). We specify the reduction rules using the ATL [8] model transformation language. Consequently, the reduction rules are written as model transformation rules. As presented in Fig. 2, a), model transformations are models themselves, conforming to their MM. They take as input one or several source models and produce as output one or several target models. In our case, Fig. 2, b) the transformation is endogenous (i.e.; the MM of the input model(s) is the same as the MM of the output model(s) - UML) and has one source (i.e.; NAL) and one target model (i.e.; DDMM). We exemplify the transformation rules in listing 1, which presents a rule that copies to the output model all classes from the input model that have at least one method.

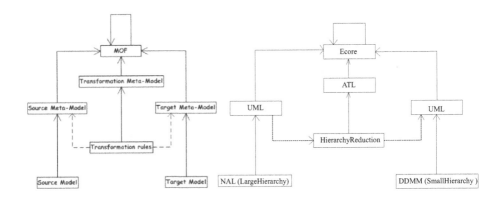

Fig. 2. a) MM-based model transformation (from [3]) and b) DDMM construction by model transformation

```
module HierarchyReductionUML; -- Module Template
create SmallHierarchyUML : UML from LargeHierarchyUML :
    UML;

rule Class {
    from
        cs : UML! Class (
            cs.ownedOperation->notEmpty())
    to
        ct : UML! Class (
            name <- cs.name,
            package <- cs.package,
            ownedOperation <- operationLst
            ),
        operationLst : distinct UML! Operation foreach
            (oper in cs.ownedOperation.asSequence())(
                name <- oper.name)
}
```

listing 1

We chose this approach because a NAL already captures a big part of the service domain, but in a much more detailed manner than necessary for a designer. By eliminating all entities that are unknown to service designers and shrinking the inheritance hierarchies, we believe we can elaborate a MM that is close to the service domain. In addition, such a MM would have the advantage of being easy to map to existing NALs. More details about this approach of constructing the DDMM by model transformation can be found in [9]. In the future, we consider enriching the DDMM obtained by reduction from NALs iteratively, by using specific domain analysis methods, such as Family-oriented Abstractions Specification and Translation [10] or Organization Domain Modeling v2 [11].

4 A Simple Graphical Telecommunications Specific Modeling Language (SGTSML)

*"A domain-specific language (DSL) is a programming language or executable specification language that offers, through appropriate notations and abstractions, **expressive power** focused on, and usually restricted to, a **particular problem domain**."*[12] The DSL development methodology has been extensively presented by [13].

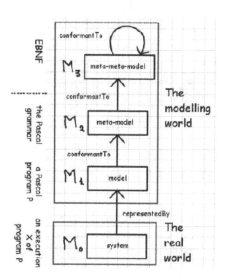

Fig. 3. Modelware and Grammarware (from [3])

On one hand, being a programming language, the definition process of a DSL has to be consistent with the definition process of any programming language. Consequently, an abstract syntax, a concrete syntax and a semantics have to be defined. On the other hand, [14] consider that *"a DSL is a set of coordinated models"*. The two points of view are not at all contradictory, as illustrated by Fig. 3, in which the correspondence between modelware and gramarware is illustrated (i.e.; to the language to describe the grammar of a programming language, in modelware it corresponds the meta-meta-model; to the grammar of the programming language it corresponds the MM and to the program itself it corresponds the model). The abstract syntax of a DSL can be modeled as the DDMM (Fig. 4), the concrete syntax can be represented as a "display surface" MM and the semantics can be obtained through a transformation model between the DDMM and, either the MM of a DSL with a precise execution, or the MM of a general purpose programming language (e.g.; Smalltalk).

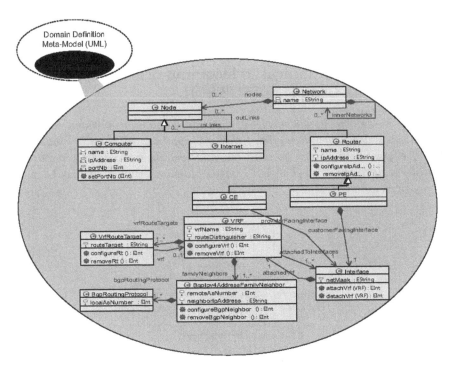

Fig. 4. Abstract Syntax of SGTSML

We tackled the construction of the DDMM in Sect. 3. For the concrete syntax (see top right filled ellipses in Fig. 1) we consider that a graphical syntax will be much easier to use by service designers, as it provides a synthetic, high-level view of the system being considered. Therefore, we defined one using TOPCASED, which has a feature that allows automatic generation of graphical editors for DSLs based on their MM. To describe the semantics of our SGTSML we decided to use the semantics of an existing general purpose programming language, Smalltalk (see right ellipses in Fig. 1). Consequently, we defined templates for code generation towards Smalltalk, using OpenArchitectureWare [15]. More details about the definition of SGTSML can be found in [6]. In the future, we intend to extend the concrete graphical syntax to represent the entire enlarged DDMM and to define a concrete textual syntax too, using tools such as TCS [16], or more classical approaches, such as compilers or translators.

5   Towards Collaborative Work and Checking Properties on Models

Using the modeling language, the designers will define a service. However, because a service is a complex entity, several designers are required to collaborate for its definition. Therefore, we must provide them with adequate communication and interaction tools. We plan to construct a knowledge base which will contain the decisions that are taken during service definition and their justifications, a design rationale system [17]. We are considering also a form of behavior modeling and model composition, but have yet to investigate and decide between UML State Machines, formal methods, ontologies or other approaches.

We are studying as well methods to ensure the models produced by service designers are valid. We envisage defining model transformations from the MM (abstract syntax) of the modeling language towards the MM of formalisms that are capable of verifying a number of properties of interest on the models defined using the modeling language. However, we have yet to identify the properties of interest and the best formalisms to check them.

6   Advantages and Disadvantages of Taking a Model-Driven Approach for Service Definition

Rapid tool prototyping. When defining a language, tools like editors, syntax checkers, compilers need to be provided together with the language. Evolving these tools together with the language can be a very time consuming task when using the classic language theory. To reduce this time, MDE proposes meta-tools: tools to define other language-specific tools. With their help, language tools can be rapidly defined and maintained during the evolution of the language. Moreover, the freed resources can be redirectioned towards other activities.

Independence from the implementation platform. The service model build using our DSML will not contain any platform details, it will be a platform independent platform (PIM). This ensures the reusability of the model, which contains only the business logic. Of course, this model needs to be implemented on several platforms, so the details of each platform are described in a platform specific model (PSM). Consequently, the PIM should contain concepts which are abstractions of those from the PSMs. This is what we are trying to ensure by building our DDMM (i.e.; the MM of the PIM) from existing NALs (i.e.; PSMs).

Iterating definition of the DDMM. The construction of the DDMM is a difficult task. It consists in extracting the abstractions of the domain, verifying that the MM is complete (i.e.; all necessary concepts and actions can be expressed), taking care that it remains in the intended scope. This is a long process, which takes years and implies many changes. Moreover, the domain itself evolves over the years. Having the flexibility of iteratively defining the DDMM ensures that the tools and the models will keep the pace with the changes in the domain.

Tool connection through interchangeable models. MDE proposes an XML representation of the models. Like in the case of web services, the models become interchangeable between different tools, programming languages. Connecting to existing model-based schedulability, performance or other property analysis tools becomes possible.

Poor meta-tool configuration power. In order to provide its most important feature - domain specificity - a DSL needs a specific concrete syntax. For this, the language meta-tools need to be highly configurable (e.g.; for a graphical syntax, allow to define the position of the pallet). This is not true for the current tools (e.g.; the icon definition problem with TOPCASED described in [6]).

7   Conclusions

Our purpose is to replace the current paper-based service design process with a more computer-aided version. For this, we prototyped a DDMM and used it to define a SGTSML. We are currently working at enlarging this DDMM through simplifications from existing NALs. Using a model-driven approach has provided us with powerful advantages. In the future, we plan to integrate support for collaborative work and for checking properties on models in the language, but have yet to investigate the best approaches.

References

1. Barrett, K., Davy, S., Strassner, J., Jennings, B., van der Meer, S., Donnelly, W.: A Model Based Approach for Policy Tool Generation and Policy Analysis. In: Proceedings of the IEEE Global Information Infrastructure Symposium (2007)
2. Fahy, C., Davy, S., Boudjemil, Z., van der Meer, S., Loyola, J., Serrat, J., Strassner, J., Berl, A., de Meer, H., Macedo, D.: Towards an Information Model That Supports Service-Aware, Self-managing Virtual Resources. In: Proc. of the 3rd IEEE internat. workshop on Modelling Autonomic Communications Environments (2008)
3. Bezivin, J.: In search of a basic principle for model driven engineering. Novatica Journal 2, 21–24 (2004)
4. Rothenberg, J.: The nature of modeling. In: Artificial Intelligence, Simulation, and Modeling (1989)
5. France, R., Rumpe, B.: Model-driven development of complex software: A research roadmap. In: FOSE 2007, pp. 37–54 (2007)
6. Chiprianov, V., Kermarrec, Y.: Model-based DSL Frameworks: A Simple Graphical Telecommunications Specific Modeling Language. In: Actes des 5 émes journées sur l'Ingénierie Dirigée par les Modéles, Nancy (2009)
7. Farail, P., Gaufillet, P., Canals, A., Le Camus, C., Sciamma, D., Michel, P., Cregut, X., Pantel, M.: The TOPCASED project: a Toolkit in Open source for Critical Aeronautic Systems Design. In: ERTS (2006)
8. Bezivin, J., Dupe, G., Jouault, F., Pitette, G., Rougui, J.: First experiments with the ATL model transformation language: Transforming XSLT into XQuery. In: 2nd OOPSLA Workshop on Generative Techniques in the context of MDA (2003)
9. Chiprianov, V., Kermarrec, Y.: An Approach for Constructing a Domain Definition Metamodel with ATL. In: Model Transformation with ATL, First International Workshop, Nantes (to be published, 2009)
10. Coplien, J., Hoffman, D., Weiss, D.: Commonality and Variability in Software Engineering. IEEE Softw 15, 37–45 (1998)
11. Simos, M., Anthony, J.: Weaving the Model Web: A Multi-Modeling Approach to Concepts and Features in Domain Engineering. In: ICSR 1998 (1998)

12. Deursen, A.V., Klint, P., Visser, J.: Domain-specific languages: an annotated bibliography. SIGPLAN Not. 35, 26–36 (2000)
13. Mernik, M., Heering, J., Sloane, A.M.: When and how to develop domain-specific languages. ACM Comput. Surv. 37, 316–344 (2005)
14. Kurtev, I., Bezivin, J., Jouault, F., Valduriez, P.: Model-based DSL frameworks. In: OOPSLA 2006, pp. 602–616 (2006)
15. Features, C.: openArchitectureWare 4.2. Technical report, Eclipse (2007)
16. Jouault, F., Bezivin, J., Kurtev, I.: TCS: a DSL for the specification of textual concrete syntaxes in model engineering. In: Proceedings of the 5th internat. conf. on Generative programming and component engineering (2006)
17. Regli, W.C., Hu, X., Atwood, M., Sun, W.: A survey of design rationale systems: Approaches, representation, capture and retrieval. Eng. with Computers (2000)

Detecting Spam at the Network Level

Anna Sperotto, Gert Vliek, Ramin Sadre, and Aiko Pras

University of Twente
Centre for Telematics and Information Technology
Faculty of Electrical Engineering, Mathematics and Computer Science
P.O. Box 217, 7500 AE Enschede, The Netherlands
{a.sperotto,r.sadre,a.pras}@utwente.nl,
g.vliek@student.utwente.nl

Abstract. Spam is increasingly a core problem affecting network security and performance. Indeed, it has been estimated that 80% of all email messages are spam. Content-based filters are a commonly deployed countermeasure, but the current research focus is now moving towards the early detection of spamming hosts. This paper investigates if spammers can be detected at the network level, based on just flow data. This problem is challenging, since no information about the content of the email message is available. In this paper we propose a spam detection algorithm, which is able to discriminate between benign and malicious hosts with 92% accuracy.

1 Introduction

Spam is a problem that all Internet users experience in their everyday lives. Symantec Corporation estimates that over 80% of all emails sent in 2008 were spam, a trend that, with a touch of irony, the company considers to be "normal" [1]. The reason we are constantly flooded with unsolicited messages is that spam is profitable. As such, spam detection is likely to remain an "open battlefield" in the coming years.

Nowadays, the most common countermeasures against spam are spam filters. Mail servers usually host the core of spam filtering operations: tools such as Spamassassin [2] reject or accept email messages based on their content. Moreover, many mail clients also locally scan the user's inbox. However, spam messages are designed to look similar to legitimate emails: examples are "phishing" emails that ask you to provide your bank details. Such camouflaging behavior reduces the effectiveness of content-based methods.

We propose a spam detection approach that does not rely on content information. More specifically, our contribution is based on network flows, defined as "a set of IP packets passing an observation point in the network during a certain time interval and having a set of common properties" [3]. These common properties typically include source/destination addresses/ports and protocol type, and they unequivocally define a flow. Flows have recently received great attention in the research community [4], since they allow scalable network monitoring of large infrastructures. Flows typically only report information about the amount of packets and bytes exchanged during a connection, but nothing about the content of the communication.

M. Oliver and S. Sallent (Eds.): EUNICE 2009, LNCS 5733, pp. 208–216, 2009.
© Springer-Verlag Berlin Heidelberg 2009

In this context, spam detection is a challenge. This paper aims to address the following question: *Is it possible to detect hosts from which spam originates by using just flow data?* More specifically, we want to investigate (a) if spam differs from legitimate SMTP traffic at the flow level and (b) how to detect spam at the flow level. The paper summarizes the results of the MSc thesis of Gert Vliek. More details about the approach can be found in [5].

The general assumption in the research community is that a spammer host will behave differently from a legitimate mail server [6,7,8]. Capturing this behavior at the network level can lead to the development of powerful tools for early spam detection, easing both the server-side load and the filtering in the client. One contribution in this field is the work of Desikan et al. [9], in which the analysis of time-evolving SMTP connection graphs helps distinguish between mail servers and spammers. A different approach is that taken by Ramachandran et al. [6]. The authors' assumption is that the network behavioral patterns of a spamming host are far less variable than the spam content itself. They therefore propose a spam detection approach based on automatic clustering and classification of sender IP addresses that show a similar behavior over a short observation time. More attention to flow approaches has been given in the works of Schatzmann et al. [7,8] and Cheng et al. [10]. In [7,8], the authors suggest that the average number of bytes, packets and bytes/packets of failed, rejected and accepted connections are flow properties suitable for the classification of spam flows. The authors rely on server logs for flow classification. On the other hand, in [10], the authors propose an alternative definition of flows that allows the stateful analysis of spam traffic. Finally, Žádník et al. [11] propose the use of classification trees for spam identification based on flow characteristic.

Compared to the previously mentioned contributions, we propose a spam detection algorithm that relies on Netflow compatible flow data and allows the detection of spamming hosts based on just network characteristics.

This paper is organized as follows. Section 2 describes SMTP traffic from a flow perspective, highlighting the differences between a normal and a suspicious host. In Section 3 we present our spam detection algorithm, followed by a validation of our approach in Section 4. Conclusions are drawn in Section 5.

2   SMTP Traffic at the Flow Level

It is a common assumption that a spamming host's behavior will differ from legitimate SMTP servers. Yet it is interesting to see if this assumption holds in real traffic.

The University of Twente, for example, relies on a system of five load-balanced mail servers, all of them having a similar behavior. Figure 1(a) shows the outgoing SMTP traffic time-series of one of them. Each time slot on the x-axis corresponds to a 5 minutes interval, for a total of five days of observation. There is one main aspect in the mail server behavior. The mail server presents a rather constant activity baseline at around 100 connections per time slot that rarely rises above 250 connections per time slot. This aspect is very significant in our case since it shows that a legitimate mail server is characterized by a steady level of usage. Figure 1(b), on the other hand, shows the outgoing SMTP traffic time series for a host known to have sent spam. Its

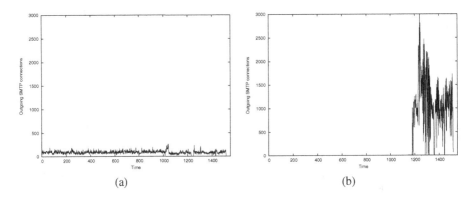

Fig. 1. Flow level behavior for a university mail server (a) and a suspicious machine (b)

network behavior is totally different from the one in Figure 1(a): the time series is characterized by sudden and prolonged activity peaks and a long period in which there is no traffic. Moreover, no usage baseline is present, at the contrary of the mail server. A deeper analysis of the spammer host behavior also reveals that there is no incoming traffic, suggesting that the host has no real traffic exchanges. This behavior is commonly observed in other hosts that have sent spam.

This example suggests that the behavior of suspicious hosts differs substantially from that of legitimate mail servers. Parameters such the incoming and outgoing traffic, as well as the widely variable level of usage can be useful in defining an algorithm for automatic spam detection.

3   An Algorithm for Spam Detection

In the previous section, we showed qualitatively that the network behavior of suspicious and legitimate hosts could be very different. We now propose an algorithm that will detect, based on just flow information, hosts that are most likely to be spammers. The algorithm consists of two main phases and a post-processing step. In the first phase, hosts that do not satisfy three basic selection criteria are filtered out. This phase aims to reduce the amount of data to be analyzed and to improve the overall performance of the algorithm. The hosts selected in the first phase are then ranked in the second phase by means of five ordering criteria according to their likelihood of being spammers. Finally, ranked hosts are once again filtered according to a post-processing criterion. The algorithm analyzes the SMTP traffic sent and received from the network that is monitored. Of course, this means spam traffic generated by a spammer outside the monitored network and targeting a different network cannot be considered for the analysis. However, the results show that it is not necessary to have a complete overview of all the traffic generated by a spammer to achieve a good detection level.

The selection and ordering criteria are explained in Sections 3.1 and 3.2, respectively. The criteria that we propose are based on the analysis of a data set of seven days of SMTP traffic captured at the University of Twente. We describe the resulting algorithm in Section 3.3.

3.1 Selection Criteria

The selection criteria allow us to concentrate, in the second phase, on a smaller subset of hosts. Therefore, in order to be further analyzed, a host has to satisfy all the selection criteria. The selection criteria aim to filter out at an early stage the majority the not-malicious clients. These criteria are defined as follows:

SC$_1$ Number of outgoing connections: We only select hosts that exhibit a certain level of activity:

$$\text{number of outgoing SMTP connections} > \theta_1 \qquad (1)$$

SC$_2$ Connection ratio: A host is suspicious if it sends far more than it receives. The connection ratio criterion is defined as:

$$\frac{\text{number incoming SMTP connections}}{\text{number of outgoing SMTP connections}} < \theta_2 \qquad (2)$$

SC$_3$ Number of distinct destinations: Criterion **SC$_1$** could also flag as suspicious a host that relies on SMTP as logging mechanism (as a printer, for instance). Such a host would probably not receive any message. Nevertheless, such host would usually report to only a limited number of destinations, while a spammer would typically diversify its destinations. A threshold for the minimum number of distinct destinations is used for discriminating these cases:

$$\text{number of distinct destinations} > \theta_3 \qquad (3)$$

3.2 Ordering Criteria

Once the suspicious hosts have been selected by applying the selection criteria, we apply the ordering criteria to rank them according to their likelihood of being spammers. While the selection criteria are combined into a binary decision, the ordering criteria yield values from a to e that are later combined into a total score for each host.

OC$_1$ Number of incoming connections: This criterion is a refinement of **SC$_2$**. We assume that spammers are not interested in receiving SMTP connections. Therefore, a host that does not have any incoming connection is more likely to be a spammer than one that has incoming SMTP traffic. The score is calculated as follows:

$$a = \begin{cases} 1 \text{ if number of incoming SMTP connections} = 0 \\ 0 \text{ otherwise} \end{cases} \qquad (4)$$

OC$_2$ Number of distinct destination: This criterion is a refinement of **SC$_3$**. We assume that a spammer would try to diversify its destinations. Therefore, hosts with a high number of distinct destinations are suspicious. We define the score b as:

$$b = \begin{cases} 1 \text{ if number of distinct destination servers} > \theta_4 \\ 0 \text{ otherwise} \end{cases} \qquad (5)$$

OC$_3$ Percentage of idle time: We assume that hosts with long idle periods are more suspicious than hosts that communicate more regularly over time. We define the score c as:

$$c = \text{percentage of idle time} \qquad (6)$$

OC$_4$ Irregularity in activity: Our studies suggest that a suspicious host tends to have a highly irregular transmission pattern. We assume that a host that has a high standard deviation σ of the number of outgoing SMTP flows per 5 minute time slot is more suspicious than one with a low one. We define the score d as:

$$d = \begin{cases} 1 \text{ if } \sigma > \theta_5 \\ 0 \text{ otherwise} \end{cases} \qquad (7)$$

OC$_5$ Number of peaks: We assume a suspicious host to show sudden traffic peaks. We define peaks as time slots where the number of outgoing connections is higher than $(\mu + k \cdot \sigma)$. μ and σ are respectively the mean and the standard deviation of the number of outgoing connections per 5 minute time slot for the host, and k is a parameter that influences the sensitivity of the measure. Hosts with a high number of peaks are therefore more suspicious. We define the score e as:

$$e = \begin{cases} 1 \text{ if } |\{\text{slots where connection rate} > (\mu + k \cdot \sigma)\}| > \theta_6 \\ 0 \text{ otherwise} \end{cases} \qquad (8)$$

3.3 The Detection Algorithm

Algorithm 1 presents the pseudocode for the detection procedure. As explained earlier, the first phase filters hosts according to the three selection criteria (lines 4 through 6). However, in order to keep the algorithm efficient, we only consider the n most active hosts, in terms of outgoing connections, that satisfy the criteria (lines 3 and 7).

In the second phase, the hosts are scored and ordered according to the ordering criteria (lines 11 through 17). For the overall score v, we calculate the average of the single scores a through e. While ranking the hosts, the algorithm also selects a subset of them that, in conjunction with the ranking, are most likely to be spammers. More specifically, only hosts that are not involved in any traffic exchange for the majority of the observation time γ are considered (line 13). This filtering permits the discrimination between hosts that have a fairly constant behavior and hosts that only transmit in bursts, as for example the hosts in Figure 1.

Finally, the algorithm only reports the m top ranked hosts (line 18). The parameter m allows tuning of the output according to the desired security level.

4 Experimental Results and Validation

Section 4.1 will describe our approach to the validation of our results. Next, in Section 4.2 we will describe our experimental setup and the results we obtained. Finally, Section 4.3 presents a study on the impact of each criterion on the performance of the algorithm.

Algorithm 1. Spam detection procedure

1: **procedure** SpamDetection(Q : host set)
2: $S_1 = \emptyset$; $S_2 = \emptyset$;
3: **for all** $x \in Q$ ordered by decreasing number of outgoing connections **do**
4:      **if** x satisfies $\mathbf{SC_1} \wedge \mathbf{SC_2} \wedge \mathbf{SC_3}$ **then**
5:          $S_1 := S_1 \cup \{x\}$;
6:      **end if**
7:      **if** $|S_1| = n$ **then**
8:          **break**;
9:      **end if**
10: **end for**
11: **for all** $y \in S_1$ **do**
12:     Compute $v := \frac{1}{5} \cdot (a + b + c + d + e)$;
13:     **if** $c > \gamma$ **then**
14:         $S_2 := S_2 \cup \{y\}$;
15:     **end if**
16: **end for**
17: Order elements in S_2 by decreasing value of v;
18: **return** top m elements in S_2;

4.1   Validation Approach

Since we based our algorithm on flows, no information about the content of the SMTP connections is available. We therefore need to rely on external services in order to evaluate our results. DNS blacklists (DNSBL) are Internet services that publish lists of offending IP addresses: in our context, IPs that have been involved in spamming activities. Spam DNSBL are repositories which content is likely to rapidly change over time: indeed, a blacklisted host can be rehabilitated if it is no longer involved in spamming activities for a sufficiently long period. Iverson [12] periodically monitors the most commonly used DNSBL and reports on their reliability.

We selected five DNSBL as trusted sources for validation: zen.spamhaus.org, bl.spamcop.net, safe.dnsbl.sorbs.net, psbl.surriel.com and dnsbl.njabl.org. We chose this set of DNSBL because they clearly indicate under which conditions a host is going to be added and removed from the list. We define a host to be *positively validated* if it has been blacklisted in at least one of the five DNSBL we are considering.

4.2   Experimental Settings and Results

We evaluate our algorithm over three data sets collected at the University of Twente: a reference data set used to developed the algorithm and two newly collected data sets referred as *Set 1* and *Set 2* in the following. Each data set spans over a period of seven days, with an average of $\sim$15M flows. The time windows over which the data sets span are not overlapping. The implementation of our approach uses SQL scripts and can process a data set in a period of 5 hours.

In our experiments, we measure the *accuracy* of the method, defined as:

$$accuracy = \frac{|\{\text{positively validated}\}|}{m} \qquad (9)$$

where m is the number of hosts reported as output by the algorithm and it can be set according to the desired security level. We decided not to compute the false positive and false negative rate since it is not possible to establish a ground truth. For the hosts that we report as suspicious and that are not listed in any DNSBL, indeed, we are unable to say if they are (a) spammers that are not yet listed (true positive) or (b) normal hosts (false positive).

Table 1. Criteria parameter settings chosen for the experiments

Parameter	Value	Parameter	Value	Parameter	Value	Parameter	Value
θ_1	200	θ_2	0.005	θ_3	5	θ_4	10
θ_5	1	θ_6	50	k	5	γ	80%

Table 1 shows which parameter values have been used in the experiments. The parameters have been manually tuned based on the statistical properties of the reference data set. We measured that only 5% of the hosts we analyzed have more than 200 connections ($\theta_1 = 200$). In a similar way, only 1% of the hosts have more than 10 distinct destinations ($\theta_4 = 10$). Less than 20% of the hosts present a standard deviation $\sigma > 1$ of the number of outgoing connections per time slot ($\theta_5 = 1$). Moreover, only 1% of the hosts have more that 50 peaks (for $k = 5$, $\theta_6 = 50$). The remaining parameters are specific to the network we are analyzing. In particular, as said in Section 2, the University of Twente relies on 5 mail servers. Therefore, we set $\theta_3 = 5$. In our network, high volume SMTP sources might receive a limited amount of incoming connections ($\theta_2 = 0.005$) and, for an observation window of seven days, spammers have shown to be idle for at least 80% of the time ($\gamma = 80\%$). Finally, the algorithm selects $n = 20,000$ hosts that satisfy the selection criteria and outputs the top $m = 100$ hosts according to the ordering criteria.

Our experimental results show that, on average, the accuracy of the system is 92%. Table 2 presents the detection accuracy for each of the considered data sets. We observe that our algorithm reaches an overall accuracy of 99% in the reference data set, while the accuracy slowly decreases in the newly collected data sets. This phenomenon suggests that the parameters chosen for our experiments might need to be periodically re-tuned according to spam flow characteristics.

4.3   Criteria Impact

In Section 3 we introduced the criteria we used in our detection algorithm. We now evaluate the impact of each single criterion to the overall detection accuracy of the algorithm. We start evaluating the impact of the only selection criteria $\mathbf{SC}_1$ and incrementally add one criterion at each run. We measure the overall accuracy on the data set

Table 2. Detection accuracy for the considered data sets

Data set	Time window	Accuracy
Reference set	18 – 24 November 2008	99%
Set 1	2–7 April 2009	96%
Set 2	8–14 April 2009	81%

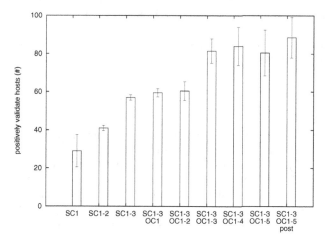

Fig. 2. Impact of the selection and ordering criteria on the overall accuracy

Set 1 and *Set 2* presented in Table 2. Figure 2 shows the average trend of the accuracy curve with respect to the number of applied criteria. The error bars indicate the standard deviation of the number of validated hosts w.r.t. *Set 1* and *Set 2*. Selection criteria SC_1 and ordering criteria OC_3 have the most impact on the accuracy measure, meaning that a high number of connections in a short period of time (bursts) is a key characteristic of a spamming host. Moreover, the accuracy measure presents an increasing trend, meaning that each criterion is beneficial to the detection process. The only exception is OC_5: in data set *Set 1*, indeed, the criterion forces a decrease of the accuracy, suggesting that under certain condition this criterion may report false positives (legitimate hosts flagged as spammers).

5   Conclusions

This paper investigates if it is possible to detect spammers at the flow level, without relying on email content. Our findings show that the network behavior of suspicious hosts differs substantially from that of a legitimate mail server, both in activity level and incoming/outgoing traffic patterns. Based on these observations, we propose a detection algorithm that makes use of just flow information. Our algorithm has been validated using trusted blacklisting services. The results show that we can detect spamming machines with a 92% accuracy for the traces on which we validate our approach, meaning that the algorithm has a low probability to report false positives (host that are not spammers, but they are flagged as such).

Our work is a first step in flow-based spam detection. In the future, we are interested in assessing the *completeness* of our system, in terms of undetected spamming hosts (false negatives). Moreover, we plan to study how our approach behaves in the presence of very peculiar services, for example a server that is only used for mailing lists. It might happen, indeed, that such systems rank high according to our algorithm, suggesting that other metrics can be added to filter them out. We are also interested in extending our approach to different scenarios, for example Botnet detection.

Acknowledgments. This research has been supported by the EC IST-EMANICS Network of Excellence (#26854).

References

1. Symantec Enterprise Security: The state of spam, a monthly report (February 2009)
2. Spamassassin (March 2009), http://spamassassin.apache.org
3. Quittek, J., Zseby, T., Claise, B., Zander, S.: Requirements for IP Flow Information Export (IPFIX). RFC 3917 (Informational)
4. Sperotto, A., Schaffrath, G., Sadre, R., Morariu, C., Pras, A., Stiller, B.: An Overview of IP Flow-based Intrusion Detection. IEEE Surverys & Tutorials (to appear, 2009)
5. Vliek, G.: Detecting spam machines, a Netflow–data based approach. Master's thesis (Feburary 2009),
   http://essay.utwente.nl/58583/1/scriptie_G_Vliek.pdf
6. Ramachandran, A., Feamster, N., Vempala, S.: Filtering spam with behavioral blacklisting. In: Proc. of the 14th ACM conference on Computer and Communications Security, CCS 2007 (2007)
7. Schatzmann, D., Burkhart, M., Spyropoulos, T.: Flow-level Characteristics of Spam and Ham. Technical Report TIK Report Nr. 291, Computer Engineering and Networks Laboratory, ETH, Zurich (August 2008)
8. Schatzmann, D., Burkhart, M., Spyropoulos, T.: Inferring Spammers in the Network Core. In: Proc. of 10th International Conference on Passive and Active Network Measurement, PAM 2009 (2009)
9. Desikan, P., Srivastava, J.: Analyzing Network Traffic to Detect E–Mail Spamming Machines. In: Proc. of the 2004 ICDM Workshop on Privacy and Security Aspects of Data Mining, PSDM 2004 (2004)
10. Cheng, B.-C., Chen, M.-J., Chu, Y.-S., Chen, A., Yap, S., Fan, K.-P.: SIPS: A stateful and flow-based intrusion prevention system for email applications. In: Li, K., Jesshope, C., Jin, H., Gaudiot, J.-L. (eds.) NPC 2007. LNCS, vol. 4672, pp. 334–343. Springer, Heidelberg (2007)
11. Žádník, M., Michlovský, Z.: Is spam visible in flow-level statistic? Technical report, CESNET 6/2008 (2008)
12. Iverson, A.: Blacklist statistic center (March 2009), http://stats.dnsbl.com/

Consistency Analysis of Network Traffic Repositories

Elmer Lastdrager and Aiko Pras

University of Twente, the Netherlands
e.e.h.lastdrager@student.utwente.nl, a.pras@utwente.nl

Abstract. Traffic repositories with TCP/IP header information are very important for network analysis. Researchers often assume that such repositories reliably represent all traffic that has been flowing over the network; little thoughts are made regarding the consistency of these repositories. Still, for various reasons, the traffic capturing process may have missed packets. For certain kinds of analysis, for example loss measurements, such inconsistencies may lead to the wrong conclusions.

This paper proposes an algorithm to detect such inconsistencies, using the idea of "fake gaps". A prototype has been developed, and used to test two well-known repositories: the WIDE and Simpleweb repositories. The paper shows that both repositories contain several inconsistencies.

1   Introduction

A network traffic repository contains network traffic gathered from one or more location(s), often a router or backbone. Captured traffic is stored in data files in a repository; typically such files contain data captured over a longer period, for example minutes, hours or even days. Repositories can store different types of network data, for example TCP/IP header files, netflow records or SNMP packets. In this paper the focus is on the most common type: TCP/IP header data.

Using a repository can be very convenient for a researcher, as gathering data yourself can be very time-consuming, or even impossible. A potential issue in using a repository, is the consistency of the traffic inside the repository. When traffic inside a repository does not completely correspond with the actual traffic that was transmitted and received, this can influence measurements, analysis and therefore also conclusions that researchers draw. Hence, it is critical to have information about the consistency of the network traffic repository, so it can be taken into account when analysing the data.

Issues with consistency of the data in repositories have been reported by M. Timmer in [1]. While using a repository, it appeared that not all data was recorded properly. Timmer introduces the term "fake gap" to represent those

M. Oliver and S. Sallent (Eds.): EUNICE 2009, LNCS 5733, pp. 217–226, 2009.
© Springer-Verlag Berlin Heidelberg 2009

parts of a TCP flow that are absent in the repository, although they were acknowledged at the TCP level. In [2] a relatively simple algorithm has been developed to find a sudden decrease in data in small intervals, which may indicate a problem with the repository. However it may very well be a temporary network problem and therefore does not necessarily affect the consistency of the repository. Although [2] has performed some initial research, the consistency analysis never exceeded a few data files. However, as researcher, knowledge about inconsistency in a repository is essential. At this moment, there are no statistics about possible inconsistency of repositories available. In this paper we will therefore analyse two well-known repositories: the WIDE and Simpleweb repositories. A tool has been developed that analyses TCP flows. We focus on TCP, because its state-full nature allows detection of fake gaps; for UDP this is, due to its stateless nature, not possible.

In this paper, the main question that will be answered is: *How can inconsistency be detected in a TCP traffic repository?*

To answer the main question, we first have a look at possible inconsistencies by answering a sub question: *What could cause inconsistencies in a TCP traffic repository?*

Next, we will focus on detecting fake gaps by introducing an algorithm. The sub question we will answer is: *How can we detect fake gaps?*

Next, we built a prototype of the algorithm to test existing repositories in order to answer the second sub question: *How consistent are today's repositories?*

It should be noted that a short version, covering roughly half of this paper, has already been published at AIMS 2009 [3]. Furthermore, an earlier version of this paper has been presented at the tenth Twente Student Conference on Information Technology [4]. That conference is an internal conference of the University of Twente, of which the proceedings have not officially been published by a real publisher.

The structure of this paper is as follows. In Section 2 we will briefly identify possible causes that could lead to inconsistent repositories. In Section 3 we will propose an algorithm to detect inconsistency and introduce the prototype we built. In Section 4 this prototype will be evaluated. In Section 5 we will discuss the results of testing two existing repositories using the prototype and finally in Section 6 we will answer our research questions, draw conclusions and discuss possible future work.

2   Causes for Inconsistency

In this Section, we will think of ways a repository can become inconsistent. We do not intend to be complete and provide an in-depth analysis. Instead, we intend to show the reader possible issues that could lead to inconsistency. Inconsistency in a repository occurs only when the recording device failed to record the actual traffic that was sent. We distinguish issues at the switch or router side (where the traffic is copied) and issues at the recording device itself.

2.1   At the Side of the Switch

For recording data, the *port mirroring* feature of a switch can be used. This is a method of recording data without interfering with the regular operation [5]. Port mirroring is used to copy all traffic from one, or more, port(s) at the switch to another port of the switch, called the *mirror port*. When the traffic from only one port is copied to the mirror port, there shouldn't be any problem as long as the bandwidth on the mirror port is greater than, or equal to, the bandwidth of the source port. However, the situation in which all traffic is copied to the mirror port is more interesting. In this case, the mirror port could be overloaded when the bandwidth used by all source ports combined is too large for it to handle. For example, a common 'mistake' is when traffic from a full-duplex 1 Gbit/sec port is mirrored to a 1 Gbit/sec monitoring port. Since the original traffic can be 1 Gbit/sec for each direction, the total amount of data the mirror port may have to forward is 2 Gbit/sec.

When traffic is dropped due to limited bandwidth of the mirror port, the recording device will record incomplete traffic and thus introduce inconsistencies. Avoiding this is relatively easy in theory, by making sure the bandwidth of the mirror port is sufficient. In practice, however, the costs of high-speed interfaces may prevent adequate dimensioning of the mirror port.

2.2   At the Recording Device

A second way a repository could become inconsistent, is when there are issues at the side of the recording device. A recording device can be a (desktop)computer or server gathering data. Commonly a recording device is connected to a router or switch using port mirroring. When it receives more packets than it can handle, the device will start dropping packets.

A study by Deri in 2004 showed that packet capture with standard (libpcap) software may result in heavy packet loss [7]. For example, Windows 2000 showed a packet loss of 32% and Linux 2.4 even over 99%. The problem, in general, are interrupts, since packet handling is performed by the kernel. For 100 Mbit/sec Ethernet cards, Linux 2.4 raised an interrupt for each received packet, putting a heavy load on the system. To overcome this problem, Deri proposed a so-called *ring buffer*, which is now part of Linux 2.6. This ring buffer contains a number of packet descriptors. In the initial state, all packet descriptors are marked as 'ready'. When a packet arrives at the network interface card (NIC), it is copied into a packet descriptor marked as ready, after which the descriptor is marked as 'used'. Instead of raising an interrupt for each received packet, an interrupt is only raised when the buffer contains a certain number of packets (or after a time-out). As a result, packet capturing performance is improved dramatically [8], since the lower number of interrupts lowers the load on the CPU, leading to less packets being dropped.

It should be noted that modern, 1 Gbit/sec Ethernet cards, have already implemented similar rings in hardware. Still new hardware developments, like for example multi-core CPUs, raise new problems. Again, software modifications, like multiple receive queues, may solve potential problems [9].

3   Detecting Inconsistency

In this Section, we will describe inconsistency called fake gaps and introduce an algorithm for detecting inconsistency. Although there may be different ways a repository can be inconsistent, we will only consider fake gaps.

3.1   Fake Gaps

In this paper's introduction, we said a fake gap to be representing those parts of a TCP flow that are absent in the repository, although they were acknowledged at the TCP level. To explain this more precisely we first have to consider a gap. To start with an example: when Alice wants to send some data to Bob, she sends ordered packets named A B C D E F. Bob may receive this as A B C E F D, but knows about the correct order and can therefore recreate the original message. This is called packet reordering. At the side of Bob, after having received C, there is a gap until D is received. In this example, the gap is filled when D is received.

We call a gap a fake gap, when one or more packets in a sequence of packets are not present, but are also not retransmitted; hence the original TCP flow is not affected. Consider Alice and Bob: Alice sends the sequence A B C D E F to Bob using TCP. Bob's network administrator records all traffic sent to Bob. According to the data recorded, Bob received A B C E F. When the connection between Alice and Bob is closed, we know Bob must have received D. We can then say that the recorded TCP flow between Alice and Bob contains a fake gap. All data was transmitted and received correctly, but the recorded data does not reflect this. Hence the recorded data is inconsistent. From now on, if we are referring to the flow of data packets within a TCP connection, we will abbreviate it to a flow.

In recorded traffic data, it is likely that there are flows that start and/or end outside the recorded time period. Therefore, detecting fake gaps in these flows is difficult. To avoid this, we only take flows into account that are sufficiently recorded. All packets of a single flow, from the first SYN-packet up to a FIN- or RST-packet should be recorded. If this is the case, we call the TCP flow a *usable flow*. Note that the final FIN-handshake can be partly outside the recorded time period.

3.2   Algorithm

In Section 3.1 we concluded fake gaps prove inconsistency. To detect this the algorithm we introduce, listed as Fig. 1, first extracts all usable flows from the complete set of packets. The second part of the algorithm loops over all usable flows. For every usable flow, it checks if there is an acknowledging packet that acknowledges a packet that has not yet been seen. If so, this indicates a fake gap and an identifier of the flow together with the packet that is used to detect the fake gap, is added to a list. So the final result of this algorithm is a list of flows combined with packets directly after the fake gaps.

```
INIT usableFlows to {}          # all usable flows found
INIT testFlows to {}            # all flows found so far
FOR each packet in data file
    IF packet is SYN
        CREATE flow from packet
        ADD flow to testFlows
    ELSE IF packet belongs to flow in testFlows
        SET flow to flowOf(packet)
        ADD packet to flow
        IF packet is FIN or RST
            REMOVE flow from testFlows
                ADD flow to usableFlows
END FOR
INIT fakeGaps to {}
FOR each flow in usableFlows
    FOR each packet in flow
        IF packet is ACK
            IF acked packets are not in this flow
                ADD tuple (flow, packet) to fakeGaps
    END FOR
END FOR
```

Fig. 1. Pseudo-code of the fake gap detection algorithm

It is important to see that this algorithm alone cannot detect the exact amount of fake gaps within the traffic dump. It can give an indication and show which usable flows are affected. If, for example, during a small interval no packets were recorded at the recording device, multiple flows can be affected by this. Our algorithm would detect a fake gap for each affected flow. We do not consider this a limitation. The results of our algorithm should provide a starting point for deep inspection of packets and flows.

3.3 Prototype

To be able to detect inconsistencies in existing repositories, we implemented the algorithm in a prototype.

Our prototype implements the algorithm in Fig. 1, but uses speed and memory optimisations. The prototype can be downloaded at [11].

As the algorithm detects fake gaps once per affected usable flow, the prototype does also. The prototype returns, once finished, a set with affected flows and a list with per fake gap the time this fake gap occured. This can be used for further analysing of the exact location of fake gaps. Our prototype tries to estimate the location of every fake gap by finding patterns in the detection times. As this is just a prototype, we consider such estimation sufficient.

Furthermore, our prototype tries to 'fix' fake gaps found, in order to continue analysing. If a fake gap is detected (e.g. a packet is expected but not seen in the rest of the flow) the prototype will report a fake gap and insert a dummy-packet.

In this way, it can continue to analyse the rest of the flow. If there is one (large) fake gap detected, there could be multiple smaller fake gaps in the data set. Therefore, the amount of detected fake gaps could be lower than the actual number. Also, the number of missing packets could be higher, since two or more packets could be missing due to a single fake gap.

The prototype has a few other limitations, which we will discuss. First of all, TCP sequence numbers are finite. If any sequence number reaches $2^{32} - 1$, it will continue with '0' [12]. The prototype does not deal with this limitation. Instead, it detects this situation, gives the user an error message and ignores the affected flow. During our research, no flows were dropped because of this limitation. As our prototype is using Java as implementation language, one may need to adjust the heap size of the Java virtual machine (JVM) to avoid crashes caused by the inability to allocate memory on the heap.

4   Evaluating the Prototype

Before the prototype that was built can be used to analyse gathered traffic from repositories, it has to be evaluated first. We have taken real life recorded traffic from the Simpleweb repository [6] and extracted a subset of packets that reflects different situations. Packet analysing software was used to manually analyse flows and extract flows from a set of traffic to be used for evaluating the prototype.

The requirements for the prototype are basically that it should find all missing packets caused by fake gaps, in usable flows and not detect false positives. The prototype should:

1. not detect any fake gap in a regular TCP flow
2. correctly handle duplicate acknowledgements
3. correctly handle packet reordering
4. correctly handle regular gaps
5. ignore all non TCP packets

We have evaluated the prototype according to these criteria. We extracted seven flows from a data file with traffic and had the prototype process them. The selected flows contained flows with fake gaps, duplicate acknowledgements, lost packets (gaps), partial handshakes and a flow without any of the above.

After having tested prototype on the extracted flows, we tested it on a small data file that was still feasible to manually inspect. We then checked whether our prototype behaved as intended according to the requirements. All files used to test out prototype can be downloaded at [11].

The processing speed of the prototype varies depending on the complexity and size of the data file. For example, it processed 2GB of data in 377 seconds. While processing, the memory usage was constantly around 50MB.

A problem we came across was a crashing JVM. After updating our JVM to the most recent one offered by Sun, most problems were over. However, there are still a few data files where the JVM crashes while running our prototype. As mentioned in section 3.3, extending the heap size of the JVM also cleared out some crashes, but unfortunately not all. The main issue seems to be that our prototype creates many classes (one for each packet), and that causes the JVM to exit with an error.

5   Analysing Repositories

We analysed two existing repositories using our prototype. The first repository we used was Simpleweb [6], maintained by the University of Twente. It was included in this paper because it is publicly available and easily accessible. We analysed a subset of data covering all 6 locations the Simpleweb repository provides, totalling to 224 data files. The second repository we included in this paper is the WIDE traffic repository [10], maintained by the MAWI working group. It contains data files with traffic of several trans-Pacific lines. We used one data file from samplepoint A to test our prototype and we analysed 27 data files from samplepoint F, which were all over 1 GB in size. We chose samplepoint F since this one is daily updated while the other samplepoints are discontinued or were not accessible. The full table of results created by our prototype can be found at [11]. Our prototype calculates fake gap statistics using various intervals. That is, fake gaps from different flows within this interval are grouped together and reported as a single fake gap. It should be noted that further research should give an indication of the exact value for the intervals we should use.

Figure 2 shows the estimated number of missing packets per repository we tested and the estimated number of fake gaps within an interval of 0.05 seconds. The left part of the graph shows the extreme values. A first observation includes the presence of fake gaps in almost all tested data files from the WIDE repository. To make comparison as clear as possible, note that only a subset of the Simpleweb data files is shown. In fact, only the 28 highest values are plotted; the remaining 196 data files are skipped. It can be observed from the raw test data, that there

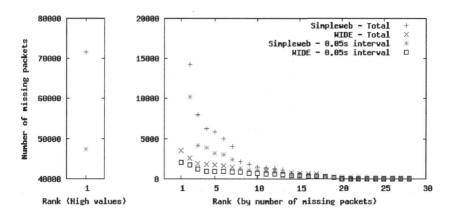

Fig. 2. Estimated number of missing packets and fake gaps. Each plotted value represents a data file.

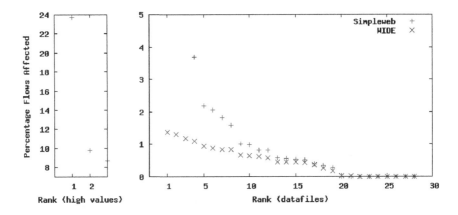

Fig. 3. Percentage of affected usable flows. Each plotted value represents a data file.

is an absence of fake gaps in 50.8% of the tested data files of the Simpleweb repository. Data files from location 2 are almost solely responsible for this. A possible explanation could be the low amount of traffic at this location.

Figure 3 plots the percentage of affected usable flows that have at least one fake gap. For the WIDE repository, on average 0.49% of the usable flows is affected by at least one fake gap. When ignoring data files without fake gaps, the average percentage of affected usable flows is 0.51%. Of the tested data files of the Simpleweb repository, an average of 0.27% of the usable flows in all data files was affected by at least one fake gap. When ignoring consistent files, the average is 0.55%. The highest value is in the file loc2-20030718-1530, where 23.72% of the flows is affected by at least one fake gap.

6   Conclusions

This paper describes our research on the consistency of network traffic repositories. Before answering the main research question, we first look at three sub questions identified in Section 1.

The first sub question, *"What could cause inconsistencies in a TCP traffic repository?"*, was answered in Section 2. To minimize the loss of packets that lead to inconsistencies, sufficient bandwidth should be present. At the recording device, customizations to the operating system and hardware could be required to keep up with large amounts of packets arriving.

The second sub question was *"How can we detect fake gaps?"*. We proposed an algorithm in Section 3, which extracts TCP flows. Then, it tries to identify fake gaps, packets that are not recorded by the recording device but were sent. The algorithm checks whether all data in the TCP flow is present by analysing TCP headers.

The last sub question, *"How consistent are today's repositories?"*, was answered in Section 5. We performed measurements on the Simpleweb [6] and

WIDE [10] repositories. We showed both repositories contain inconsistencies. In the Simpleweb repository an average of 0.27% of the investigated TCP flows was affected by at least one fake gap. For the WIDE repository, this average was 0.49%. The research covered a substantial subset of data from both repositories. We analysed 28 data files from the WIDE repository and 224 data files from the Simpleweb repository.

Going back to the main research question, *"How can inconsistency be detected in a TCP traffic repository?"*, we can now conclude detecting inconsistency is possible by using the proposed algorithm, which detects fake gaps. The knowledge that a repository is not always consistent is very important for research where it is critical to have all data recorded, like research on packet loss. For this kind of research, it is recommended to take possible inconsistency in the repository into account and, if no statistics are present, analyse the repository data before using it.

Future research could include extending the proposed algorithm to support TCP flows that are not completely present in the data file. This research can be used together with algorithms like the one described in [2], which checks for anomalies in traffic rate, to find the exact locations of fake gaps. This can, in turn, be used to draw conclusions about non-TCP traffic, thereby getting a better overview of the consistency of a network traffic repository.

Acknowledgments. This research work has been supported by the EC IST-EMANICS Network of Excellence (#26854).

References

1. Timmer, M.: How to identify the speed limiting factor of a TCP flow, http://dacs.ewi.utwente.nl/assignments/completed/bachelor/reports/B-assignment_Timmer.pdf (retrieved at October 5, 2008)
2. Slomp, G.: Consistency of repositories. Presented at 8th TSConIT, http://referaat.cs.utwente.nl/new/paper.php?paperID=377 (retrieved at October 5, 2008)
3. Lastdrager, E.E.H.: Consistency of network traffic repositories - an overview. In: Proceedings of 3rd Conference on Autonomous Infrastructure, Management and Security, AIMS 2009 (2009)
4. Lastdrager, E.E.H.: Consistency analysis of network traffic repositories. Presented at 10th TSConIT, http://referaat.cs.utwente.nl/new/paper.php?paperID=464 (retrieved at February 20, 2009)
5. Wessels, D., Fomenkov, M.: Wow, that's a lot of packets. In: Proc. Passive and Active Measurements Workshop, PAM (2003)
6. van de Meent, R., Pras, A.: Simpleweb/University of Twente – Traffic Measurement Data Repository, http://traces.simpleweb.org (retrieved on October 5, 2008)
7. Deri, L.: Improving Passive Packet Capture: Beyond Device Polling. In: Proceedings of 4th International System Administration and Network Engineering Conference, SANE (October 2004)
8. Wu, W., Crawford, M., Bowden, M.: The performance analysis of linux networking - Packet receiving. Computer Communications 30(5), 1044–1057 (2007)

9. Deri, L.: Towards 10 Gbit NetFlow Monitoring Using Commodity Hardware. Presentation at the joint Emanics / IRTF-NMRG workshop on NetFlow/IPFIX for network management,
   `http://www.ibr.cs.tu-bs.de/projects/nmrg/meetings/2008/munich/`
   (retrieved on March 1, 2009)
10. Cho, K., Mitsuya, K., Kato, A.: Traffic data repository at the WIDE project. In: Proc. USENIX Annual Technical Conference, p. 51 (2000)
11. Lastdrager, E.E.H.: Prototype and results,
    `http://www.vf.utwente.nl/~lastdragereeh/referaat`
12. Postel, J.: RFC 793: Transmission Control Protocol, Internet Engineering Task Force (1981)

Author Index

Agustí, Ramón   178
Alff, Patrick D.   199
Awang, Azlan   138

Barisch, Marc   188
Bertrand, Gilles   21
Bolea, Liliana   178

Calveras, Anna   168
Casadevall, Fernando   128
Catalan, Marisa   168
Chiprianov, Vanea   199

Dañobeitia, Borja   118
Duarte Murta, Cristina   108

Emstad, Peder J.   1

Fehér, Gábor   51
Femenias, Guillem   118
Ford, Alan   98

Garcia-Palacios, Emi   31
Gáspár-Papanek, Csaba   69
Gergely, Viktor   51
Gómez, Carles   168
Gyarmati, László   59

Haidine, Abdelfattah   158
Hauger, Simon   148
Horváth, Dániel   11
Hu, Guoqiang   1
Hurley, John   31

Jiang, Yuming   1

Kalogiros, Costas   98
Kapitány, Gábor   11
Kermarrec, Yvon   199
Kögel, Jochen   188
Kostopoulos, Alexandros   98

Lagrange, Xavier   138
Lahoud, Samer   21

Lastdrager, Elmer   217
Lehnert, Ralf   158
Leonardi, Emilio   41
Ludovici, Alessandro   168
Lukovszki, Csaba   11

Maciel, Joylan Nunes   108
Meier, Sebastian   188
Mellia, Marco   41
Meo, Michela   41
Moldován, István   11
Molnár, Miklós   21

Nevin, Anne   1

Paradells, Josep   168
Pérez-Romero, Jordi   178
Petróczi, Attila István   69
Plósz, Sándor   11
Pras, Aiko   208, 217

Renault, Éric   88
Riera-Palou, Felip   118
Rodrigues, Emanuel B.   128
Ros, David   138

Sadre, Ramin   208
Sallent, Oriol   178
Sezer, Sakir   31
Sousa, Pedro   78
Sperotto, Anna   208
Sulaiman, Samer   158

Teuchert, Domenic   148
Texier, Géraldine   21
Traverso, Stefano   41
Trinh, Tuan Anh   59
Tuerk, Stefan   158

Vliek, Gert   208

Walker, Michael L.   128

Zeghlache, Djamal   88